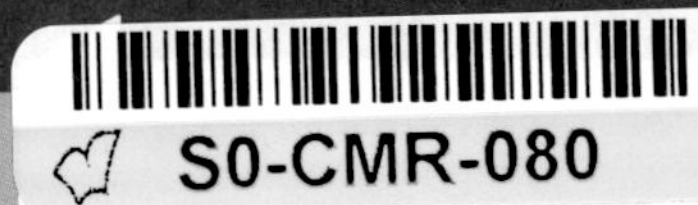

KEYSTONE Finish Line

Biology

Acknowledgments

Illustrations: Pages 10, 15, 16, 17, 19, 20, 22, 30, 40, 59, 63, 71, 79, 85, 92, 98, 104, 106, 108, 109, 116, 118, 120, 125, 126, 148, 172, 176, 188, 197, 198, 204, 206: John Norton; Pages 12, 14: Zeke Smith; Page 18 *digestive system*: Laurie Conley; Page 179: Image used under Creative Commons from "Voyage of the Beagle" as found on http://darwin-online.org.uk/converted/published/1845_Beagle_F14_fig07.jpg; Page 208: Cindy Shaw

Photos: Cover and title page: *Great blue heron eating a brook trout* www.shutterstock.com, cappi thompson; Page 15: *red blood cells* Lawrence Berkeley National Lab; *nerve cells* National Heart, Lung, and Blood Institute, National Institutes of Health, and the US Department of Health and Human Services; *plant cells* www.en.wikipedia.org; Page 29: image used under Creative Commons from Cory; Page 31: J. Schmidt, National Park Service; Page 89: *air conditioning unit* www.shutterstock.com, ARENA Creative, *furnace* www.shutterstock.com, Viacheslav Lopatin; Page 146: Used with permission of UW Cytogenetics/Wisconsin State Laboratory of Hygiene © Board of Regents of the University of Wisconsin System; Page 160: Olaf Leillinger/Wikipedia; Page 170: Raimond Spekking/Wikipedia (CC-BY-SA-3.0); Page 185: *Battus philenor* © Jarek Tuszynski/Wikimedia Commons/CC-BY-SA-3.0, *Limenitis arthemis astyanax* Saxophlute, *Limenitis arthemis arthemis* D. Gordon E. Robertson

ISBN 978-0-8454-7599-7

Contents

Introduction to Keystone Finish Line Biology 5

Module A—Cells and Cell Processes

Unit 1 Basic Biological Principles 7

Lesson 1 Unifying Characteristics of Life BIO.A.1.1.1, BIO.A.1.2.1 8

Lesson 2 Organization of Multicellular Organisms BIO.A.1.2.2 15

Unit 2 The Chemical Basis for Life 25

Lesson 1 Unique Properties of Water BIO.A.2.1.1 26

Lesson 2 Organic Molecules: Lipids and Carbohydrates BIO.A.2.2.1, BIO.A.2.2.2, BIO.A.2.2.3 33

Lesson 3 Organic Molecules: DNA and Proteins BIO.A.2.2.2, BIO.A.2.2.3 42

Lesson 4 Enzymes BIO.A.2.3.1, BIO.A.2.3.2 48

Unit 3 Bioenergetics 55

Lesson 1 ATP and Cellular Respiration BIO.A.3.1.1, BIO.A.3.2.1, BIO.A.3.2.2 56

Lesson 2 Photosynthesis BIO.A.3.1.1, BIO.A.3.2.1, BIO.A.3.2.2 62

Unit 4 Homeostasis and Transport 67

Lesson 1 Membranes of the Cell BIO.A.4.1.1, BIO.A.4.1.3 68

Lesson 2 Passive Transport BIO.A.4.1.2 75

Lesson 3 Active Transport BIO.A.4.1.2 83

Lesson 4 Homeostasis BIO.A.4.2.1 89

Module A Review—Cells and Cell Processes 97

Module B—Continuity and Unity Of Life

Unit 5 Cell Growth and Reproduction 105

Lesson 1 Genes and Protein Synthesis BIO.B.1.2.2, BIO.B.2.2.1, BIO.B.2.2.2 106

Lesson 2 The Cell Cycle, DNA Replication, and Mitosis BIO.B.1.1.1, BIO.B.1.2.1 114

Lesson 3 Genes, Alleles, and Meiosis BIO.B.1.1.2, BIO.B.1.2.2 122

Unit 6 Genetics 131
Lesson 1 Genes and Inheritance BIO.B.1.2.2, BIO.B.2.1.1 132
Lesson 2 Mutations and Chromosome Abnormalities BIO.B.2.1.2, BIO.B.2.3.1, BIO.B.3.1.3 141
Lesson 3 Genetic Engineering BIO.B.2.4.1 148

Unit 7 Theory of Evolution 159
Lesson 1 Mechanisms of Evolution BIO.B.3.1.1, BIO.B.3.1.2, BIO.B.3.1.3 160
Lesson 2 The Evidence for Evolution BIO.B.3.2.1 169
Lesson 3 Scientific Terminology BIO.B.3.3.1 179

Unit 8 Ecology 187
Lesson 1 Ecosystems and Biomes BIO.B.4.1.1, BIO.B.4.1.2 188
Lesson 2 Ecosystem Interactions BIO.B.4.2.1, BIO.B.4.2.2 196
Lesson 3 Cycles of Matter BIO.B.4.2.3 204
Lesson 4 Ecosystem Response to Change BIO.B.4.2.4, BIO.B.4.2.5 211

Module B Review—Continuity and Unity of Life 227

Glossary 239

Welcome to Keystone Finish Line Biology

This book was written to help you get ready for the Keystone Biology Exam. The best way to prepare for and succeed on the test is to review the ideas and practice the skills you will need for it.

Keystone Finish Line Biology contains lessons to help you review key information relevant to the topics of biology tested on the Keystone Biology Exam. Each lesson includes examples to remind you what a concept means or show how a skill is used. On the right side of many lesson pages is a sidebar containing definitions of words you might not know or remember and facts that are related to the main idea of the lesson. After each lesson, there are sample test questions to help you practice what you have reviewed.

Like the actual Keystone Exam, the practice pages include two different kinds of questions. Some of these questions will be easy, others will make you think carefully, and some will present a challenge. You should do these questions on your own if possible, just as if you were taking the real test.

- One type of question found in this book is **multiple choice.** These questions present four answers to choose from. Be sure to read all of the answer choices carefully before selecting one. Even if you are not sure of the correct answer, you can often use the process of elimination to discard incorrect choices. Multiple-choice questions are worth one point on the exam.
- The other type of question is **constructed response.** These are open-ended items that can be answered in more than one way. You must answer these questions in writing, using your own words. Constructed-response items generally have two or three parts, and require you to think in greater detail about several related aspects of a concept or process. They are worth up to three points on the exam.

  To answer a constructed response item, follow the item instructions *exactly.* Ask yourself, "Am I answering the question that is being asked? Have I included everything I need to include, but not included information that is not asked for?" Always think about what you will say before writing your explanation, so that your thoughts are clear and organized. Of course, be sure to write legibly.

Each lesson contains at least one sample of each type of question. A box under the sample item explains how to think about the question so that you can answer it correctly. At the end of each unit, independent practice questions of both types give you the opportunity to try out the skills you have reviewed on your own.

The units are grouped into two modules. Following each module is a review section of practice problems that cover all the concepts and skills addressed in that module's lessons in a mixed order. The module review includes both types of questions, multiple choice and constructed response.

Short passages accompany some of the questions you will see. These passages provide information that you use to answer the question. The information may include text, a diagram or illustration, or a table or graph. The question or group of questions that follows might be about the information itself, or about how the information can be applied.

This workbook was created to give you some practice for the Keystone Biology Exam. It will help you remember the science concepts you have learned, and allow you to practice the relevant skills. It will also give you the chance to answer the same kinds of questions you will see on the test. Good luck!

Module A
Cells and Cell Processes

Unit 1
Basic Biological Principles

At the foundation of biology are some basic biological principles. This unit will help you review the underlying characteristics of life, the levels of organization that organisms exhibit, and the structures and functions that make up those levels.

1 Unifying Characteristics of Life All organisms share some basic characteristics of life. In this lesson, you will review the characteristics that define organisms as living things. You will also review the cell as the basic building block of life. Whether simple prokaryotic cell or differentiated eukaryotic cell, every cell has structures with specific functions.

2 Organization of Multicellular Organisms One defining characteristic of life is having levels of biological organization. Every level is a system with a specific structure and function. In this lesson, you will review the levels that make up an organism: cell, tissue, organ, organ system, and organism. You will also review how the structures that make up these levels function and interrelate.

Unifying Characteristics of Life

BIO.A.1.1.1, BIO.A.1.2.1

Earth is home to a great variety of **organisms,** from tiny single-celled bacteria to complex animals and plants. It may be difficult, at first, to see what all these organisms have in common, but all life on Earth shares several unifying characteristics.

An **organism** is a living thing, such as an animal, plant, fungus, protist, or bacteria.

Characteristics of Life

A closer look reveals that all organisms are composed of one or more **cells,** the basic building blocks of life. A cell is the smallest living unit of any organism, and has specific parts that allow it to carry out life processes. An organism may be **unicellular** or **multicellular.**

A **cell** is the basic unit of life.

A **unicellular** organism, such as bacteria, has a single cell to carry out all life functions.

Multicellular organisms, such as animals and plants, may have trillions of cells with specialized functions within that organism's life cycle. The cells work together to carry out the organism's life functions.

In addition to being composed of cells, all living organisms share the following characteristics and abilities:

- **Obtaining and using energy—**All organisms must obtain energy in some form, whether they absorb sunlight (like plants) or ingest other organisms to gain the energy stored in their molecules (like animals).
- **Maintaining a stable internal state—**Organisms and their cells function best at certain temperatures, pH levels, solute concentrations, and other conditions. They must keep levels from falling too low or rising too high. This process is called **homeostasis.**
- **The ability to grow—**Even single cells grow larger, and multicellular organisms grow by dividing, that is, duplicating, their cells many times over.
- **The ability to reproduce—**Almost all of the organisms in a species are able to reproduce. For unicellular organisms, reproduction consists of cell division.
- **Responding to stimuli in the environment—**A *stimulus* is a change (for example, in temperature or color) that an organism can detect. Responses may take different forms. Some are behavioral. For example, a rabbit may run away from a predator. Some plants move their leaves to face the incoming sunlight. Other responses do not involve movement. For example, some plants produce poisonous chemicals when insects begin to eat their leaves. To respond to changing conditions, organisms must be able to sense their environment. Many plants and animals can sense changes in light, temperature, and gravity.

Homeostasis is the process of maintaining a stable internal environment.

Both unicellular and multicellular organisms may reproduce sexually or asexually. For example, yeast is a single-celled fungus that sometimes reproduces sexually. Many plants can reproduce asexually as well as from seeds.

In low-light environments, eye pupils dilate to allow more light to pass into the eye. Describe **two** characteristics of life exhibited by this example.

Pupil dilation is a response to a stimulus—low light—in the environment. This response requires the use of energy. Pupil dilation is also an example of homeostasis, as constant light levels in the eye are maintained.

Characteristics of All Cells

All organisms consist of cells, and all cells share several characteristics that are essential to life. The **plasma membrane,** or *cell membrane,* forms the outside layer of a cell. It separates the cell from its environment and regulates the exchange of material into and out of the cell.

A **plasma membrane** is a molecular bilayer that encloses a cell.

Cytoplasm is the substance that fills the cell's internal volume. It is composed mostly of water.

DNA is the molecule that stores genetic information, which allows the cell to pass it on to future generations. Genes are temporarily copied as RNA and brought to the ribosomes.

DNA and RNA are both **nucleic acids,** biological macromolecules that act as blueprints to convey genetic information.

Ribosomes are the smallest organelles within the cell and many of them are found throughout the cytoplasm. They decode the genetic information in mRNA and assemble amino acids into proteins.

Ribosomes are made up of protein and RNA. They are not enclosed by membranes.

Which structure is **not** present in all organisms?

A a cell wall

B a plasma membrane

C genetic material

D cytoplasm

All cells contain a plasma membrane, cytoplasm, and some form of genetic material, so choices B, C, and D are incorrect. Cell walls are found in plants, fungi, and bacteria, but not in animals. Therefore A is the correct choice.

Viruses contain genetic information, but because they lack ribosomes and other cell structures, they are not considered organisms.

Prokaryotic and Eukaryotic Cells

Prokaryotes and eukaryotes are the two main types of cells. **Prokaryotes** are unicellular organisms that lack membrane-bound organelles. This means that their DNA is not contained within a nuclear membrane, but is instead found directly in the cytoplasm. Prokaryotes are the oldest type of cell, originating about 3.5 billion years ago. They include common bacteria and bacteria-like cells (archaea) that are found in extreme environments.

A **prokaryotic** cell is much smaller and simpler than a eukaryotic cell, lacking a nucleus and other membrane-bound organelles.

Membrane-bound means being enclosed within a membrane inside the cytoplasm.

Eukaryotes are much more complex cells, normally larger than prokaryotic cells. They originated about 1.5 billion years ago. They have membrane-bound organelles located within the plasma membrane. Their DNA is contained within a nucleus. A *cytoskeleton,* or protein scaffold, helps to maintain the structure of these large cells. Eukaryotes include protists, fungi, animals, and plants. They may be either unicellular or multicellular.

All multicellular organisms are **eukaryotes,** so all multicellular organisms have cells with nuclei and membrane-bound organelles.

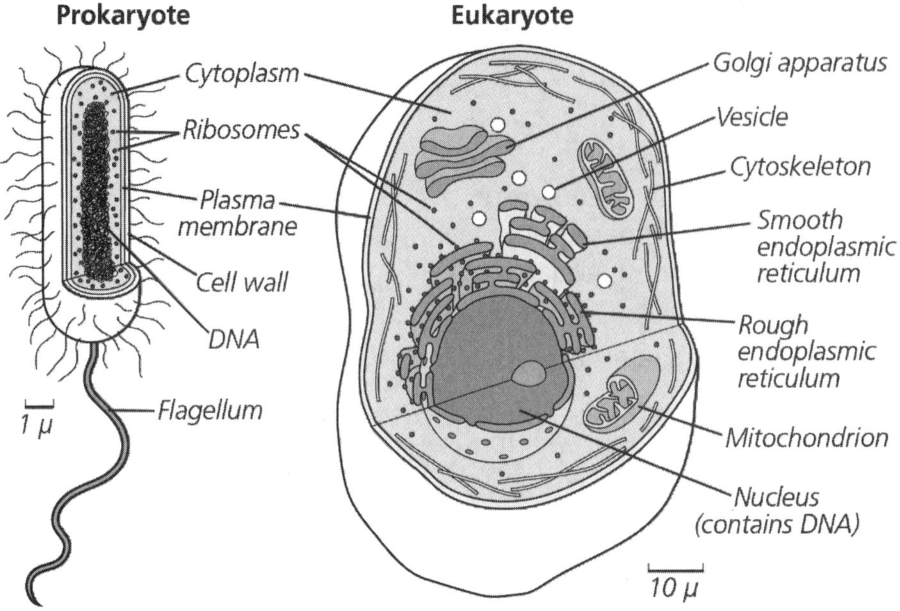

The simpler prokaryotic cell originated earlier than the complex eukaryotic cell.

Prokaryotic cells are generally smaller than eukaryotic cells because they are less complex, have less material inside them, and have limited ways to transport materials into and out of the cell efficiently. This table compares them.

PROKARYOTIC CELLS VERSUS EUKARYOTIC CELLS

	Prokaryotic Cell	Eukaryotic Cell
Nucleus	No	Yes
Cell Number	Unicellular	Unicellular or multicellular
DNA	Circular chromosome found in cytoplasm	Linear chromosomes contained in nucleus
Examples	Bacteria	Plants, animals, fungi, protists
Plasma Membrane	Yes	Yes
Membrane-bound Organelles	No	Yes
Ribosomes	Yes, small	Yes, large
Cell Wall	Yes	Present in plants and fungi
Cell Diameter	1–10 micrometers (μm)	10–100 micrometers (μm)

A micrometer (μm) is equal to 1×10^{-6} meter.

Describe two similarities and two differences between prokaryotes and eukaryotes.

There are many answers to this question. Similarities include the presence of genetic information (DNA), cytoplasm, a plasma membrane, and ribosomes in both types of cells. Differences include the lack of a nucleus in prokaryotes, the size difference between eukaryotes and prokaryotes, and the addition of membrane-bound organelles such as mitochondria and chloroplasts in eukaryotes.

Organelles of the Eukaryotic Cell

The eukaryotic cell contains a variety of membrane-bound **organelles** with very specific functions. The **nucleus** contains the cell's genetic information (DNA), packaged as chromosomes. **Mitochondria** are the powerhouses of the cell. These organelles synthesize the energy-rich ATP molecules required to carry out life processes.

Like all cells, eukaryotic cells contain ribosomes. Some ribosomes float unattached in the cytoplasm; they produce proteins used within the cell. Other ribosomes are attached to the exterior membrane of the **endoplasmic reticulum (ER),** a membrane-rich organelle that surrounds the nucleus. These ribosomes produce proteins that will be transported outside the cell. The endoplasmic reticulum wraps "packages" of these proteins into membrane *vesicles* and releases them. The **Golgi apparatus** absorbs and tags these vesicles with an "address" so they can be secreted by the cell for use elsewhere in the organism.

A eukaryotic cell produces and secretes a protein. Trace the path of the protein through the cell's organelles, starting with the original genetic information for the protein.

The genetic information for the protein is stored in the nucleus. It is transported to the ribosomes attached to the rough ER (where proteins bound for "export" are assembled). Once made, the protein is packed into a vesicle that travels to the Golgi apparatus. Then, it is "tagged" and sent to the plasma membrane, where it leaves the cell.

Animal and Plant Cells

Animal and plant cells have many of the same organelles, such as the plasma membrane and the nucleus. However, there are some differences. **Chloroplasts** are plant organelles that capture the energy of sunlight and transform it into chemical energy, like simple sugars. Chloroplasts contain the pigment *chlorophyll,* which absorbs the energy of sunlight much like a solar panel.

An **organelle** is a specialized part of a cell with a specific function.

The **nucleus** is an organelle that contains the genetic material of a eukaryotic cell.

Mitochondria are membrane-bound organelles where energy transformation takes place.

There are two kinds of **endoplasmic reticulum,** rough and smooth. Rough ER has ribosomes attached to the surface and produces proteins. Smooth ER is involved in the production of fatty acids and lipids. No ribosomes are attached to smooth ER.

A *vesicle* is a small membrane sac inside the cell, which may contain material for transport.

The **Golgi apparatus** is an organelle that processes materials for release from the cell.

Chloroplasts are plant organelles that transform sunlight into chemical energy.

Chlorophyll is the pigment that makes plants green.

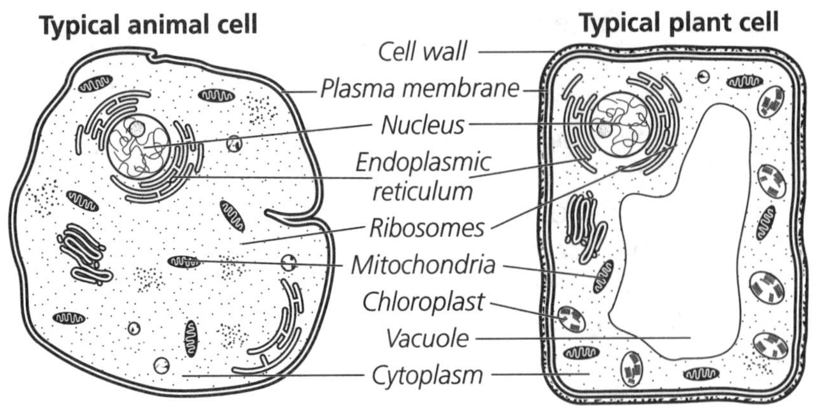

Each organelle in a cell has a specific function.

Surrounding the plasma membrane of the plant cell is a rigid *cell wall,* which supports and gives structure to plant bodies. The large *central vacuole* is an organelle that stores water, nutrients, wastes, and other material. While animal cells may contain smaller vacuoles, they lack the large central vacuoles of plant cells. When filled with liquid, the plant cell's vacuole exerts pressure against the cell wall. This makes the plant rigid.

In addition to animals and plants, eukaryotes include fungi and protists, such as paramecia. Fungi and protists may share some of the characteristics of plants or animals, or may have unique characteristics. Fungi have cell walls, but they are composed of chitin rather than cellulose, as in plants.

The plant *cell wall* is a structure on the outside of the plasma membrane. It is made of cellulose.

The large *central vacuole* stores water, nutrients, and other material in a plant cell.

Plant cells contain some organelles not found in animal cells. Describe **two** organelles that play major roles in plant cells but not animal cells.

One structure found in plant cells but not in animal cells is a cell wall, a stiff outer layer that surrounds the plasma membrane and gives a cell rigidity and strength. Another structure is a chloroplast, an organelle where photosynthesis occurs. A third structure is the vacuole. Although small vacuoles can be found in other types of cells, a large central vacuole plays a major structural role in plant cells. It also stores water and nutrients for the cell. These roles require them to be much larger in plant cells than in animal cells.

IT'S YOUR TURN

Please read each question carefully. For a multiple-choice question, circle the letter of the correct response. For a constructed-response question, write your answers on the lines.

1 A mitochondrion produces ATP for energy. A plant's leaves turn toward the direction of sunlight. A bacteria cell secretes a waste product through its plasma membrane. Which characteristic of life do **all** of these examples describe?

A growing and reproducing

B obtaining and using energy

C response to external stimuli

D maintenance of homeostasis

2 Which do the cells of an *E. coli* bacterium and an elephant have in common?

A ribosomes to assemble proteins

B mitochondria to produce energy

C chloroplasts found around the vacuole

D chromosomes located in the cytoplasm

3 A cell from which organism would **most likely** be smallest?

A a sugar maple tree

B a five-spotted ladybug

C a *Saccharomyces* yeast

D a *Lactobacillus* bacterium

4 Which statement correctly pairs the organelle with its function?

A The vacuole stores genetic information.

B The chloroplast synthesizes proteins from amino acids.

C The nucleus absorbs the sun's energy for photosynthesis.

D The plasma membrane controls the flow of materials into the cell.

Use the diagram below to answer questions 5 and 6.

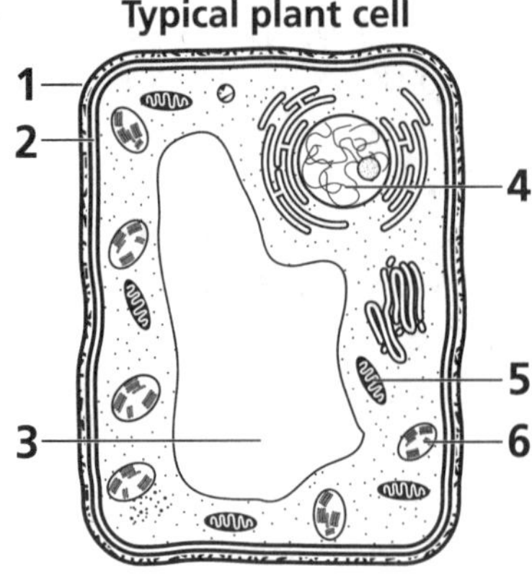

5 Which structure contains the cell's genetic material?

A structure 2

B structure 4

C structure 5

D structure 6

6 Refer to the diagram above to answer the following questions.

A Identify structure 1 and describe its main function.

____

____

B Identify structure 3 and describe its main function.

____

____

C A wilted houseplant is watered. Explain how structures 1 and 3 work together to cause a change in the plant.

____

____

____

____

Organization of Multicellular Organisms

BIO.A.1.2.2

All organisms are systems, with parts that work together to help them live, grow, and reproduce. Each of these parts has a structure that helps it to carry out its function. The parts of a multicellular organism can be examined at different levels. The simplest level is the cell, while the most complex is the individual organism.

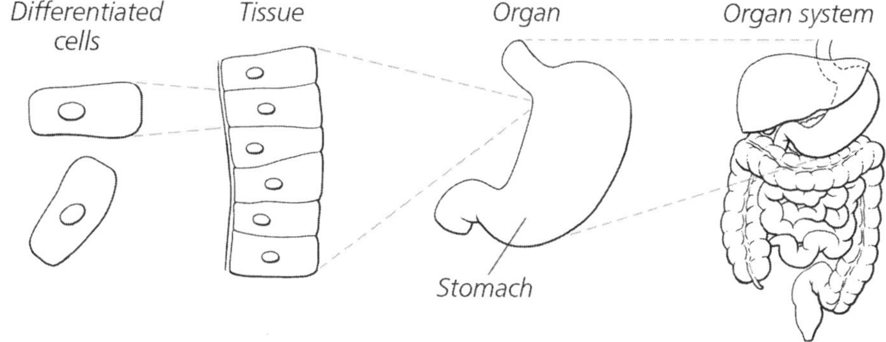

The human digestive system has different levels of organization.

An object's *structure* is the arrangement of its parts. Its *function* is its specific activity or role.

An organism's cells make up its tissues. Tissues compose organs. Different organs work together as organ systems.

Cells and Tissues

The basic structural unit of a living thing is the cell. Cells themselves are tiny systems with organelles and membranes that allow them to carry out life processes. The individual cells in a multicellular organism do not carry out every life function of the organism. Instead, different cells perform different jobs. They are *differentiated,* or specialized to perform particular functions.

Differentiated cells are specialized to perform particular functions within a multicellular organism.

In mammals, red blood cells are specialized to deliver oxygen to body tissues. Red blood cells are small, round disks that are thin and flexible. Their shape allows them to move easily through even the narrowest blood vessels. In contrast, nerve cells have long, thin branches that extend from the main part of the cell. These structures help them deliver information from one part of the body to another.

Animal red blood cells

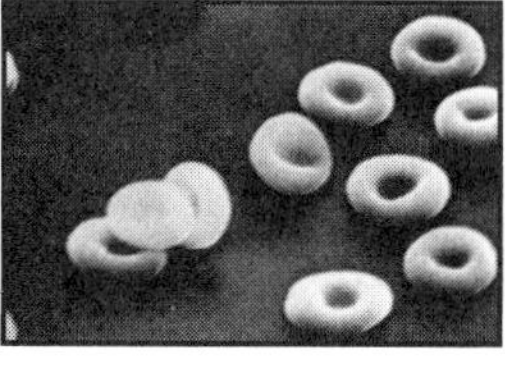

Animal nerve cells

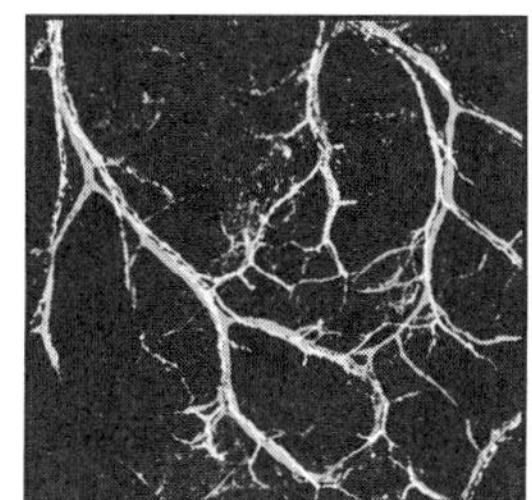

Plant support cells

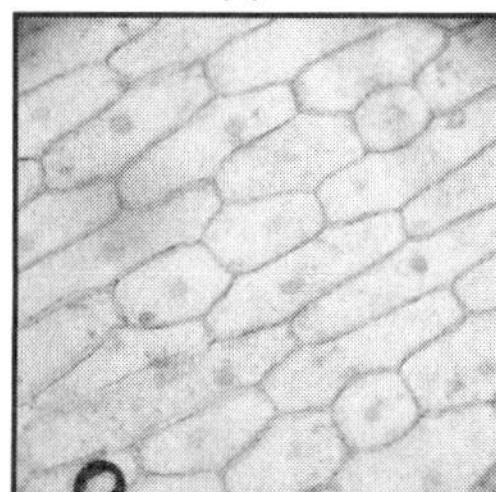

In multicellular organisms, cells are differentiated because they have specialized functions.

Cells form tissues. A **tissue** is a group of similar cells that share a structure and function. For example muscle tissues are made up of very long, thin cells that can *contract,* or shorten, to allow movement. Groups of muscle cells work together to move the body.

Epithelial tissues cover body surfaces in animals. The outer layer of skin is epithelial tissue made up of small, flat interlocking cells. This epithelial tissue encloses and protects the organism. *Connective tissues* hold organs in place and attach epithelial tissue to other tissues.

A **tissue** is a structure made of similar cells that perform a specific function.

Epithelial cells form sheets of tissue that enclose or line body parts. Epithelial tissue may have one or many layers.

Fat and bone are *connective tissues.* Blood is a form of connective tissue, even though it is a fluid.

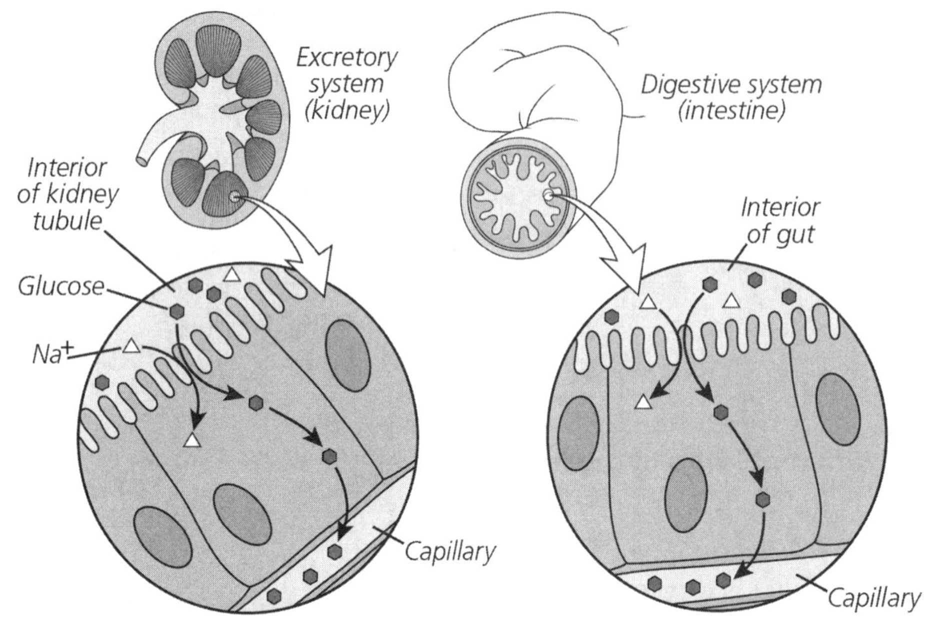

Capillaries are the narrowest blood vessels, with walls only one cell thick. Substances in the blood move across capillary walls, into and out of cells.

The image above shows cells from two different organ systems. These specialized cells form tissues that line the kidney tubule and intestine. How do the cells' similar structures help them to carry out their functions?

The function of the cells is to absorb dissolved minerals and nutrients and allow them to cross into the circulatory system. Both cells have a surface with projections of the plasma membrane. This aids in absorption by increasing the surface area over which solutes may cross into the cell.

Organs and Systems

Within a multicellular organism, different types of tissues can form an **organ.** For example, the stomach is an organ that *digests,* or breaks down, food. Muscle tissues in the stomach help mix food with gastric juices. Epithelial tissues in the inner lining of the stomach secrete acidic fluids that aid in digestion. Other tissues secrete mucus to protect the stomach from being harmed by these acids, and blood supplies oxygen to stomach tissues.

An **organ** is a structure, made up of two or more tissue types, that performs a specific job.

Glands in the stomach lining secrete strong acids. Gastric (stomach) acid has a pH between 1 and 3.

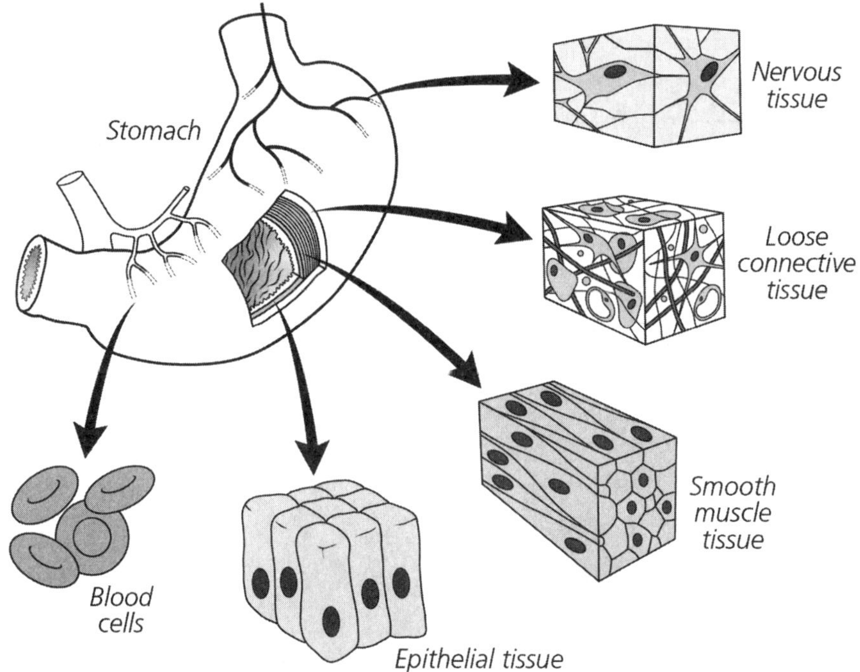

The stomach is an organ made up of various kinds of tissue.

Muscle tissues may be under voluntary control or involuntary control, as with the smooth muscle lining the stomach.

Organs form **organ systems,** groups of related organs that work together to do a particular job. For example, the human *digestive system* includes the mouth, esophagus, stomach, intestines, gallbladder, liver, and pancreas. These organs work together to break down food into small molecules.

After food is digested, blood vessels in the intestines absorb useful molecules. These molecules are transported to cells in every part of the body, where they are used for energy and as raw materials to repair and build new cells.

In a complex multicellular organism, organ systems function to meet the basic needs of cells throughout the body. Recall that cells are specialized and cannot carry out all life functions on their own. They rely on the body's systems to meet some of their needs. Functions of organ systems include the following:

- Exchanging materials with the environment
- Transporting materials to and from cells
- Allowing movement
- Storing nutrients for later use
- Responding to stimuli

An **organ system** is a group of organs that work together to perform a specific function.

Human organ systems include:

- Nervous
- Endocrine
- Skeletal
- Muscular
- Integumentary
- Immune
- Circulatory
- Respiratory
- Digestive
- Urinary
- Reproductive

In a unicellular organism, a single cell would carry out all of these functions.

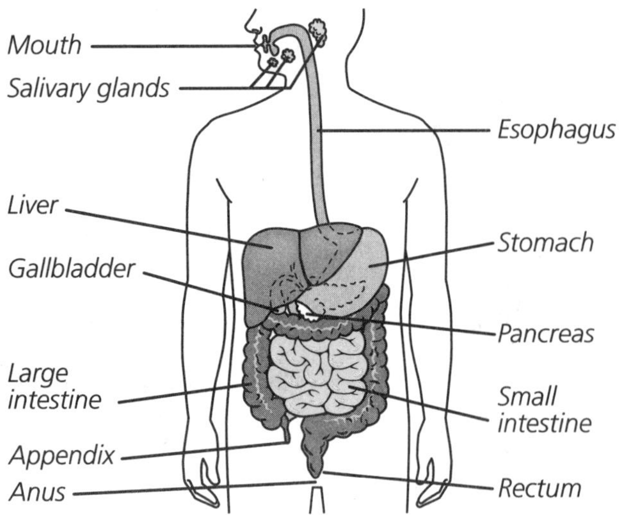

The diagram above shows the digestive system. How do the organs of the digestive system work together to carry out the function of digestion?

The mouth moistens and breaks down ingested food, which is carried to the stomach by the esophagus. There, it is broken down by stomach acids and released into the small intestine. The pancreas and liver secrete substances into the small intestine to help complete digestion. Then, the digested nutrients and minerals are absorbed into the body by the small intestine. Any undigested material passes into the large intestine, where water is reabsorbed and bacteria convert some of the waste into vitamins.

Interrelated Organs Systems

An organ system may be dedicated to a single function or share multiple functions with other systems. For example, the main functions of the *respiratory system* are to bring oxygen into the body and to remove the carbon dioxide produced by cells from the body. The organs of the respiratory system work together to accomplish these functions.

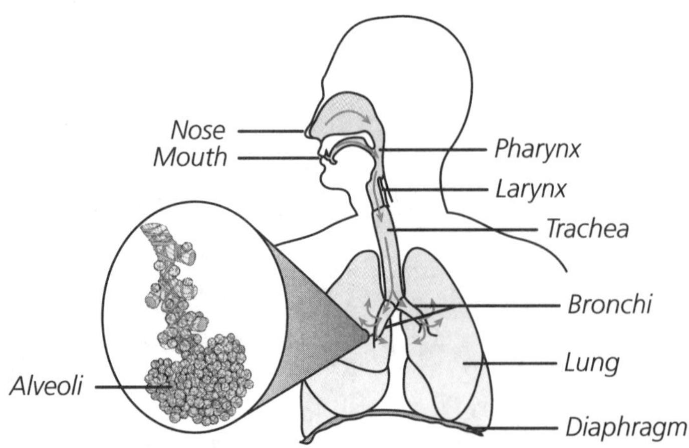

The diaphragm contracts to expand the lungs, causing air to move through the nose and mouth and into the trachea and bronchi. The bronchi branch into smaller tubes that lead to microscopic, sac-like *alveoli* in the lungs.

Oxygen moves from the alveoli into the surrounding capillaries. At the same time, carbon dioxide moves from the capillaries into the alveoli and is exhaled. This process is called *gas exchange.*

Gas exchange refers to the movement of carbon dioxide and oxygen between an organism and its environment. Because most cells of a multicellular organisms are not in direct contact with the environment, gas exchange is a function of organ systems.

Capillaries are part of the *circulatory system,* which includes the heart, blood, arteries, and veins. This system transports oxygen, nutrients, carbon dioxide, and metabolic wastes throughout the body. The diagram shows the main parts of the circulatory system. Notice that there are two circulatory pathways: one between the right side of the heart and the lungs, and another between the left side of the heart and the body.

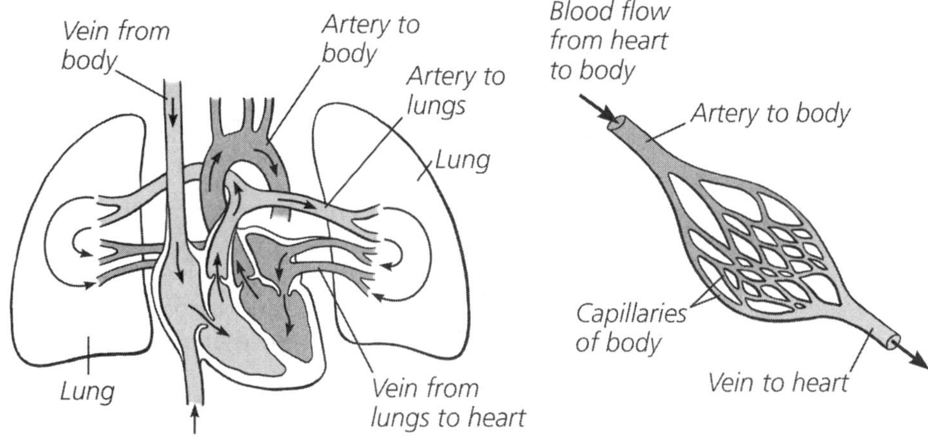

All veins carry blood toward the heart. All arteries carry blood away from the heart.

Just as the respiratory and circulatory systems work together, so do other organ systems. The *muscular system* consists of muscles, organs that can contract in response to a nerve signal. Contracting muscles can exert forces on the bones they are attached to, allowing the organism to move. Muscles work in opposing pairs. One muscle in a pair causes motion in one direction around a joint. Its partner causes motion in the opposite direction, as shown below.

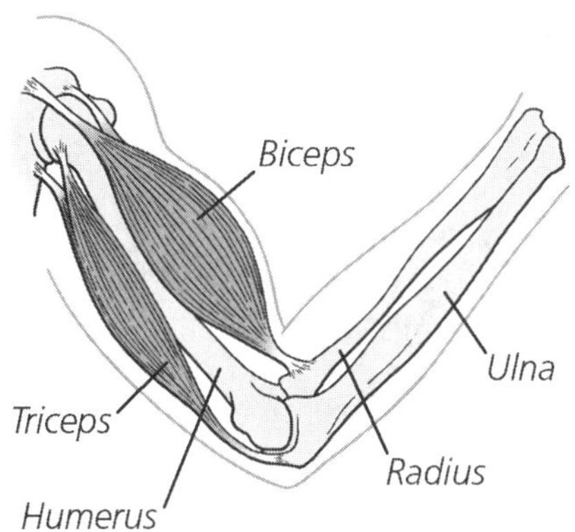

Bones are part of the skeletal system.

Muscles exert force by contracting, not by lengthening. Muscles work in opposing pairs to move the bones of the body.

Skeletal muscle tissue is under voluntary control. You can decide whether to move these muscles.

Describe how two or more organ systems work together to provide cells with needed oxygen and remove carbon dioxide they produce.

The respiratory system functions to bring oxygen into the body and expel carbon dioxide. Gas exchange occurs in the alveoli, where dissolved oxygen enters the capillaries and carbon dioxide in the capillary blood crosses into the lungs. Capillaries are part of the circulatory system, which transports blood to all the cells of the body. When blood from the lungs is pumped to cells and tissues, gases are again exchanged with the cells.

Structure and Function in Plants

The structures of plant cells, tissues, and organs help them to carry out their specific functions. Plant *vascular tissues* are made of differentiated cells that stack together to form tube-like structures. This structure allows them to transport food, water, and minerals throughout the plant body.

In a plant leaf, the inner mesophyll cells carry out **photosynthesis.** The upper layer of the leaf is transparent, so light can pass through them to the cells beneath. The wax cuticle keeps water in the leaf. The underside of a leaf contains *stomata,* openings that allow water vapor and other gases in and out of the plant.

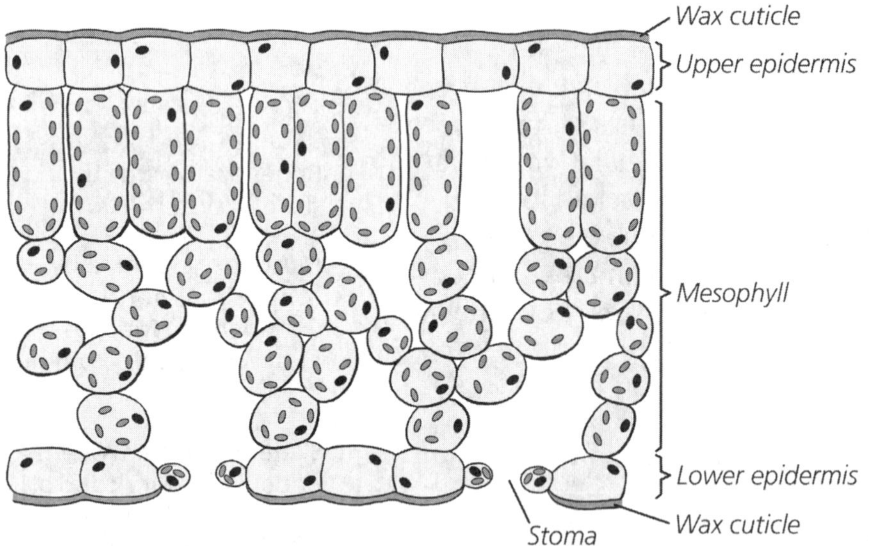

The specialized structures of leaf cells and tissues help them carry out specific functions.

Without *vascular systems* to transport material, plants would grow no taller than mosses.

Photosynthesis is the process of using the energy from sunlight to convert water and carbon dioxide to glucose and oxygen.

A *stoma* (pl. *stomata*) is an opening that allows gases such as oxygen, carbon dioxide, and water vapor in and out of the leaf. Guard cells on either side of the stoma regulate the size of the opening.

The prefix *meso-* means "middle."

Many trees in temperate environments have broad, flat leaves. How does this leaf structure support the function of obtaining energy?

A A flatter surface allows more oxygen to enter the leaf.

B A flatter surface allows more water to be retained in the leaf.

C A larger surface area allows more light to reach the mesophyll.

D A larger surface area allows more room for photosynthetic cells.

Plants obtain energy from sunlight, which passes through the upper layers of a leaf. A broad, flat leaf has a large surface area, which provides more room for sunlight to enter the leaf. Thus, the shape of the leaf is suited for collecting the necessary amount of sunlight. A flatter, broader surface contains more stomata, allowing more oxygen to enter the leaf. However, oxygen is not a form of energy, so choice A is incorrect. A flatter surface makes water conservation more difficult, so choice B is incorrect. Compared to a thicker leaf of the same volume and a smaller surface area, one with a larger surface area does not have more room for mesophyll cells. Therefore, choice D is incorrect. The upper layers of a leaf allow sunlight to pass through and reach the middle layer, where photosynthesis takes place. A broad, flat leaf has a large surface area, which provides more area over which sunlight may enter the leaf and reach the mesophyll beneath. Choice C is correct.

IT'S YOUR TURN

Please read each question carefully. For a multiple-choice question, circle the letter of the correct response. For a constructed-response question, write your answers on the lines.

1 Which sequence is arranged from simplest to most complex?

A squamous cell → epithelial tissue → skin → integumentary system → human

B squamous cell → skin → integumentary system → epithelial tissue → human

C human → integumentary system → squamous cell → skin → epithelial tissue

D human → squamous cell → skin → epithelial tissue → integumentary system

2 Two types of tissues that compose the stomach organ are epithelial and connective. Which function of epithelial tissues distinguishes them from connective tissues?

A They support and link to other tissues.

B They churn and move food through the stomach.

C They transmit messages rapidly through the body.

D They line the inner and outer surfaces of the stomach.

Use the diagram below to answer question 3.

ORGAN SYSTEMS IN A FISH

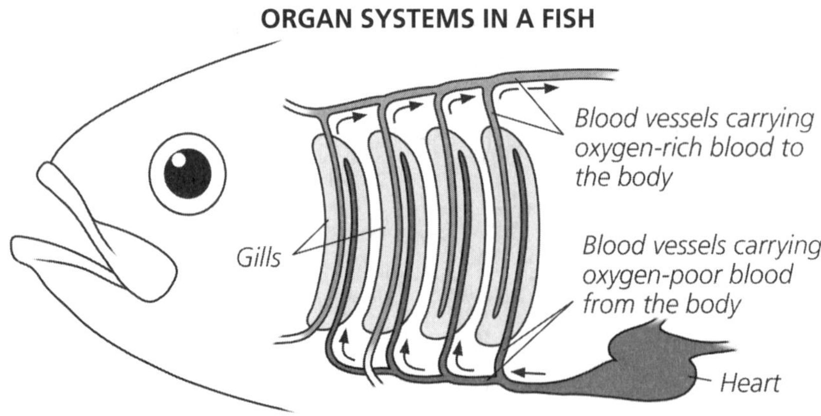

3 What function do these organ systems in the fish perform together?

A digestion

B locomotion

C obtaining energy

D exchanging gases

Use the diagram below to answer question 4.

FRESHWATER PROTIST

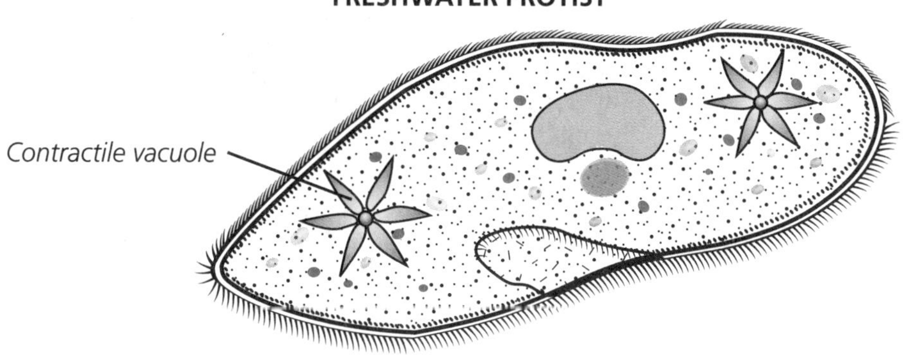

4 The diagram shows a single-celled freshwater protist. The contractile vacuole pumps water out of the cell.

A Describe how the function of the contractile vacuole helps the protist stay alive.

____

____

____

____

B Describe how the same function is carried out in animals. Identify at least one organ or system involved in this function.

____

____

____

____

C Describe how the same (or a similar) function is carried out in plants. Identify at least one organ, structure, or cell type involved in this function.

____

____

____

____

Use the diagram below to answer question 5.

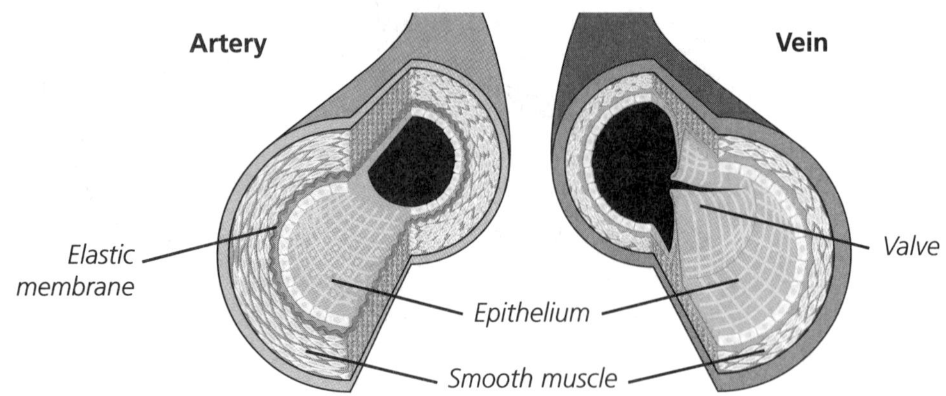

5 The heart pumps blood forcefully through the arteries, which branch into smaller and smaller vessels until they form the smallest vessels, the microscopic capillaries. Minerals, nutrients, and dissolved gases pass between capillary blood and the cells of the body. After capillary networks pass through tissues, these vessels merge to form veins, which return the blood to the heart. The diagram above shows cross sections of an artery and a vein.

A Describe how the structures of arteries are specialized for their particular function.

____

____

____

____

B Describe how the structures of veins are specialized for their particular function.

____

____

____

____

C Describe how the function of capillaries is made possible by their structure.

____

____

____

____

Module A
Cells and Cell Processes

Unit 2
The Chemical Basis for Life

Life processes depend on particular molecules and their chemical interactions. This unit will help you review the molecules important to life and the structures and functions of four categories of biological macromolecules.

1 Unique Properties of Water The unique properties of water support life on Earth. In this lesson, you will review the chemical and physical properties that make this molecule so important to living organisms.

2 Organic Molecules: Lipids and Carbohydrates The chemistry of living things is based on carbon. In this lesson, you will review the structure and function of the carbon atom and the characteristics that make it ideal for the formation of biological macromolecules. You will also review the structures and functions of lipids and carbohydrates.

3 Organic Molecules: DNA and Proteins Biological macromolecules include DNA and proteins. In this lesson, you will review the structures and functions of proteins and nucleic acids.

4 Enzymes Enzymes function as catalysts to regulate specific biochemical reactions. In this lesson, you will review what enzymes are, how they carry out their function, and the specific factors that limit their function.

Unique Properties of Water

BIO.A.2.1.1

Life on Earth, as we know it, could not exist without water. Water is one of the most important, stable, and abundant molecules found in living things. The many millions of reactions that take place in the cell involve substances dissolved in water.

The Molecular Structure of Water

Many of water's properties are a result of its molecular structure. A water molecule consists of two hydrogen atoms and one oxygen atom, held together by *covalent bonds.* This type of bond forms between atoms that share electrons. However, the atoms in a covalent bond do not always share electrons equally. In water, the oxygen atom pulls on the electrons more strongly than the hydrogen atoms do. This unequal sharing describes a polar covalent bond.

Because electrons spend more time near the oxygen atom, they give this part of the water molecule a partial negative charge. The hydrogen atoms, in contrast, gain partial positive charges. Although the entire molecule is neutral, different parts of it carry different charges. For this reason, water is described as a *polar* molecule.

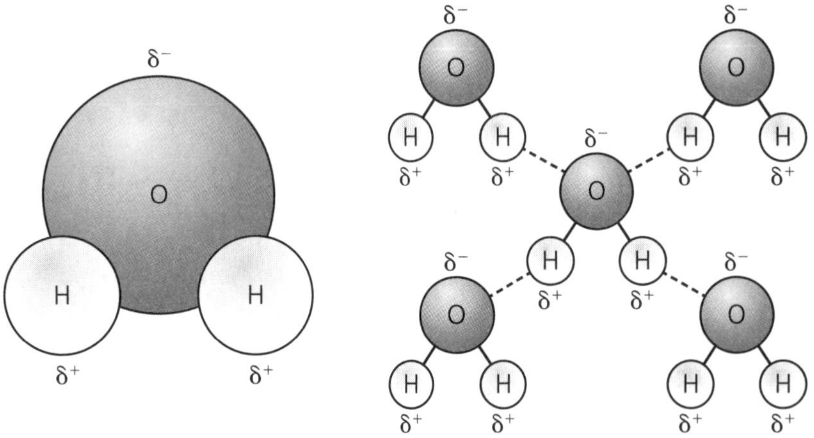

A water molecule has partially charged regions, which form hydrogen bond interactions between molecules.

Because they are polar, water molecules form *hydrogen bond interactions* with each other. In a volume of water, the positive regions of one water molecule attract the negative region of a neighboring water molecule. Hydrogen bond interactions are responsible for many of the unique and important properties of water.

Most of an organism's cells are made up of water. The average human body is up to 65% water.

Covalent bonding occurs when atoms share electrons.

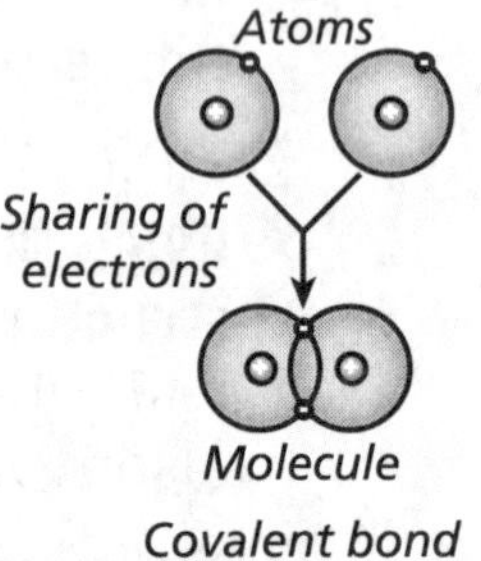

Covalent bond

Remember that electrons are negatively charged.

A *polar* molecule has regions of opposite partial charge. It is called *partial* because it is not the full charge that results when an electron is completely gained or lost.

Opposite charges attract. Like charges repel.

A *hydrogen bond* is not a true bond, like the covalent bonds between atoms. For this reason, it is called a *bond interaction.*

Explain why two water molecules probably will **not** occur as shown in the diagram below.

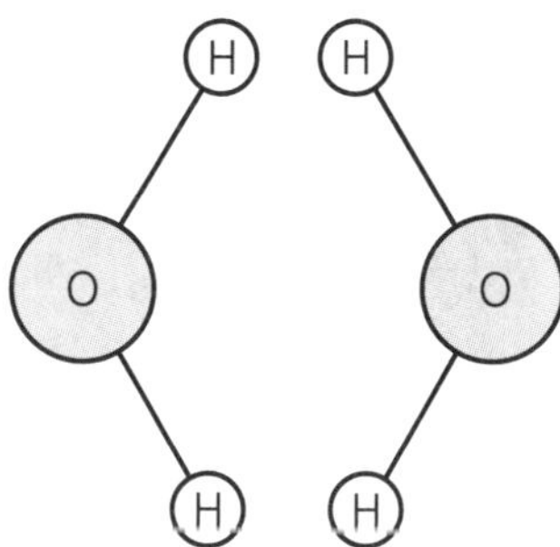

The partial positive charges of the hydrogen atoms repel each other, making it unlikely that water molecules will be arranged in this way. The opposite partial charges of the hydrogen and oxygen atoms attract each other, and so these regions will likely be found together between water molecules.

Water, the (Nearly) Universal Solvent

Table salt is an *ionic* compound, meaning that it is composed of two ions with opposite charges (Na^+, Cl^-). When mixed with water, a salt crystal dissolves into charged ions as water molecules surround them. The ability of water to dissolve ionic compounds is essential to life. The proper concentrations of ions such as calcium, potassium, sodium, and chloride are essential to the functioning of cells.

Because water is a polar molecule, it also dissolves other polar molecules. Many important molecules in the cell are polar. Because water can dissolve many different polar and ionic substances, it is known as the *universal solvent.* The rule of solubility is that "like dissolves like." Table sugar is a common example of a polar molecule, which dissolves easily in water.

However, some substances do not dissolve easily in water. **Lipids** are composed of nonpolar molecules and are therefore insoluble in water. Lipids make up the plasma membrane of the cell, creating an effective barrier to the surrounding watery environment.

An *ion* is an atom with a positive or negative charge.

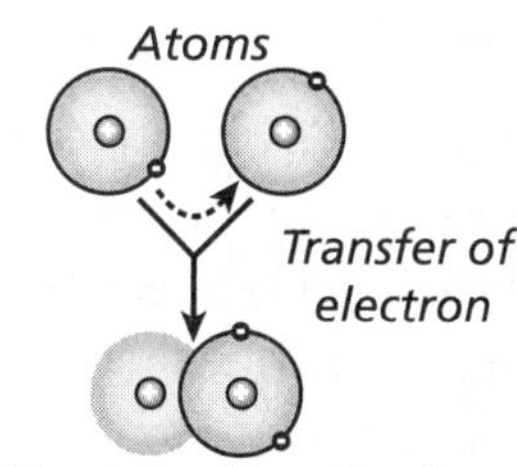

Solubility is the ability of one substance, the *solute,* to dissolve in another substance, the *solvent.*

Lipids include fats and oils and are nonpolar. Nonpolar molecules may be described as *hydrophobic,* or "water-fearing."

Salt is dissolved by water, resulting in positive sodium ions and negative chlorine ions. Which diagrams shows how water molecules orient themselves around the ions?

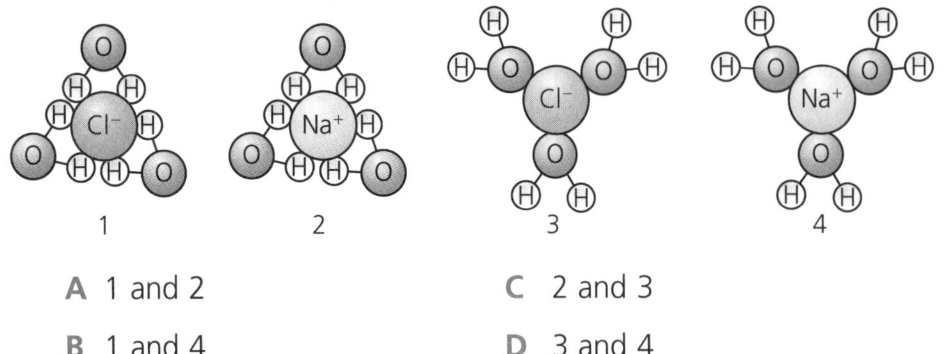

A 1 and 2

B 1 and 4

C 2 and 3

D 3 and 4

The partial positive region of the water molecule will be attracted to the negative chlorine ion (Cl^-). The hydrogen atoms have a partial positive charge. The partial negative region of the water molecule will be attracted to the positive sodium ion (Na^+). The oxygen atom has a partial negative charge. Choice B, diagrams 1 and 4, is correct.

Adhesion and Cohesion

Hydrogen bonding interactions between water molecules give water the property of **cohesion.** That is, water sticks to itself. Cohesion causes high *surface tension,* meaning that more force is required to break the surface of a liquid. You have probably seen droplets or beads of water form from moisture in the air. Water forms beads because surface tension resists other forces, such as gravity, that work to break the surface.

In contrast, **adhesion** is the tendency of water to stick to substances other than itself. Adhesion is due to hydrogen bonding interactions between water molecules and non-water molecules. For example, water will adhere to the sides of a glass tube, forming a *meniscus.*

Thanks to cohesion and adhesion, tall plants are able to move water from their roots to the tops of their shoots, defying gravity. Plants conduct water through interconnected, tube-like cells. When water on an upper leaf evaporates, the water just below it is pulled up to take its place. All the water molecules, down to the roots, are pulled along, too. This movement of water is caused by cohesion between water molecules and the adhesion of water to the cell walls. The ability of a liquid to flow against gravity in a narrow space, such as a thin tube, is called *capillary action,* or *capillarity.*

Cohesion is the tendency of water molecules to attract each other and stick together.

Surface tension helps keep the surface of water intact.

Adhesion is the tendency of water molecules to stick to other surfaces.

A *meniscus* is a curve of water near the surface due to the adhesive force between the water molecules and the container.

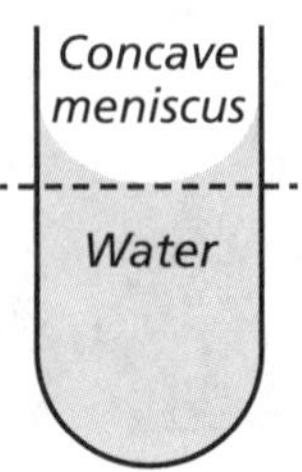

The ability of the water strider insects shown here helps them to escape predators. Using the properties of water, explain how this is possible.

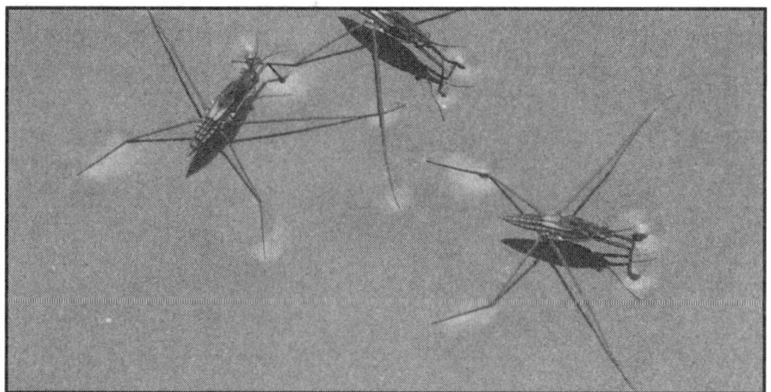

Water has high cohesion due to hydrogen bonding interactions. This results in a high surface tension. The weight of the water strider is not great enough to overcome the surface tension of the water. However, the weight of a larger predator would be great enough to overcome this force, causing the predator to sink into the water.

Water and Heat Energy

If you have visited the beach on a summer day, the water may have felt cooler or hotter than the air. Water has a high capacity to absorb and retain heat, known as **specific heat.** Compared to other substances, water requires more heat energy for its temperature to change. Early in the summer, ocean water has not absorbed enough heat for its temperature to rise very much. Water also releases heat energy slowly. Late in the summer, ocean water will be warm because it has not cooled as quickly as the rest of the environment.

Bodies of water absorb and release heat slowly, creating a more moderate environment for organisms. This same property of water makes it easier for an organism to control its body temperature. A large amount of heat can be gained or lost before body temperature changes. Cold-blooded animals can absorb enough heat during the day to last them through the night. Warm-blooded animals can more easily maintain a constant internal temperature.

When a liquid absorbs enough heat, it begins to evaporate, changing to a gas. The amount of heat needed for water to evaporate, its *heat of vaporization,* is high. When people perspire, water on the skin absorbs heat as it evaporates. This is why sweating is such an effective way of cooling down.

Similarly, water must lose a large amount of heat before it freezes. This is water's *heat of fusion.* This means that, even if the temperature of the air changes drastically, water will resist the change and provide a more stable environment for aquatic organisms. Organisms can lose large amounts of heat before they freeze.

Specific heat is the amount of heat energy needed to increase the temperature of one unit of a substance.

Note that temperature is not the same thing as heat. Adding equal amounts of heat to different substances can have different effects on their temperatures.

Water has one of the highest specific heat capacities of any substance. For example, it takes five times as much heat to raise the temperature of a gram of water by 1°C as it does for a gram of sand.

Remember that animal cells are about 65% water.

Heat of vaporization is the heat absorbed when water changes from liquid to vapor.

Heat of fusion is the heat released when liquid water freezes to ice.

Scientists debate whether dinosaurs were warm-blooded or cold-blooded. One position is that some dinosaurs were "accidentally" warm-blooded due their large size. Explain how this could be possible.

Animal bodies are 65% water. Because water can retain heat well, a large animal would have a large reserve of heat in its body. Once warm, the dinosaur body would remain warm for a long period.

Water and Density

Water has one more unusual property: it has a greater *density* as a liquid than as a solid. When liquid water reaches its **freezing point,** the water molecules arrange themselves into an orderly structure, leaving more space between them. The same amount of matter takes up more volume (space), making it less dense.

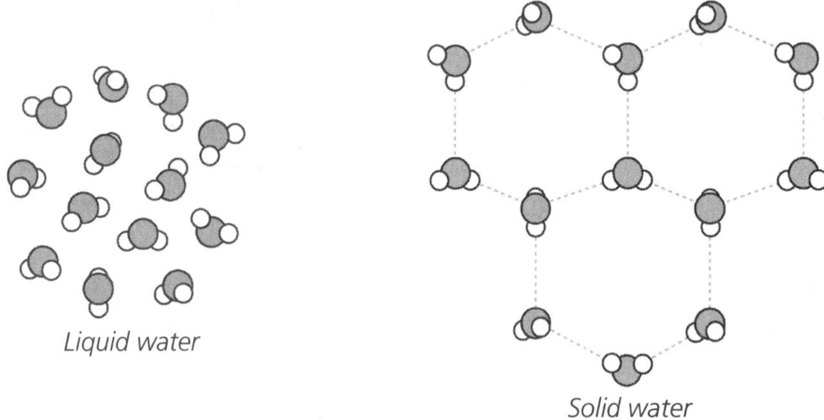

Molecules of liquid water and of ice (solid water) differ in the amount of space between them.

Because ice is less dense than liquid water, it floats on the surface of ponds and other bodies of water. As temperatures drop in winter, streams and lakes freeze from the top, down. The less-dense ice remains above the denser liquid water. It also acts as an insulating barrier for the water below it. It is therefore possible for smaller bodies of water not to freeze completely and for aquatic organisms to survive cold winters.

Density is the mass of a substance divided by its volume:

$$\text{Density} = \frac{\text{mass}}{\text{Volume}}$$

For equal masses, a less-dense substance takes up a larger volume.

Most substances are less dense as liquids than solids. Water is an exception.

Think of a bottle of oil-and-vinegar salad dressing. The less-dense oil floats above the denser vinegar.

Freezing point is the temperature at which a liquid becomes a solid. The freezing point of water is 0°C, or 32°F. This is also called its *melting point.*

When leafy, green vegetables are frozen and then thawed, their texture changes. Explain why freezing causes this change.

Plant cells contain a high percentage of water, particularly in the central vacuole. When frozen, the density of the water decreases and the ice takes up a larger volume inside the cell. This causes the cell wall to burst and results in leafy vegetables losing their "crunch."

IT'S YOUR TURN

Please read each question carefully. For a multiple-choice question, circle the letter of the correct response. For a constructed-response question, write your answers on the lines.

1 Which property of water molecules explains the other properties listed below?

A adhesion

B cohesion

C hydrogen bond

D polar covalent bond

2 One property of water that makes it unique is its density. Which example describes a result of this property?

A Polar bears float on ice floes to hunt for food.

B Trees transport water from their roots to their leaves.

C Water strider insects walk on the surface of pond water.

D Plants receive enough light to grow under the surface of a lake.

Use the picture below to answer question 3.

3 The picture shows water droplets hanging on the tips of pine needles. How do the physical properties of water result in the image shown?

A Cohesion allows droplets to form, and adhesion keeps the droplets on the needles.

B Adhesion allows droplets to form, and cohesion keeps the droplets on the needles.

C Cohesion allows droplets to form, and capillarity keeps the droplets on the needles.

D Adhesion allows droplets to form, and capillarity keeps the droplets on the needles.

4 **Which statement correctly describes one way that the properties of water affect heat and temperature?**

A Water retains more heat than other materials, making coastal ecosystems warmer year-round.

B Water absorbs heat when it freezes, helping to insulate lakes and ponds from cold temperatures.

C Water absorbs heat when it changes to vapor, helping to keep animals cool through perspiration.

D Water retains less heat than other materials, keeping aquatic ecosystems cooler than those on land.

5 **A tree absorbs water from its roots and loses water that evaporates from leaves. Inside the tree, capillary action allows water to flow upwards through tissue called *xylem*, which is composed of tubes made from cell walls.**

A **Identify and explain how two (2) properties of water contribute to capillary action within the xylem.**

____

____

____

____

____

____

B **A tree can experience *cavitation*, which occurs when a bubble of air forms inside a xylem tube. Explain how cavitation affects a tree's ability to conduct water.**

____

____

____

____

Organic Molecules: Lipids and Carbohydrates

BIO.A.2.2.1, BIO.A.2.2.2, BIO.A.2.2.3

You may have heard the phrase "carbon-based life form." Actually, all life on Earth is carbon based because this element forms the compounds that make up cells and organisms. **Organic compounds** contain carbon and hydrogen, often along with oxygen, nitrogen, phosphorus, or other elements.

Organic compounds contain carbon atoms bonded to hydrogen atoms.

The Uniqueness of Carbon

When atoms share electrons, they form covalent bonds. Elements differ in the number of covalent bonds they can form. Think of drink cup holders with different numbers of slots for cups. A hydrogen atom is a single cup holder—it can form just a single covalent bond with another atom. An atom of oxygen can form up to two bonds; it is a two-cup holder. A carbon atom is a deluxe cup holder with four slots—the most of any element!

Covalent bonds may be single, double, or triple bonds. In a single bond, one pair of electrons is shared between the atoms. In a double bond, two pairs are shared, and three pairs are shared in a triple bond.

A carbon atom is most stable when all four of its slots are filled. The simplest organic molecule, methane, is a carbon atom singly bonded to four hydrogen atoms. Single bonds fill all four slots. But carbon can also form double or triple bonds. A carbon atom doubly bonded to two oxygen atoms forms carbon dioxide. Carbon can even form a triple bond, as in the acetylene molecule. Notice that the hydrogen atoms in acetylene fill the remaining slots for each carbon atom.

BONDS IN CARBON MOLECULES

Compound	Formula	Molecule
Methane	CH_4	H, C, H, H, H
Carbon dioxide	CO_2	O, C, O
Acetylene	C_2H_2	H, C, C, H

Carbon is unique in that a single atom can form up to four covalent bonds.

The diagram shows part of a carbon compound. Its hydrogen atoms are not shown. How many hydrogen atoms are needed to make up one molecule of the compound?

$$C = C - C$$

A 5

B 6

C 7

D 8

The left-hand carbon forms one double bond. It can therefore form two single bonds with hydrogen atoms. The central carbon forms a double and a single bond. It is able to form one more single bond to a hydrogen atom. The right-hand carbon atom forms a single bond with the central carbon and has the capacity for three more single bonds. The total number of hydrogen atoms is 2 + 1 + 3 = 6, choice B.

Carbon's unique structure allows the formation of **macromolecules,** large, complex molecules such as lipids, carbohydrates, proteins, and nucleic acids.

Macromolecules are large, complex molecules made of chains of smaller molecules.

Lipids: Fats and Oils

Lipids include fats, oils, waxes, and sterols (such as cholesterol). Fats and oils share the same basic structure: *fatty acid* "tails" connected to a single *glycerol* molecule. A fatty acid is a long chain of carbon atoms connected to each other by single or double bonds. Lipids consist almost entirely of carbon and hydrogen atoms, with very few oxygen atoms.

Because lipids are nonpolar molecules, they are not soluble in water.

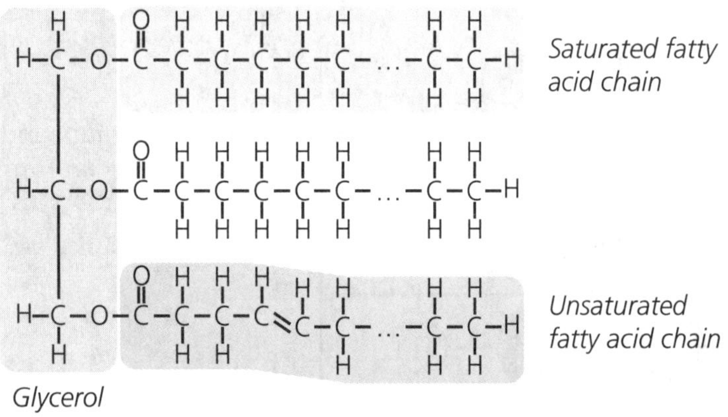

Saturated fatty acid chain

Unsaturated fatty acid chain

Glycerol

This lipid molecule consists of glycerol attached to three fatty acid chains. Note the difference between the saturated and the unsaturated fatty acids.

In fats and oils, a single *glycerol* molecule is attached to three long *fatty acid* chains. Because they are not made up of repeating subunits, lipids are not considered polymers.

Fatty acids may be saturated or unsaturated. In a saturated fatty acid, the carbon atoms have the maximum number of single bonds (and hydrogen atoms). An unsaturated fatty acid has fewer than the maximum number of bonds. That is, it has one or more double bonds.

Lipids have the following important functions:

- **Energy storage—**Organisms may convert other organic molecules to lipids for long-term storage. For example, your body's *adipose* tissue is made up of cells with special compartments that store lipids.
- **Cell membranes—**Phospholipids help to form the plasma and organelle membranes of the cell. A phospholipid contains a polar phosphate group attached to glycerol.
- **Insulation and protection—**Fats help to insulate the body and provide vital cushioning to major organs. Waxes coat and protect some organisms.
- **Chemical messengers—**Another class of lipids, the *sterols,* act as chemical messengers or hormones. Cholesterol is the basic molecule from which estrogen, progesterone, and testosterone are made.

A double bond causes a fatty acid chain to kink or bend. This makes the lipid more likely to melt at room temperature. Explain whether fats (solids at room temperature) or oils (liquid) are more likely to have saturated fatty acids.

While a saturated fatty acid chain is straight, an unsaturated fatty acid chain has a double bond, which causes it to bend. This makes it more difficult for the lipid to take on a rigid, tightly packed, solid form. Since fats tend to be solid at room temperature, they are more likely to have fully saturated fatty acids. Oils tend to have unsaturated fatty acids.

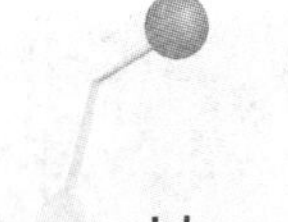

Fats and oils provide 9 Calories of energy per gram. Unsaturated fats are thought to be healthier than saturated fats.

Adipose tissue is the tissue found in your body that helps to store "fat."

Some insects have a waxy coating to keep them from getting wet in rainy weather. Plant leaves have a waxy cuticle to prevent water loss.

Sterols are lipid molecules that act as chemical messengers within your body.

Phospholipids

The plasma membrane is made up of *phospholipids*. Two fatty acid chains make up the nonpolar "tails" while the phosphate group is the polar "head." The lipids in cell membranes make them impermeable to water; water cannot cross the membrane directly, but must go through special protein channels.

Phospholipids **are the major component of cell membranes. Because the lipid portion is nonpolar, it is impermeable to water.**

Polar phosphate head

Glycerol

Nonpolar fatty acid tail

A phospholipid molecule consists of a polar "head" region and a nonpolar "tail."

The plasma membrane is made up of a phospholipid bilayer, or two sheets of phospholipids. Given the structure of a phospholipid, how are these sheets arranged in the plasma membrane?

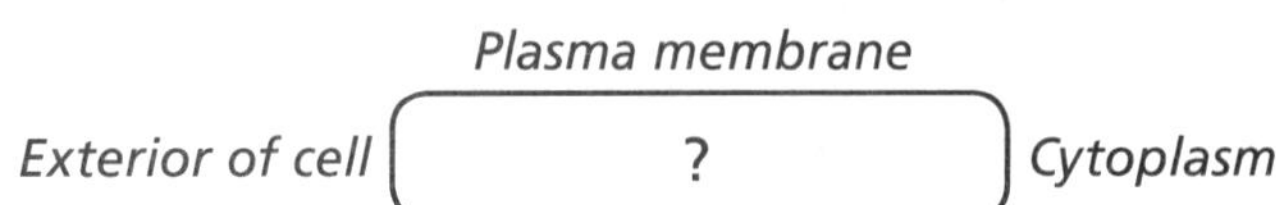

A head•tail—head•tail

B head•tail—tail•head

C tail•head—tail•head

D tail•head—head•tail

Both the exterior of the cell and the cytoplasm are water solutions. Therefore, the polar phosphate "heads" will be oriented toward the outer sides of the membrane. The nonpolar, hydrophobic fatty acid "tails" will be on the inside of the membrane, away from water. Choice B is correct.

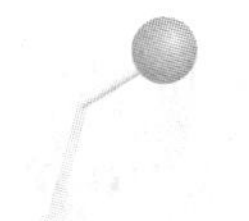

Carbohydrates

Carbohydrates consist of carbon, hydrogen, and oxygen, in a 1:2:1 ratio. Glucose, the compound used by cells for energy, is the simplest type of carbohydrate, a *monosaccharide.* Monosaccharides with six carbon atoms all have the molecular formula $C_6H_{12}O_6$. The carbon and oxygen atoms often form the basic structure, a ring. Monosaccharides also include the *isomers* fructose and galactose.

Glucose *Fructose*

Glucose and fructose are six-carbon monosaccharides.

The table sugar you're familiar with is a *disaccharide* called sucrose. Disaccharides consist of two monosaccharides joined in a double-ring structure. In the case of sucrose, the monosaccharides are glucose and fructose.

A **carbohydrate** is a macromolecule made of carbon, hydrogen, and oxygen, that cells use for energy.

A gram of carbohydrate provides 4 Calories of energy.

Carbohydrates contain proportionally more oxygen than lipids do. The generic formula for a monosaccharide is $C_nH_{2n}O_n$.

Isomers have the same molecular formula but different arrangements of atoms.

Two monosaccharides join to form a *disaccharide.*

Polysaccharides

Small organic molecules such as monosaccharides may be linked up in chains of many hundreds to create much larger macromolecules. These basic building block units are **monomers,** and they join together to form large *polymers.* Glucose is an important monomer. Many glucose molecules link together to form *polysaccharides,* such as starch, glycogen, and cellulose.

Starch is a complex carbohydrate produced by plants to store energy. Starch molecules may be extremely long, straight chains of glucose, or chains with multiple branches. Sources of starch include wheat, rice, and potatoes.

Glycogen is the human body's equivalent of starch, found in the liver and muscles. Glycogen is broken down into glucose when energy is required. It is more highly branching than plant starch, and forms around a central kernel of protein.

Cellulose is a structural carbohydrate that makes up plant cell walls. It functions to strengthen and support the plant cell. This polysaccharide can be broken down by very few organisms.

Monomers are smaller building block molecules that combine through chemical reactions to form large polymers.

Polysaccharides include glycogen, starch, and cellulose. Glycogen has chains that branch off in many directions, while starch is more linear.

Like lipids, carbohydrates also have many different functions:

- **Cellular respiration—**Carbohydrates are digested to glucose, which enter cells to be used in cellular respiration.
- **Energy storage—**Glycogen and starch store energy for animals and plants, respectively. Glycogen in the muscles and liver can be broken down into glucose. Plant starches, such a wheat, potatoes, and corn, can be ingested for energy.
- **Structure—**Cellulose strengthens the plant cell walls.

Because of how the glucose monomers are linked, cellulose is not digestible by most animals. It is therefore a good source of indigestible fiber in the diet.

Compare 100 Calories' worth of table sugar and 100 Calories' worth of baked potato.

Table sugar is a disaccharide while potato consists of a polysaccharide, starch. Starch is a macromolecule. Both are similar in that they are composed of monosaccharides. Both contain glucose, although table sugar also contains fructose. Both are carbohydrates and provide 4 Calories per gram. Both consist of the elements carbon, hydrogen, and oxygen.

Reactions That Make or Break Macromolecules

In organisms, specific chemical reactions join monomers together and break polymers apart. The first is called *dehydration synthesis,* and it occurs when two monomers join together. For monosaccharides, two –OH groups join together, losing two hydrogen atoms and one oxygen atom. The two monomers are now linked and one molecule of water (H_2O) is created. Multiple rounds of dehydration synthesis create large macromolecules from small monomers. This reaction also joins fatty acids to a glycerol molecule, which has three –OH groups.

Dehydration synthesis joins monomers together to form large polymers. Water is produced as a by-product of the reaction. Some textbooks call this a *condensation reaction.*

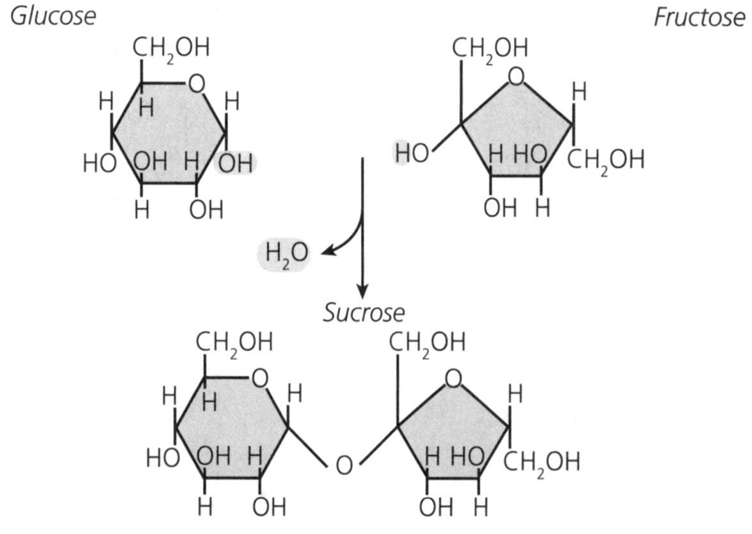

Glucose

CH_2OH O H H H HO OH H OH H OH

Fructose

CH_2OH O H HO H HO CH_2OH OH H

H_2O

Sucrose

CH_2OH O H H H HO OH H O CH_2OH O H H HO CH_2OH H OH OH H

In these diagrams, the carbon atoms are not all labeled. They also occur at any unlabeled angles between straight lines.

Dehydration synthesis produces sucrose from glucose and fructose. It also produces a water molecule.

When organisms need to break down polymers into monomers, they use a chemical reaction called *hydrolysis*. A molecule of water is used to add back the –OH group and hydrogen atom to the monomers. As a result, the chemical bond between the monomers is broken. Hydrolysis is the reverse of dehydration synthesis.

Hydrolysis reactions break down polymers into smaller monomers. The root term *hydro* means "water" and *lysis* means "to loosen or release."

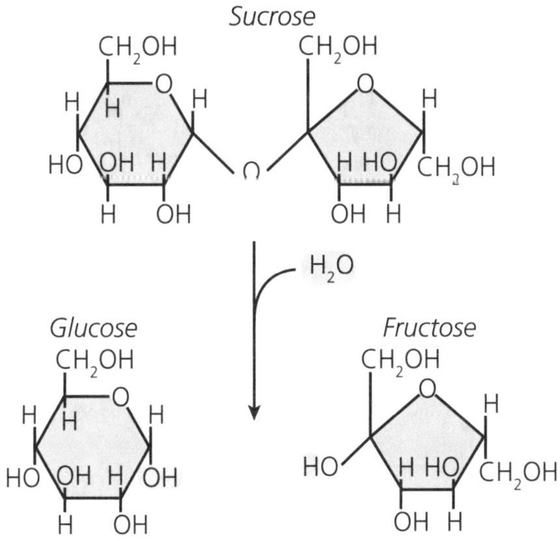

Sucrose

H_2O

Glucose

Fructose

Water is required for the hydrolysis of sucrose.

In a cell, 132 glucose monomers are joined to form a straight chain of starch. Explain how the number of water molecules changes.

Dehydration synthesis joins monomers together to form polymers, producing water. If 132 monomers are joined, the dehydration synthesis reaction must occur 131 times. Therefore, 131 new water molecules form.

IT'S YOUR TURN

Please read each question carefully. For a multiple-choice question, circle the letter of the correct response. For a constructed-response question, write your answers on the lines.

1 A single atom of carbon is joined to a hydrogen atom. What is the maximum number of double bonds the carbon atom may yet form?

A 1

B 2

C 3

D 4

2 Which of the following types of compounds is unlike the other three?

A wax

B saturated fat

C phospholipid

D polysaccharide

3 Which of the following is **not** created as a result of dehydration synthesis?

A cellulose

B disaccharide

C glucose

D water

Use the diagram below to answer question 4.

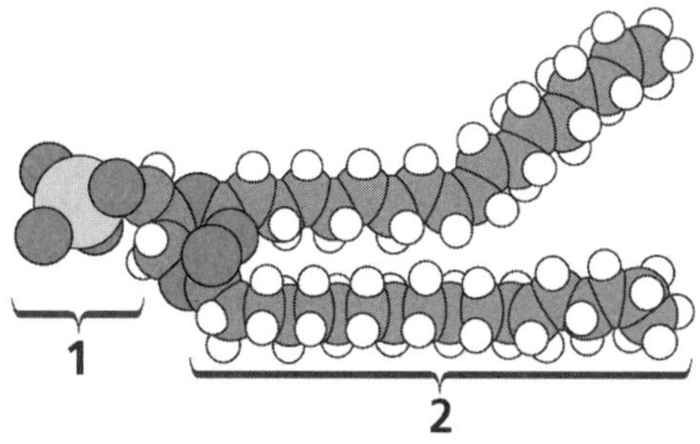

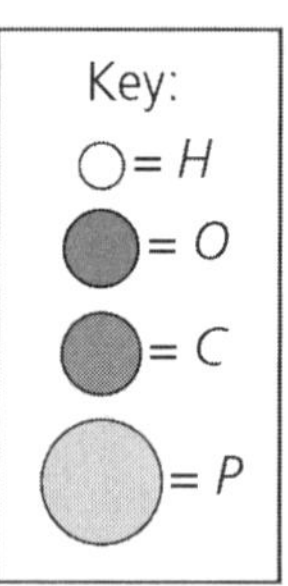

4 The diagram shows a molecule with regions numbered 1 and 2. Which statement correctly describes the molecule?

A Region 1 is composed of fatty acids and is polar.

B Region 1 is composed of phosphate and is nonpolar.

C Region 2 is composed of phosphate and is polar.

D Region 2 is composed of fatty acids and is nonpolar.

5 Lipids, such as fats and oils, play important roles in living organisms. Carbohydrates also carry out essential functions in living things.

A Describe the general structure of a fat or oil molecule.

B Describe how the structures of fats and oils differ from the structure of carbohydrates.

C Describe how a function of fats and oils is similar to a function of carbohydrates.

LESSON 3 Organic Molecules: DNA and Proteins

BIO.A.2.2.2, BIO.A.2.2.3

The major classes of macromolecules are carbohydrates, lipids, nucleic acids, and proteins. Nucleic acids and proteins play very active roles in the structure and function of cells. Both types of molecules are polymers made up of similar, but not identical, monomers.

Some macromolecules are polymers made up of repeating subunits called monomers.

Nucleic Acids: DNA and RNA

Some of the most important polymers in living cells are the **nucleic acids,** DNA and RNA. These polymers are made up of monomers called *nucleotides.* Each nucleotide consists of three parts: a phosphate group, a 5-carbon sugar, and a variable nitrogenous base. As a result, instead of being exactly identical, the nucleotides come in four different varieties or "flavors": adenine (A), cytosine (C), guanine (G), and thymine (T). (RNA has uracil, U, instead of thymine.) Like letters of an alphabet making up a story, the four nucleotides allow RNA and DNA to encode information—genetic information.

A **nucleic acid,** DNA or RNA, is a macromolecule that carries genetic information.

DNA is deoxyribonucleic acid and **RNA** is ribonucleic acid.

Nucleotides are the building blocks, or monomers, of nucleic acids. They are composed of carbon, hydrogen, nitrogen, oxygen, and phosphorus.

The nitrogenous bases of nucleotides vary. They determine whether each nucleotide is an A, T, C, or G.

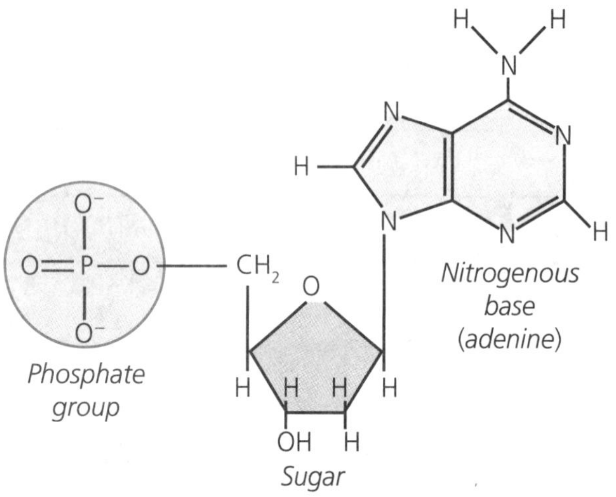

Nucleotides all have three similar components: a sugar, a phosphate group, and a variable nitrogenous base.

The nucleotides that make up DNA differ slightly from those in RNA in several ways:

- **5-carbon sugar—**RNA nucleotides contain ribose instead of deoxyribose.
- **Uracil—**This nucleotide is used in RNA instead of thymine.
- **Double vs. single strand—**While DNA is usually found as a double-stranded molecule, RNA is usually a single strand.

Deoxyribose and ribose are 5-carbon sugars, or monosaccharides.

A nucleic acid polymer is made by joining the phosphate group of one nucleotide to the sugar of a second nucleotide, through a dehydration synthesis reaction. This forms a chain of repeating phosphate groups and 5-carbon sugars. The nitrogenous bases are not involved in forming the chain, but simply jut out from one side of it.

Nucleic acids have a phosphate-sugar backbone. The nucleotide monomers are joined by dehydration synthesis.

The bases do, however, participate in another, critical type of bonding: nucleotides form hydrogen bonds with other nucleotides. Hydrogen bonding between two DNA strands forms the DNA double strand. However, for this to occur, the two strands must be *complementary*. That is, each type of nucleotide must pair with its "partner" type on the other strand: A with T and G with C. The same type of hydrogen bonding allows RNA to pair with DNA. In this case, uracil (U) bonds with adenine (A). Hydrogen bond interactions between the complementary bases bind the nucleic acid strands together.

In *complementary* DNA strands, the A of one strand forms a hydrogen bond with the T of the opposite strand. C and G also pair in this way. In RNA, U takes the place of T.

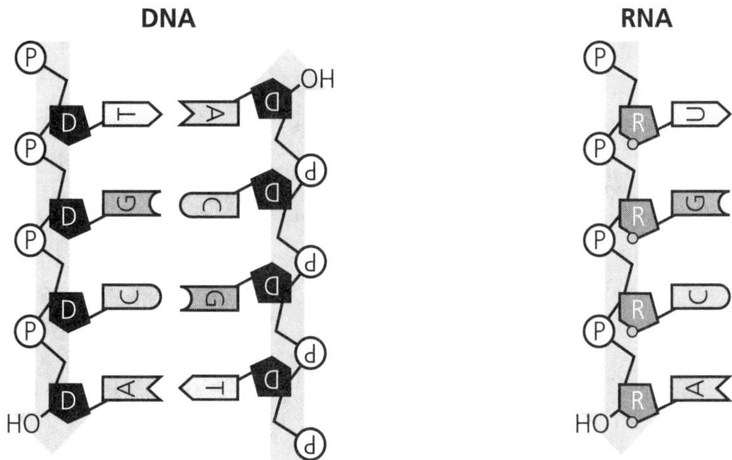

Both DNA and RNA share a phosphate-sugar backbone. DNA is usually found as a double strand. Its nitrogenous bases pair with complementary bases on the partner strand.

Hydrogen bond interactions hold the two strands of DNA together to form the double strand. These bonds are easily broken and reformed, allowing the DNA strands to be easily separated whenever necessary.

Nucleic acids have the following functions:

- **Encoding genetic information**—DNA encodes the genetic information of the cell. It makes up the chromosomes found in the nucleus. Genes provide specific instructions for making the proteins the organisms need to carry out all of life's chemical reactions and cellular functions.
- **Protein synthesis**—RNA transports genetic information to ribosomes for the production of proteins.
- **Composing ribosomes**—These organelles are made up of RNA and proteins.

Which is **not** found in both RNA and DNA?

A ribose sugar

B phosphate group

C nitrogenous base

D guanine nucleotide

Both DNA and RNA contain phosphate groups, nitrogenous bases, and guanine nucleotides; choices B, C, and D are incorrect. Choice A is correct because the ribose sugar is found only in RNA molecules.

Proteins

Proteins are important polymers that perform a variety of functions within living organisms. Proteins help living organisms to catalyze reactions, transport molecules, copy and synthesize DNA, and communicate between cells.

Proteins consist of long, straight chains of *amino acid* molecules linked together. Amino acids are all composed of the same amino, carboxyl, and central carbon structure. Like nucleotides, however, amino acids are not all identical. The R group is the variable part of the monomer. Most cells use 20 different amino acids.

Peptide bonds join amino acids through dehydration synthesis reactions. Notice how a water molecule is formed from the –OH group of one monomer and the hydrogen atom of the next monomer. A single *polypeptide* chain can be many hundreds of amino acids in length.

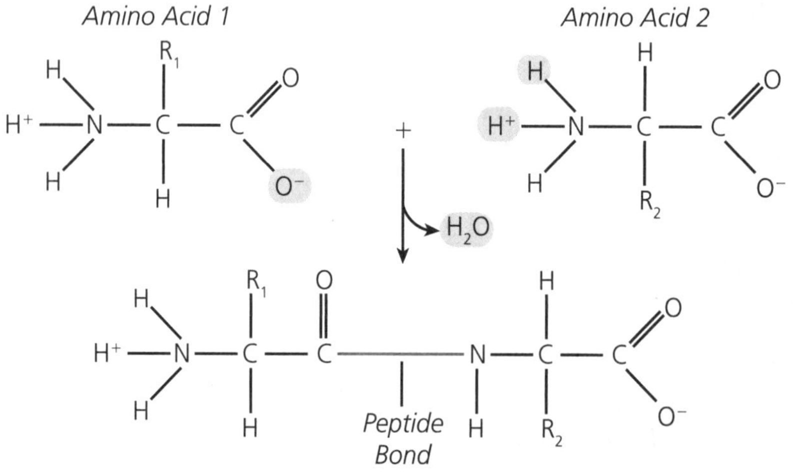

Amino Acid 1

Amino Acid 2

H_2O

Peptide Bond

Two amino acids join to form a peptide bond through dehydration synthesis. A water molecule is a by-product.

Proteins are macromolecules that perform structural and regulatory functions for cells.

Amino acids are the building blocks, or monomers, of proteins. Amino acids contain nitrogen, as well as carbon, hydrogen, and oxygen.

Some R groups are polar; others are nonpolar.

A *peptide bond* joins amino acids.

Dehydration synthesis reactions join amino acids to make peptides.

Dehydration reactions break down peptides into amino acids.

However, polypeptide chains do not branch; they are single lines of amino acids, similar to a necklace made of beads. In order to give proteins the three-dimensional structure needed to function, polypeptide chains must bend and fold in various ways. One or more polypeptides, folded into a specific three-dimensional structure, make up the protein.

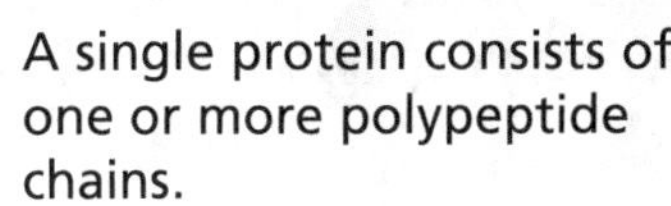

A single protein consists of one or more polypeptide chains.

Proteins have important roles in the following:

- **Cell structures—**Proteins provide much of the structure of the cell, making up the cytoskeleton of eukaryotic cells.
- **Animal structures—**Proteins make up hair, nails, and muscles.
- **Cell function—**Proteins in the cell membrane help determine which substances enter or exit the cell.
- **Enzymes—**Some proteins are enzymes, which help carry out specific chemical reactions. Without enzymes, many of the reactions within the cell would not occur quickly enough to support life.

Explain how many thousands of different types of proteins, with diverse structures and functions, can be assembled from just 20 types of amino acids.

Amino acids are building blocks that can be joined together in many different combinations and sequences to make up polypeptide chains of different lengths. These polypeptides can join together in different ways and take on different three-dimensional structures to form proteins. Therefore, a great variety of proteins can be assembled from just 20 types of amino acids.

IT'S YOUR TURN

Please read each question carefully. For a multiple-choice question, circle the letter of the correct response. For a constructed-response question, write your answers on the lines.

1 Which term refers to the molecule shown?

A nucleotide

B amino acid

C polypeptide

D nitrogen base

2 Which pair of terms is **not** correctly matched?

A deoxyribose: RNA

B polypeptide: protein

C nitrogenous base: DNA

D amino acid: polypeptide

Use the diagram below to answer question 3.

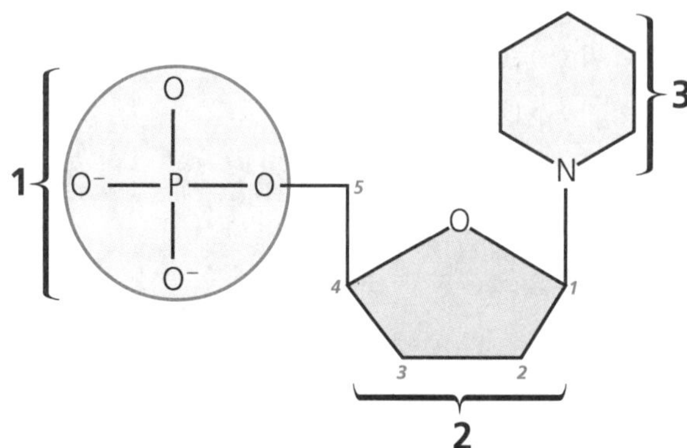

3 Which statement about the part of the molecule labeled 3 is correct?

A It comes in twenty different varieties.

B It is the same for all monomers of this type.

C It participates in hydrogen bond interactions.

D It forms the backbone of a nucleic acid strand.

4 Which does **not** describe a function of proteins?

A They encode genetic information.

B They allow muscle cells to contract.

C They help to carry out chemical reactions.

D They make up structures that support the cell.

5 Proteins and nucleic acids play important roles in the cell.

A Compare the structure of proteins with the structure of nucleic acids.

___

___

___

___

B Describe how the monomers that make up nucleic acids contribute to their function.

___

___

___

___

C Describe how the monomers that make up proteins contribute to their function.

___

___

___

___

Enzymes

BIO.A.2.3.1, BIO.A.2.3.2

Proteins play many roles in the cell. Some proteins function as **enzymes.** Enzymes allow reactions to occur at rates of thousands of times per second. Without enzymes, necessary chemical reactions would not occur at the rate that is required for life.

Enzymes are protein catalysts.

Enzymes and Activation Energy

Enzymes function as **catalysts,** greatly speeding up the rate of a chemical reaction. Unlike a product of a reaction or the raw material for a reaction, the enzyme is not used up or changed as the reaction proceeds.

Catalysts are substances that speed up chemical reactions, without being changed or used up.

The graphs below compare the energy of the starting *reactants,* or raw materials, with that of the final *products.* As the reactants are changed to products, they take on an intermediate form. This form has a greater amount of energy than either the products or reactants. Unless this *activation energy* is added, the reaction cannot proceed.

In a reaction, *reactants* are chemically changed to *products.*

Enzymes work by lowering the activation energy of a chemical reaction. With a lower activation energy, the reactants can be changed to products at a much faster rate.

The energy required for chemical reaction to convert reactants to products is called the *activation energy.* Enzymes reduce the activation energy.

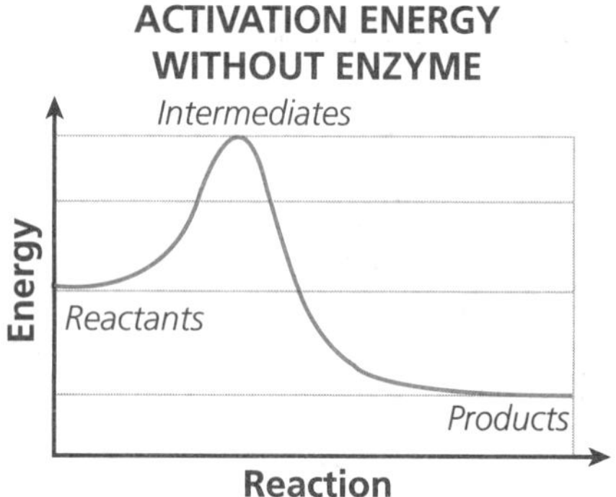

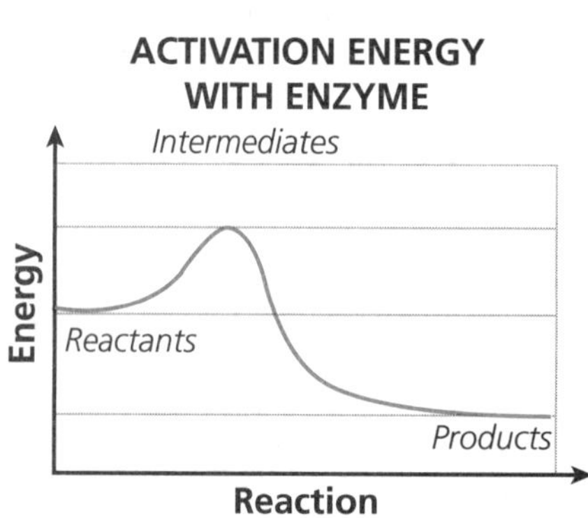

How does the energy of a reaction change when it is catalyzed by an enzyme?

A The energy of the products increases.

B The energy of the products decreases.

C The energy of the intermediates increases.

D The energy of the intermediates decreases.

Choices A and B are incorrect because the energy of the reactants and products does not change. An enzyme lowers the activation energy of a reaction, which is the energy required to form the intermediates. In a catalyzed reaction, the intermediates can form with less energy.

Enzyme Specificity

An organism can have thousands of enzymes, each one specific to a different reaction. An enzyme acts on the reactant, or starting material of a reaction. This substance is called a *substrate.* Enzymes are highly specific for the substrates they bind. For example, sucrose (table sugar) must be digested into monosaccharides so that our cells can absorb it. The enzyme sucrase speeds up this chemical reaction, but will not affect the breakdown of lactose (milk sugar).

sucrose → glucose + fructose

The shape of an enzyme is what makes it specific to one substrate and not any others. Enzymes are proteins, and proteins are folded into complex, three-dimensional structures. An enzyme's structure has a deep fold or pocket on its surface, to which a substrate molecule attaches. These folds are called *active sites.* Binding with the active site causes the substrate to be converted to products.

A substrate binding to the active site of an enzyme is analogous to a key fitting into a lock. The enzyme catalyzes the reaction only if the shape of the substrate fits the active site. A substrate can also *induce* the enzyme to fit. When the right substrate enters the active site, the enzyme's shape changes slightly as the substrate bonds with the active site.

The *substrate* is the substance that the enzyme helps to react. Enzymes are *substrate-specific.*

Enzyme names often end in the suffix *-ase.*

Sucrose and lactose are both disaccharides made up of two monosaccharides.

The *active site* is the region on an enzyme to which the substrate binds. Binding catalyzes the change from substrate to product. Active site bonds are very temporary.

The older lock-and-key model and the newer induced-fit model are two ways of describing how a substrate binds to an enzyme.

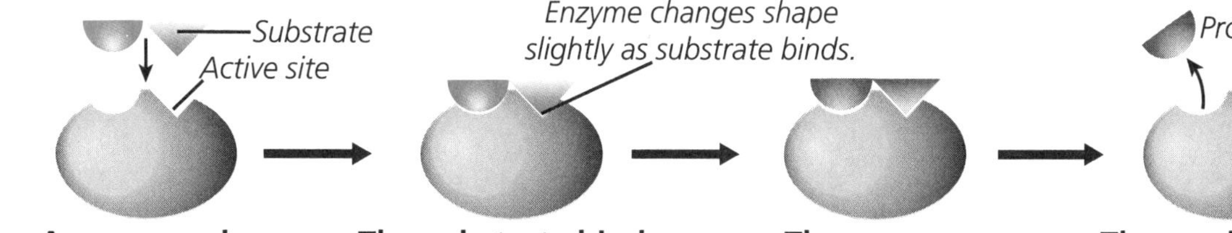

An enzyme is specific to a substrate. **The substrate binds to the active site.** **The enzyme catalyzes the reaction.** **The products of the reaction are released from the active site.**

Some enzymes have evolved from enzymes with different substrates and functions. Which amino acids in the enzyme most likely changed during the course of this evolution?

Because the active site plays such an important role in substrate specificity and enzyme function, amino acids making up this part of the protein are most likely to have changed.

Enzymes and Optimal Conditions

An enzyme functions best at an optimal temperature and pH level. Its reaction rate slows if it is placed in less-than-optimal conditions. This is because enzymes are proteins, macromolecules with complex, highly folded, three-dimensional structures. An enzyme's ability to catalyze a reaction depends on its structure. When conditions disrupt an enzyme's structure, the enzyme's activity is affected.

The reaction rate refers to how fast or slow the reaction occurs.

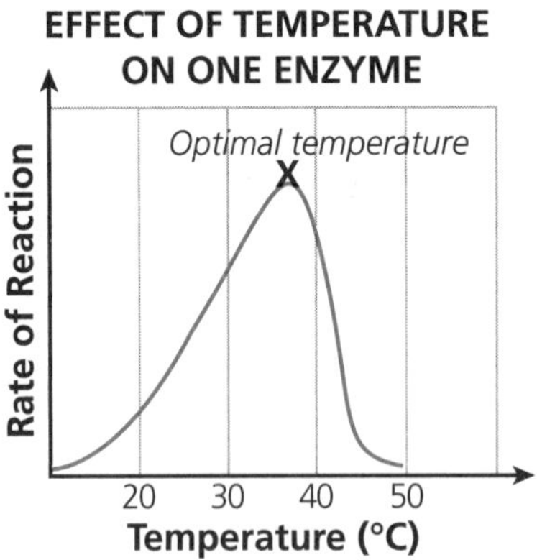

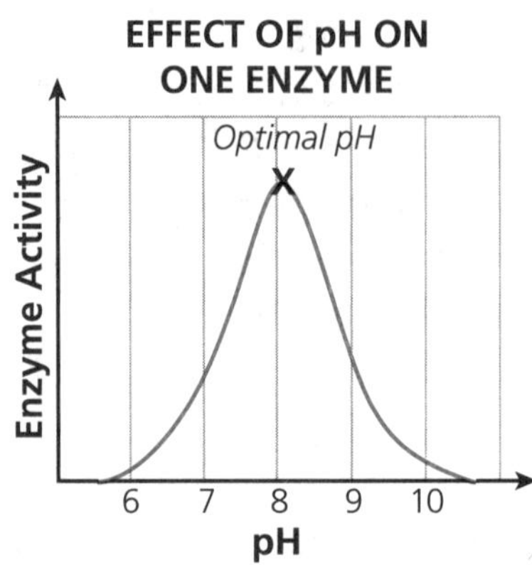

On the pH scale, 0 to 6 is acidic, 7 is neutral, and 8 to 14 is basic.

Different enzymes function best in different conditions. The optimum temperature for enzymes in the human body, for example, is about 37°C (98.6°F). Similar enzymes in a cold-water fish function best at lower temperatures.

Temperatures or pH levels that are too high or low can cause an enzyme to *denature.* A denatured enzyme no longer functions. Denaturation may be permanent or may be reversible if conditions change.

Denaturation is the process of an enzyme becoming inactive due to factors that alter the enzyme's structure.

A denatured enzyme does not catalyze a reaction.

Thermophilic bacteria live in hot springs with temperatures of 70°C (158° F). Water this hot would instantly scald your skin. A scientist collects these bacteria to be cultured in a laboratory. Explain what the scientist would need to do to ensure a healthy culture.

Because the bacteria are adapted to hot temperatures, their enzymes function optimally in these conditions. To culture the bacteria in a laboratory, the scientist would need to grow them in a solution at 70°C.

Enzyme and Substrate Concentrations

It seems obvious that adding more substrate to an enzyme will result in more product (that is, enzyme activity increases). Is this always the case? The graph on the next page shows that increasing the concentration of substrate does increase enzyme activity—up to a point. Then, the activity levels off.

Suppose enough substrate is added to fill all the active sites of all the enzyme molecules. Any additional substrate will not be catalyzed because there are no available active sites. At this point, increasing substrate concentration will have no effect on the rate of enzyme activity. It is limited by enzyme concentration.

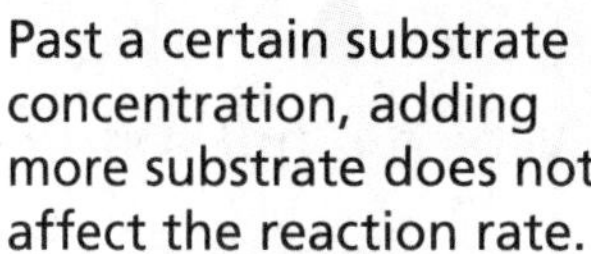

Past a certain substrate concentration, adding more substrate does not affect the reaction rate.

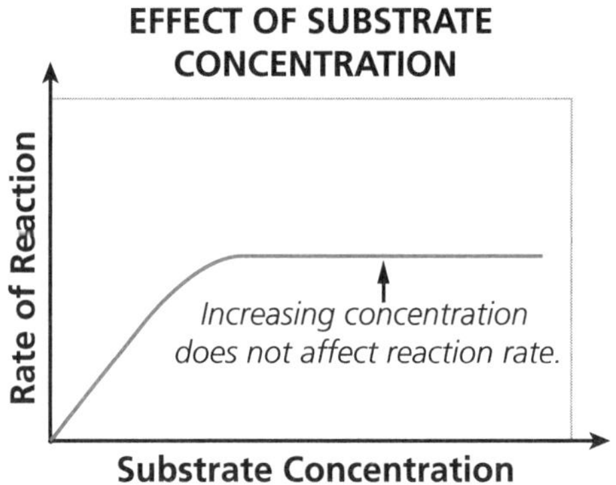

Similarly, if the concentration of enzyme that is added to the substrate increases, the reaction rate will also increase. This then levels off above a certain enzyme concentration. At this point, all the substrate molecules are bound to enzyme. Increasing enzyme concentration will have no effect on activity—there is no substrate available for them to catalyze.

Past a certain enzyme concentration, adding more enzyme does not affect the reaction rate.

In an experiment, test tubes are filled with equal enzyme concentrations and different substrate concentrations. As substrate concentration increases, the reaction occurs at a faster rate. However, after a certain concentration, the reaction rate remains the same. Can you change the quantities in the test tube to obtain more product?

Yes. The rate of reaction is limited by the availability of enzyme. There is more substrate than enzyme. Adding additional enzyme to the test tube will catalyze the extra substrate and increase the reaction rate.

IT'S YOUR TURN

Please read each question carefully. For a multiple-choice question, circle the letter of the correct response. For a constructed-response question, write your answers on the lines.

1 Which is **not** a structural feature of an enzyme?

A protein

B substrate

C active site

D amino acid

2 Organisms produce hydrogen peroxide (H_2O_2), a by-product of metabolism that is toxic to cells. The catalase protein catalyzes the reaction shown below.

$$2H_2O_2 \rightarrow 2H_2O + O_2$$

Which statement describes the reaction?

A Water is the substrate.

B Hydrogen peroxide is the enzyme.

C Catalase is consumed by the reaction.

D Oxygen gas is a product of the reaction.

3 **The enzyme lactase catalyzes the breakdown of lactose (milk sugar) to glucose and galactose. Students set up a beaker with milk and lactase enzyme. Which describes how the concentrations of these substances will change?**

A The concentration of lactase will decrease, and the concentration of galactose will increase.

B The concentration of galactose will decrease, and the concentration of glucose will increase.

C The concentration of galactose will increase, and the concentration of lactase will remain the same.

D The concentration of lactose will increase, and the concentration of glucose will remain the same.

4 **A reaction tube is set up at 37°C with twice as much substrate as enzyme. The pH level of the solution is 5. The reaction rate is measured. Which of the following changes will not affect the rate of the reaction?**

A increasing the pH level

B increasing the temperature

C increasing the enzyme concentration

D increasing the substrate concentration

Use the graph below to answer question 5.

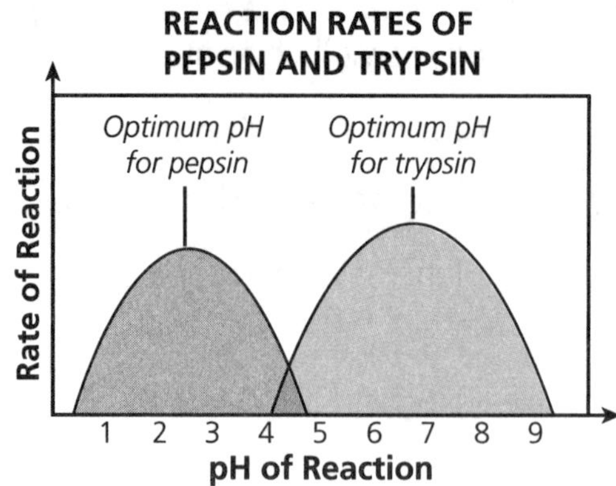

5 The graph shows the rate of enzyme activity in relation to pH for two enzymes—pepsin and pancreatic trypsin. Both enzymes break down proteins in food. Pepsin works within the stomach. Trypsin works in the small intestine.

A What does the graph indicate about the pH of the stomach and small intestine?

____

____

____

____

B The contents of the stomach are released into the small intestine. How does this affect the function of the pepsin that is included with the stomach contents?

____

____

____

____

C What is the advantage to having two different protein-digesting enzymes, rather than just one?

____

____

____

____

Module A
Cells and Cell Processes

Unit 3
Bioenergetics

Among the most important processes carried out at the cellular level is transformation of energy. This unit will help you review the energy transformations that take place during cellular respiration and photosynthesis.

1 ATP and Cellular Respiration ATP is a compound central to the processing of energy by the cell. In this lesson, you will learn about ATP's role in obtaining and transforming energy and how it changes during biochemical reactions. You will also review transformation of energy during cellular respiration and the role mitochondria play.

2 Photosynthesis Energy transformations also take place in photosynthesis. In this lesson, you will review the transformation of energy during photosynthesis, the specific cell structures in which it takes place, and how the process compares with the process of cellular respiration.

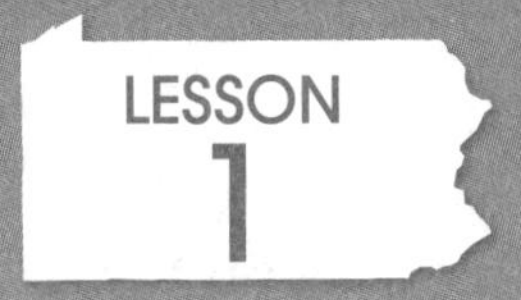

ATP and Cellular Respiration

BIO.A.3.1.1, BIO.A.3.2.1, BIO.A.3.2.2

Millions of chemical reactions are carried out continuously in the body's cells. Some reactions release energy, but many reactions consume energy. How does a cell provide the energy to power its metabolic reactions?

Some chemical reactions release energy. Others absorb energy, storing it in the products in the form of chemical energy.

The Role of ATP

A reaction that consumes energy takes lower-energy reactants and changes them into higher-energy products. The atoms are the same, but the amount of energy in the products is higher. This added energy must have a source.

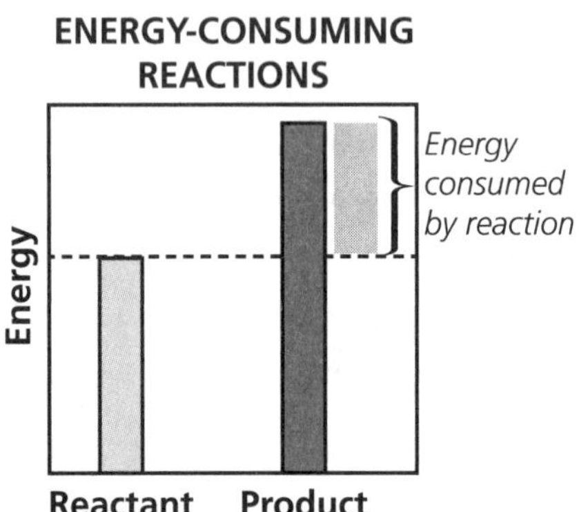

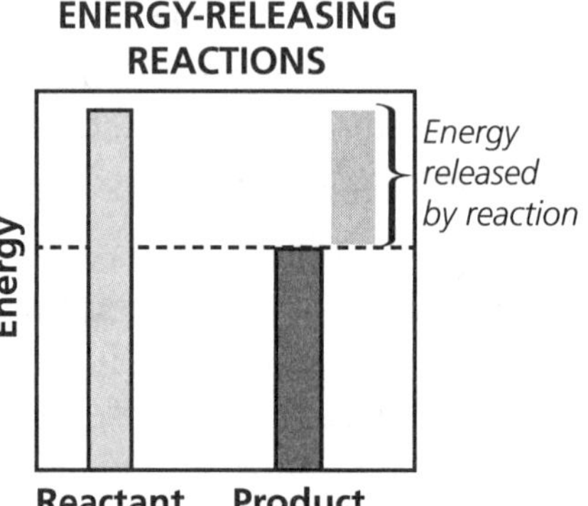

**Some reactions require energy (left).
Others release energy (right).**

The energy changes shown in the graphs are distinct from the activation energy needed to drive a reaction, which is not shown. Enzymes help reactions to occur faster, but do not provide energy for them.

Some reactions do the opposite—they form lower-energy products, releasing some of the chemical energy stored in the reactants. Fortunately, these two types of reactions can be paired. The energy released by one reaction is used in the other.

An important energy-releasing reaction involves **adenosine triphosphate,** or **ATP.** A molecule of ATP includes three phosphate groups. When the end phosphate group is removed, energy is released. This energy helps to power many of the reactions that are essential to life.

ATP, adenosine triphosphate, is a small, soluble molecule that provides energy to reactions throughout the cell. For this reason, ATP is known as the "energy currency" of cells.

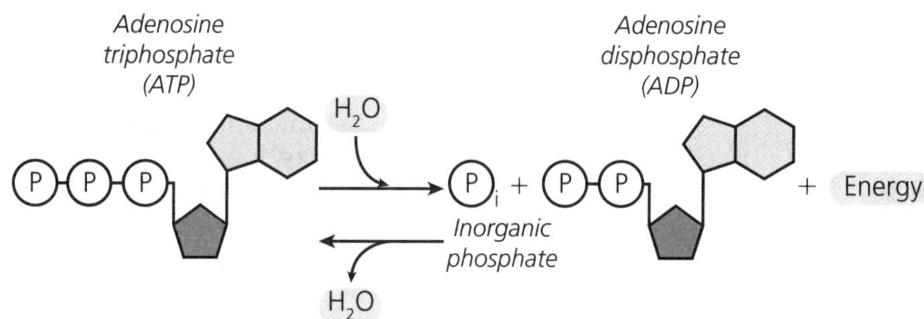

ATP is hydrolyzed to form ADP and a phosphate group. ADP and phosphate can be combined to form ATP.

ATP is broken down by hydrolysis to form ADP (adenosine diphosphate) plus a phosphate group. These products can be joined together again, by dehydration synthesis, into ATP. ATP is continuously broken down and re-formed in living cells.

The bond that attaches the last phosphate group to the ATP molecule releases energy when broken. Some of this energy is released as heat.

ATP is broken down into ADP and a phosphate group. These products can then be reassembled to form more ATP.

ATP is changed to ADP by hydrolysis; ADP is changed back to ATP by dehydration synthesis reactions.

Which comparison between ATP and ADP is correct?

A ATP stores less chemical energy than ADP and phosphate.

B ATP stores more chemical energy than ADP and phosphate.

C Less energy is used to form ATP than is released from ATP hydrolysis.

D More energy is used to form ATP than is released from ATP hydrolysis.

Choices C and D are incorrect because the energy used to form ATP must be equal to the energy released upon ATP hydrolysis. (Note that some of the released energy is lost as heat.) ATP is a carrier of stored chemical energy. It releases this energy upon hydrolysis to ADP and phosphate. ATP stores more chemical energy than the products it forms. Therefore, choice B is correct and choice A is incorrect.

The First Stage of Cellular Respiration

ATP is continuously produced and consumed in the cell. Without a constant supply of ATP, the cell would not be able to perform all of the functions it needs to survive. The energy required to reassemble ATP is supplied by **cellular respiration.** This process breaks down organic molecules, such as glucose, that originate in food. The net equation for aerobic respiration is shown below. Notice that it requires oxygen and produces carbon dioxide.

$$\underset{\text{(glucose)}}{C_6H_{12}O_6} + \underset{\text{(oxygen)}}{6O_2} \longrightarrow \underset{\text{(carbon dioxide)}}{6CO_2} + \underset{\text{(water)}}{6H_2O}$$

The word *respiration* also refers to breathing, which takes oxygen into the body and expels carbon dioxide.

Food provides organisms with a source of chemical energy.

Respiration takes place in three distinct stages. Each stage releases a bit more of the chemical energy stored in a glucose molecule. The first stage takes place in the cytoplasm of the cell. Glucose molecules are broken down into smaller molecules during *glycolysis.* Oxygen is not involved in this process, and only two molecules of ATP are assembled from the energy released from a glucose molecule.

The equation on page 57 shows *aerobic respiration,* or respiration that involves oxygen. Other forms of cellular respiration occur without use of oxygen. They are called *anaerobic respiration.* One type of anaerobic respiration is fermentation. During fermentation, organisms carry out glycolysis, but not the later stages that occur in aerobic respiration. Fermentation converts glucose into ethanol and carbon dioxide, or into lactic acid. Anaerobic respiration releases less of the energy (ATP) stored in glucose than aerobic respiration does.

Aerobic **cellular respiration** breaks down glucose and oxygen to form carbon dioxide and water. The reaction is a net reaction, or the sum of many separate reactions occurring in the cell. The production of water and carbon dioxide, and the use of oxygen, all take place at different stages.

Glycosis means "the splitting of sugar." It is the first stage of respiration. It takes place in the cell's cytoplasm.

Aerobic means "requiring air or oxygen." The prefix *an-* means "not." *Anaerobic respiration* takes places without oxygen. A type of anaerobic respiration is *fermentation.* Fermentation by yeast and bacteria is used in food making.

Which types of respiration are useful in increasing the amount of gas in a food product?

A fermentation producing lactic acid only

B fermentation producing carbon dioxide and ethanol only

C aerobic respiration and fermentation producing lactic acid

D aerobic respiration and fermentation producing carbon dioxide and ethanol

Choices A and C are incorrect because lactic acid fermentation does not produce a gas. Choice D is incorrect because aerobic respiration uses as many oxygen gas molecules as the carbon dioxide molecules it produces. Only fermentation producing ethanol and carbon dioxide, which does not consume oxygen, can increase the amount of gas. Choice B is correct.

Respiration in the Mitochondria

The later stages of respiration take place in the **mitochondria** of eukaryotic cells. This organelle has two membranes. The outer membrane surrounds the organelle and separates it from the rest of the cell. The inner membrane is folded over many times, creating a larger surface area inside the mitochondrion. Because reactions occur on the inner membrane, a high surface area allows more reactions to take place at once.

Mitochondria are organelles in animal and plant cells that produce energy (ATP) for the cell.

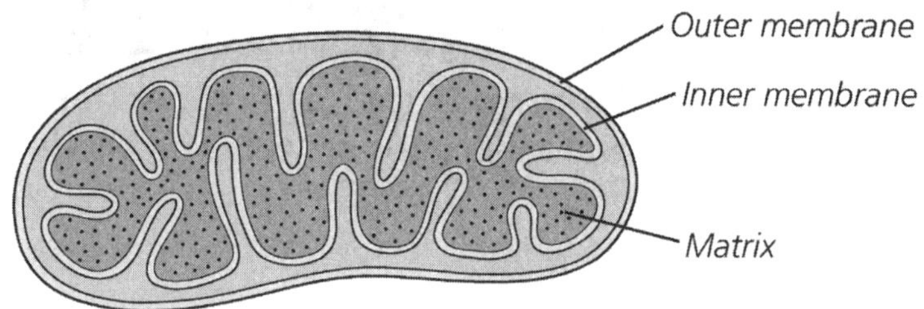

The second and third stages of aerobic respiration take place in the matrix of the mitochondria.

The mitochondrial matrix is where the second stage of aerobic respiration, the *citric acid cycle*, takes place. Enzymes in the matrix help to break down the products of glucose in a series of chemical reactions. The carbon compounds from glucose are converted to carbon dioxide. This releases even more energy from these compounds. However, most of the ATP is still to be produced.

The first two stages have been building up hydrogen (H^+) ions in the matrix. In the third stage of respiration, these ions flow across the inner membrane. As they do so, they power an enzyme called ATP synthase, which is attached to the inner membrane. This enzyme synthesizes ATP from ADP and phosphate. As ions exit the matrix, ATP is produced.

The table shows the number of ATP molecules produced at each stage of aerobic cellular respiration.

STAGES OF AEROBIC CELLULAR RESPIRATION

Stage	Description	Number of ATP per Glucose
I	Glucose is broken down.	2
II	Carbon compounds are converted to CO_2.	2
III	ATP synthase produces ATP.	32–34
Total		36–38

Explain how the structure of the inner mitochondrial membrane aids in the function of the mitochondrion.

In cellular respiration, most of the ATP is produced when ions flow across the inner mitochondrial membrane, powering ATP synthase. This enzyme synthesizes ATP from ADP and phosphate. Having a larger surface area for these processes to occur increases the rate of ATP production. The highly folded structure of the membrane increases its surface area.

All eukaryotes, including plants, fungi, animals, and protists, contain mitochondria. These organelles may have originated as free-living prokaryotes that found a home in a eukaryotic cell.

The *citric acid cycle* is also called the *Krebs cycle.* It breaks down the carbon compounds from glucose to form carbon dioxide.

The matrix and inner membrane of the mitochondria are important sites of ATP production.

Think of the glucose molecule as a wet sponge. Each stage of respiration squeezes a bit more water (energy) out of the sponge.

Most of the ATP is produced in the third stage of respiration.

IT'S YOUR TURN

Please read each question carefully. For a multiple-choice question, circle the letter of the correct response. For a constructed-response question, write your answers on the lines.

Use the diagram below to answer question 1.

Adenosine triphosphate (ATP)

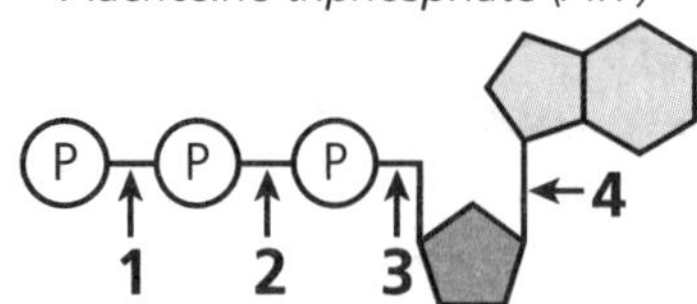

1 The breaking of which bond powers reactions in the cell?

A bond 1

B bond 2

C bond 3

D bond 4

2 Which pair of molecules are broken down by the cell to release energy?

A ADP and glucose

B ATP and glucose

C ATP and carbon dioxide

D ADP and carbon dioxide

3 Which pair of compounds are raw materials for cellular respiration?

A glucose and ATP

B oxygen and glucose

C carbon dioxide and ATP

D carbon dioxide and oxygen

4 Which does **not** take place in the mitochondria of the cell?

A Carbon dioxide is produced.

B Hydrogen ions cross a membrane.

C Glucose is broken down into organic compounds.

D The ATP synthase enzyme combines ADP and phosphate.

5 In which organism does respiration **not** take place in the mitochondria?

A bacteria

B maple tree

C seaweed

D yeast

6 You are preparing for a marathon. The night before the race, you eat a large bowl of pasta and a baked potato. Both are high in carbohydrates. During the race, you begin to feel hot and thirsty. You drink an energy drink to help you cool down.

A Explain how your meal helps you to prepare to supply energy to your muscle cells during the marathon.

____

____

____

____

B Explain why you begin to feel hot during the race, in terms of energy and cellular respiration.

____

____

____

____

C During intense effort, muscle cells may switch to anaerobic respiration. Describe what you should do to avoid this during the race.

____

____

____

____

Photosynthesis

BIO.A.3.1.1, BIO.A.3.2.1, BIO.A.3.2.2

You may obtain energy by eating a bowl of macaroni and cheese. Similarly, a fungus may obtain energy from the tree stump it slowly digests, and a protist may obtain it from the bacterium it engulfs. What is the source of this food energy? Some organisms, including plants, algae, and certain prokaryotes, make their own food via photosynthesis.

Photosynthesis and Cellular Respiration

Photosynthesis is a process that converts light energy from the sun into chemical energy stored in compounds such as glucose.

Photosynthetic organisms use the energy in sunlight to produce glucose and oxygen from carbon dioxide and water. The net equation for photosynthesis requires six molecules of carbon dioxide (CO_2) and six molecules of water (H_2O). It produces one glucose molecule ($C_6H_{12}O_6$) and releases six molecules of oxygen (O_2) to the environment. The chemical equation below describes what happens during photosynthesis.

$$\underset{\text{(carbon dioxide)}}{6CO_2} + \underset{\text{(water)}}{6H_2O} + \underset{\text{(sunlight)}}{\text{energy}} \longrightarrow \underset{\text{(glucose)}}{C_6H_{12}O_6} + \underset{\text{(oxygen)}}{6O_2}$$

The glucose made from photosynthesis provides the plant with energy. Plants can use this chemical energy right away, or store the sugars as starches for later use. Like animals, plants carry out **cellular respiration.** In fact, photosynthesis and aerobic respiration may be considered opposite processes. The chemical equation below shows aerobic respiration.

$$\underset{\text{(glucose)}}{C_6H_{12}O_6} + \underset{\text{(oxygen)}}{6O_2} \longrightarrow \underset{\text{(carbon dioxide)}}{6CO_2} + \underset{\text{(water)}}{6H_2O}$$

Which of the following **best** explains the relationship between photosynthesis and cellular respiration?

A Both produce carbon dioxide and oxygen.

B Both require energy from the sunlight to occur.

C The products of one are the reactants of the other.

D A plant can carry out either one process or the other.

Photosynthesis is a biological process in which light energy is used to produce glucose. Photosynthesis uses up carbon dioxide and water and produces oxygen.

Some ATP is also produced directly by photosynthesis.

Glucose produced by photosynthesis may be broken down in **cellular respiration,** providing energy for the plant. It may also form the cellulose that strengthens plant cell walls or be stored in a macromolecule such as starch for later use.

Plants increase the net supply of oxygen because they produce more oxygen via photosynthesis than they consume in cellular respiration.

Choice A is incorrect because photosynthesis produces only oxygen, while cellular respiration produces only carbon dioxide. Choice B is incorrect because cellular respiration does not require sunlight to occur. Choice D is incorrect because a plant has the capability to complete both photosynthesis and cellular respiration. Choice C is correct because the products of photosynthesis are used as reactants for cellular respiration and vice versa.

Chloroplasts and Photosynthesis

Photosynthetic eukaryotic cells contain organelles called **chloroplasts.** A chloroplast has two membranes that surround the stroma, or inner fluid. In the stroma are stacks of "disks" known as thylakoids. The membranes of the thylakoids are important in photosynthesis. They contain *chlorophyll,* the pigment that can capture the energy in sunlight. This energy drives the chemical reactions of photosynthesis.

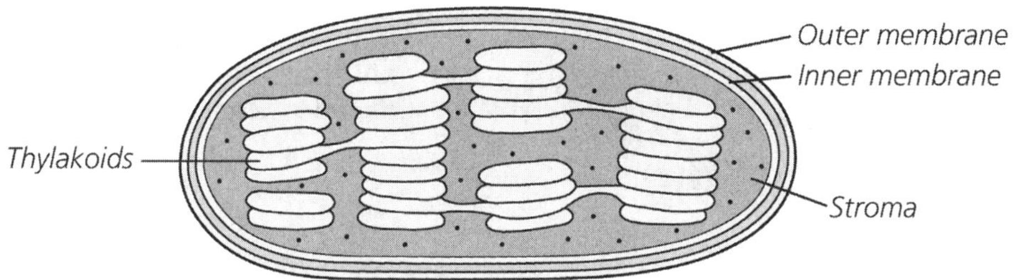

Glucose is produced in the chloroplasts of plant cells.

In most plants, photosynthesis takes place primarily in the leaves. Therefore, leaf cells need carbon dioxide and water as raw materials for photosynthesis. Leaves take in carbon dioxide from the atmosphere through openings called *stomata* (singular, *stoma*), which are small pores on the underside of the leaf. Plants open their stomata to take in carbon dioxide and release oxygen. They can close them to prevent water loss when temperatures are high.

Most plants take in water from the soil through roots anchored in the ground. This water travels to the cells in their leaves through tube-like vascular tissues.

When temperatures become too warm, leaves close their stomata to conserve water. How will high temperature **most likely** affect the rate of photosynthesis?

When temperature is high, stomata close to prevent water loss from the plant. This reduces the plant's ability to take in carbon dioxide for photosynthesis. Therefore, the rate of photosynthesis is likely to decrease in higher temperatures.

Chloroplasts are the organelles where photosynthesis takes place in eukaryotic cells.

Chlorophyll is a green pigment that captures the energy in sunlight. Pigments are molecules that absorb visible light. Chlorophyll gives leaves their green color.

Chloroplasts surround the large central vacuole of a plant cell.

Plant vascular tissue consists of *xylem* (for water and minerals) and *phloem* (for sap).

Two Stages of Photosynthesis

Photosynthesis has two stages, which occur in different parts of the chloroplast. The first stage consists of the *light-dependent reactions.* Sunlight energizes chlorophyll. This leads to a series of chemical reactions that harness the energy necessary for the next stage of photosynthesis. This first stage

- uses chlorophyll and other molecules built into the thylakoid membranes,
- captures energy from sunlight,
- produces ATP and other energy-rich molecules,
- splits water molecules (the hydrogen atoms and electrons are needed in the next stage), and
- releases oxygen gas from the leaf.

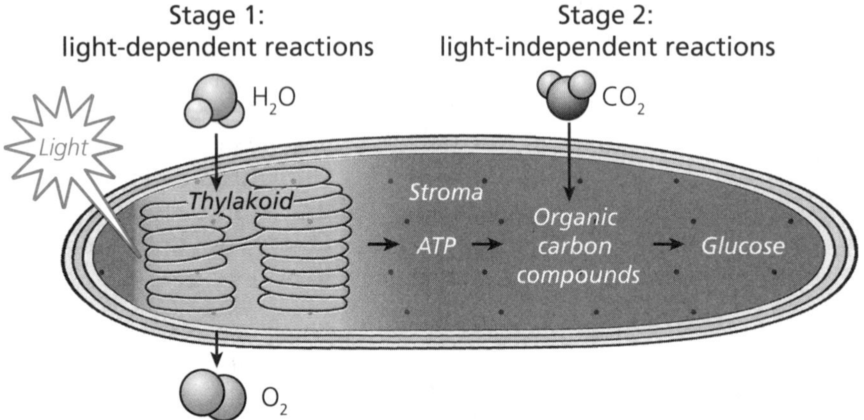

Photosynthesis involves both light and dark reactions.

The second stage of photosynthesis, the *light-independent reactions,* requires no light, but does use the products that were obtained in the first stage. This stage

- takes place in the stroma of the chloroplast,
- depends on energy from light-dependent reactions,
- uses the hydrogen atoms and electrons obtained from water in the first stage, and
- converts carbon dioxide into organic molecules such as glucose.

The *light-dependent reactions* of photosynthesis take place in the thylakoid membranes, which contain chlolophyll.

The rate of photosynthesis can be influenced by light intensity, air temperature, carbon dioxide levels, and water availability.

In the first stage, water molecules are split to form oxygen gas.

In the second stage of photosynthesis, carbon dioxide is consumed.

The *light-independent reactions* of photosynthesis are also called the *Calvin cycle* or the *dark reactions,* because they use light indirectly.

Organic compounds contain carbon and hydrogen. They are used to build glucose and other important molecules.

Scientists supply plants with water molecules containing a heavier-than-usual oxygen isotope, oxygen-18. Which of the products of photosynthesis will contain this isotope? Explain.

The oxygen released by the light-dependent reactions will contain the oxygen-18 isotope. Oxygen gas is produced by splitting the water molecule. The oxygen is released; it is not incorporated into organic carbon compounds.

IT'S YOUR TURN

Please read each question carefully. For a multiple-choice question, circle the letter of the correct response. For a constructed-response question, write your answers on the lines.

1 Which is a difference between photosynthesis and cellular respiration?

A Photosynthesis can produce glucose without oxygen.

B Photosynthesis occurs only in plants, and respiration occurs only in animals.

C Cellular respiration stores energy, but photosynthesis releases energy.

D Cellular respiration releases oxygen, but photosynthesis releases carbon dioxide.

2 Which statement describes what occurs in the stroma of the chloroplast?

A Oxygen is released.

B Carbon dioxide reacts.

C Water molecules are split.

D Chlorophyll absorbs energy.

3 How would the environment change if there were fewer plants to carry out photosynthesis?

A It would have more oxygen.

B It would have more glucose.

C It would have more ATP energy.

D It would have more carbon dioxide.

4 Which pair of compounds are both products of photosynthesis?

A water and glucose

B oxygen and glucose

C glucose and carbon dioxide

D oxygen and carbon dioxide

5 The law of conservation of energy states that energy cannot be destroyed or created. It can only change in form and move from place to place. An ATP molecule in an animal cell is used for energy.

A Explain how the energy reached the ATP molecule from its original source.

____

____

____

____

____

____

B Describe how energy changed in form from its original source to the ATP molecule.

____

____

____

____

C Explain how the energy changes when the ATP molecule is converted to ADP and phosphate.

____

____

____

____

Module A
Cells and Cell Processes

Unit 4
Homeostasis and Transport

To maintain life, organisms must regulate the balance of materials inside and outside of the cell. This is accomplished by the transport of materials through the plasma membrane. This unit will help you review the structures and processes by which cells maintain homeostasis.

1 Membranes of the Cell Particular cell structures are involved in the transport of materials into, out of, and throughout a cell. In this lesson, you will review the structure of the plasma membrane and its regulatory function. You will also review how other membrane-bound organelles facilitate the transport of materials within a cell.

2 Passive Transport Some materials are transported into, out of, or throughout a cell by passive mechanisms. In this lesson, you will review the processes of diffusion, osmosis, and facilitated diffusion and how specific membrane-bound organelles facilitate these processes.

3 Active Transport Other materials are transported into, out of, or throughout a cell by active mechanisms. In this lesson, you will review the processes of pumps, endocytosis, and exocytosis and how specific membrane-bound organelles facilitate these processes.

4 Homeostasis Organisms use particular mechanisms to maintain homeostasis, the biological balance between their internal and external environments. In this lesson, you will learn how organisms maintain homeostasis through mechanisms such as thermoregulation, water regulation, and oxygen regulation.

Membranes of the Cell

BIO.A.4.1.1, BIO.A.4.1.3

The **plasma membrane** surrounds the cytoplasm of a cell, controlling what enters and exits. The plasma membrane is *semipermeable,* meaning that some substances cross more easily than others and certain substances cannot move across it at all. An effective plasma membrane allows essential materials to move into the cell and metabolic wastes to pass out of it.

The Phospholipid Bilayer

The plasma membrane and the membranes of organelles share a basic molecular structure. They consist of two layers of *phospholipids,* arranged into sheets, called a *bilayer.* Each phospholipid has a polar "head" region and two nonpolar "tails." The heads are *hydrophilic* while the tails are *hydrophobic.* These properties of the phospholipids determine how they are arranged in the bilayer. The hydrophilic heads line the outside of the membrane, facing both the intracellular cytoplasm and the extracellular fluid. The hydrophobic tails in each layer face each other, avoiding the watery environment.

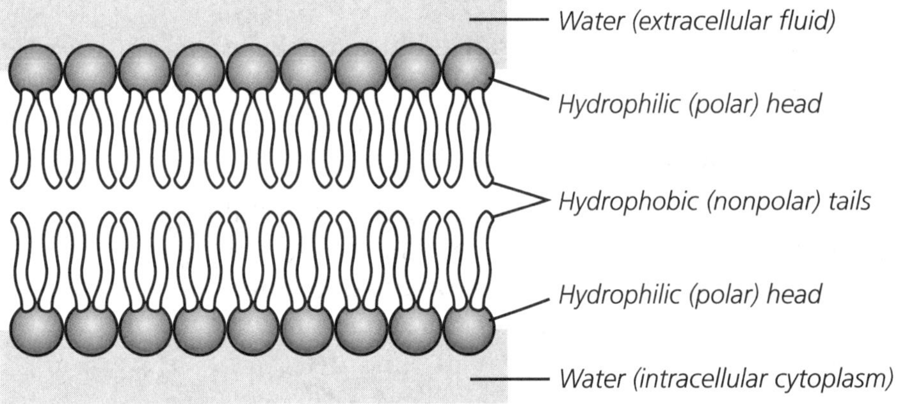

The phospholipid bilayer has a nonpolar hydrophobic center.

The middle section, made up of fatty acids, is nonpolar and hydrophobic. The physical properties of this middle section determine how easily different substances may move across the membrane. Therefore, small, nonpolar molecules such as dissolved oxygen (O_2) are able to pass easily through the membrane. Ions and polar molecules, however, are repelled by the nonpolar tails. The membrane is less permeable or completely impermeable to these substances. In addition, macromolecules are simply too large to fit through the bilayer.

The **plasma membrane** is sometimes called the *cell membrane.*

A *semipermeable* membrane allows some substances to cross more easily than others. It is **impermeable** to certain substances, which cannot pass through.

The plasma membrane is called a *bilayer* because it is made up of two layers of phospholipids.

Phospholipids are organic macromolecules. A single molecule has a phosphate "head" region and long fatty acid "tails."

Polar = *hydrophilic* = water-seeking
Nonpolar = *hydrophobic* = water-avoiding

The phosphate head is hydrophilic. It faces outwards. The fatty acid tails are hydrophobic. They are sandwiched in the center.

In animal cells, cholesterol is also found within the hydrophobic center of the bilayer. It helps to make the membrane more rigid.

The principle that "like dissolves like" applies to the bilayer. Polar molecules and ions are repelled by the nonpolar region.

Ions are charged atoms, such as calcium (Ca^{2+}).

Which of the following should pass **most** easily through the plasma membrane?

A a protein

B a small lipid

C a sodium ion

D a water molecule

Proteins, choice A, are macromolecules and cannot easily fit through the membrane. Sodium ions, choice C, are charged and are therefore repelled by the nonpolar tails of the phospholipids. Similarly, water molecules, choice D, cannot cross easily because they are polar. (Water does penetrate the bilayer, but it does so relatively slowly.) Small lipids, choice B, are nonpolar and can therefore cross the bilayer easily.

Membrane Proteins

Although water is a polar molecule and moves slowly across the phospholipid bilayer, it can still move in and out of the cell quite easily. This is due to another component of the plasma membrane, *membrane proteins*. One type of membrane protein is called an *aquaporin*. This protein channel is shaped like a tube with a hydrophilic center, which water molecules can pass through easily. The more aquaporins a cell has in its membrane, the more permeable it is to water. Aquaporin is just one type of membrane protein.

Membrane proteins are found throughout the lipid bilayer. They may be located on one side of the plasma membrane or span across it.

The structure of the cell membrane is described by the fluid mosaic model. A mosaic is an artwork made up of many separate pieces that form an image. Membrane proteins move fluidly among the phospholipids.

Carbohydrates can attach to membrane proteins or lipids, creating glycoproteins and glycolipids. These act as "self-markers" for body cells, so that the immune system does not attack them.

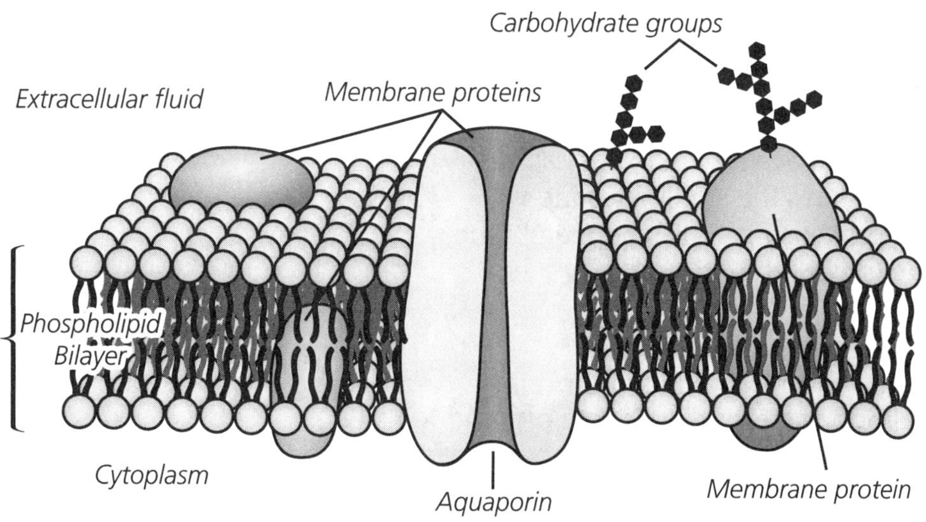

Membrane proteins throughout the phospholipid bilayer are essential to the function of the cell membrane.

Plasma membrane proteins have several different functions.

- They help to stabilize and shape the membrane.
- Proteins on the outer surface allow the cell to be recognized by other cells, such as those of the immune system.
- Outer surface proteins act as receptors to which hormones and other molecules or ions may attach. Once a substance attaches, the receptor responds by causing changes inside the cell.
- Proteins that span the membrane help to transport ions and polar molecules into and out of the cell.

Proteins are made up of different amino acids. The R group of an amino acid gives it specific properties, making it small or large, polar or nonpolar. Where are the nonpolar amino acids in an aquaporin protein most likely to be found?

A along the inner tube of the channel

B in a band around the outside of the channel

C on the end of the protein that faces the cytoplasm

D on the end of the protein that faces the extracellular fluid

Nonpolar amino acids are hydrophobic and will be attracted to the nonpolar central region of the phospholipid bilayer. Choices A, C, and D are incorrect because these regions of the channel are in contact with water. Amino acids here must be polar and hydrophilic. Choice B is correct; the amino acids in the middle of the protein's exterior are nonpolar. This region is in contact with the fatty acid tails of the bilayer.

Cells in the body have different combinations of proteins on their plasma membranes. These membrane proteins help to determine cells' specialized functions. For example, a cell that makes up estrogen-sensitive tissue will have receptors for estrogen on its surface. In contrast, a cell that lines the small intestine will have numerous glucose transport proteins in its plasma membrane, allowing it to absorb glucose from digested food.

The tongue is lined with taste buds, which detect the components of food and relay this information to the brain. What type of membrane protein do taste bud cells rely on, and how do they help these cells carry out their function?

Cells of the taste buds contain receptors for substances in foods. When a chemical in food binds to a receptor, this type of membrane protein causes changes in the cell that result in a signal being sent to the brain.

Membranes Inside the Cell

Although the plasma membrane is vital to the cell, membranes inside the cytoplasm are very important, too. Many of the organelles in a eukaryotic cell are surrounded by their own membranes. For example, the chloroplasts and mitochondria each have a double membrane, composed of an outer and inner membrane. This is evidence that these organelles were once free-living organisms, "captured" by a primitive eukaryotic cell (**endosymbiosis**). In addition, the highly folded inner membrane of mitochondria and the thylakoid membranes inside chloroplasts help these organelles to carry out their functions.

In addition, membranes make up the nucleus, endoplasmic reticulum (ER), and Golgi apparatus inside the cell. These are sometimes considered a single, interconnected system called the *endomembrane system.*

Endosymbiosis is a theory that early eukaryotic cells were formed from simpler prokaryotes.

Membranes in mitochondria and chloroplasts are essential to their function.

The nuclear membrane is sometimes called a *nuclear envelope.* The nuclear envelope, ER, and Golgi body make up the *endomembrane system.*

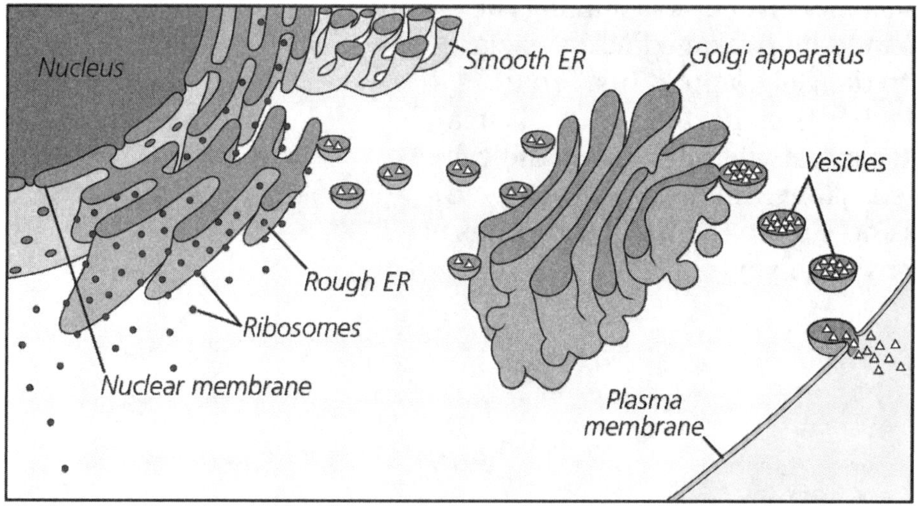

The nuclear envelope, endoplasmic reticulum, Golgi apparatus, and vesicles work together to transport material within the cell.

The parts of the endomembrane system work together for a particular purpose. The nucleus and ER membranes are connected and located close together, making it easy for mRNA to travel from the nucleus to the ribosomes of the rough ER, which assemble proteins. Similarly, the smooth ER synthesizes molecules such as fatty acids and hormones. The substances made by the rough and smooth ER are usually destined for outside the cell or for the plasma membrane. However, they must first be modified and packaged by the Golgi apparatus.

The rough ER has ribosomes bound to it, while smooth ER does not.

The ER is often compared to a manufacturing plant or factory, and the Golgi apparatus to a shipping warehouse that packages the goods and sends them to their destinations.

To reach the Golgi apparatus, substances from the ER are packaged into *vesicles,* sections of membrane that bud off the ER and form sacs. These vesicles move through the cytoplasm and fuse with the membrane of the Golgi apparatus. This organelle further modifies the materials and prepares them for transport. Finally, they are packaged into vesicles that bud off the opposite surface of the Golgi apparatus and transport the material toward the plasma membrane of the cell.

A *vesicle* is a small, temporary membrane sac in the cytoplasm. Vesicles form from sections of organelle or plasma membrane that "bud off."

Vesicles can also fuse with membranes of the cell. The vesicle then becomes part of the membrane.

Proteins that will be used by a cell are assembled by free ribosomes in the cytoplasm. Proteins that will be exported from a cell or are destined for the plasma membrane are assembled by the ribosomes of the rough ER. Explain why proteins are assembled in different places.

The ER works with the Golgi apparatus to export proteins out of the cell or to the plasma membrane. Assembling the proteins in the ER allows them to be packaged into vesicles that transport the proteins to the Golgi apparatus. From there, the proteins can be further transported to the plasma membrane. In contrast, proteins that will be used by the cell do not need to be transported. Therefore, they will not need to be packaged into vesicles and sent to the Golgi apparatus. They can be produced directly in the cytoplasm.

IT'S YOUR TURN

Please read each question carefully. For a multiple-choice question, circle the letter of the correct response. For a constructed-response question, write your answers on the lines.

1 Why is the phospholipid bilayer only partially permeable to water?

A Water is repelled by the polar tails of the phospholipid.

B Water is repelled by the polar head of the phospholipid.

C Water is repelled by the hydrophobic tails of the phospholipid.

D Water is repelled by the hydrophobic head of the phospholipid.

2 Which is **not** a component of the plasma membrane?

A fatty acids

B phosphates

C amino acids

D nucleic acids

3 The calcium ion passes easily through the membrane of one cell but cannot cross the membrane of a second cell. Which part of the plasma membrane allows this substance to cross?

A Carbohydrate groups on the membrane allow the ions to cross.

B The fatty acid tails of the phospholipids allow the ions to cross.

C Protein channels in the plasma membrane allow the ions to cross.

D Phosphate groups of the phospholipid bilayer allow the ions to cross.

4 The chart below lists three kinds of molecules. Fill in the chart based on the ability of a molecule to pass through the phospholipid bilayer of the plasma membrane.

Molecule	Is the plasma membrane permeable to this molecule? Explain the reasoning behind your answer.
Cl^- (Chlorine Ion)	
O_2 (Oxygen)	
Starch (polysaccharide)	

5 A particular cell produces 1) a cell receptor protein, 2) a protein that makes up the cytoskeleton of the cytoplasm, and 3) a hormone that will be secreted into the bloodstream.

A Identify where the cytoskeleton protein will be synthesized. Explain your answer.

B Identify where the hormone will be synthesized. Explain your answer.

C Identify where a cell receptor protein will be assembled and describe how it will reach its final destination.

Passive Transport

BIO.A.4.1.2

The plasma membrane is an area of constant movement as molecules are shuttled back and forth in a variety of ways. Without this movement of molecules, wastes would build up inside the cell and needed materials would not enter it. The movement of substances may be driven by differences in their **concentration** inside and outside the cell.

In addition to the plasma membrane, cell membranes surround the organelles of eukaryotic cells and make up most of the ER and Golgi apparatus. Transport processes are therefore important within the cell.

Concentration refers to the amount of a substance (a solute) dissolved in a given volume of water or other solvent.

Concentration Gradient

When a dissolved substance is more concentrated in one area than in an adjacent area, it forms a **concentration gradient.** For example, in the diagram below, there is more dissolved solute at one corner of the solvent, and far less everywhere else. Notice how the concentration changes over time.

A **concentration gradient** is a gradual difference in the concentration of a substance in a solution as a function of distance.

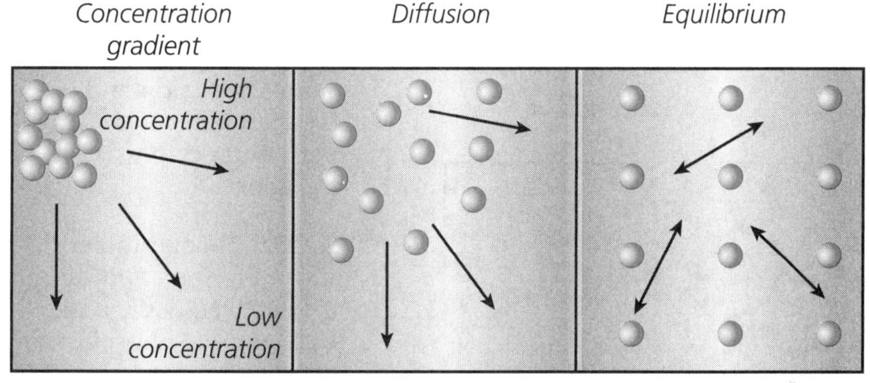

Diffusion moves a dissolved substance *down* its concentration gradient.

Molecules and ions in a solution are constantly in motion. Because of this, they will naturally move from the more-concentrated region to the less-concentrated regions. This movement "down" the concentration gradient is called **diffusion.** Diffusion does not require any energy *input* to occur. It happens whenever a concentration gradient exists.

Eventually, enough of the substance will have diffused that its concentration is equal everywhere throughout the solution. It has reached a state of *equilibrium.* Even though molecules may move in any direction, there is no overall movement in any single direction.

Because the particles that make up a substance have energy, they are always in motion.

Diffusion is the movement of molecules or ions *down* a concentration gradient. It stops when *equilibrium* is reached.

Glucose is added to water and the solution is stirred until the glucose is evenly distributed throughout. Will diffusion occur within the solution? Explain.

Diffusion will not occur in the solution once its concentration is equal throughout. Diffusion requires a concentration gradient to occur.

Passive Transport

What happens when a concentration gradient occurs across a cell membrane? If the membrane is permeable to the substance, the substance will move across the membrane, toward the side of lower concentration, due to simple diffusion. Recall that diffusion requires no energy input, and that the net movement of particles stops once equilibrium is reached.

Any type of cellular transport that does not require some form of energy input is called **passive transport.** There are several types of passive transport. Diffusion across a membrane is the simplest type. Small, nonpolar molecules cross the phospholipid bilayer most easily, slipping between the phospholipids and crossing into or out of the cell.

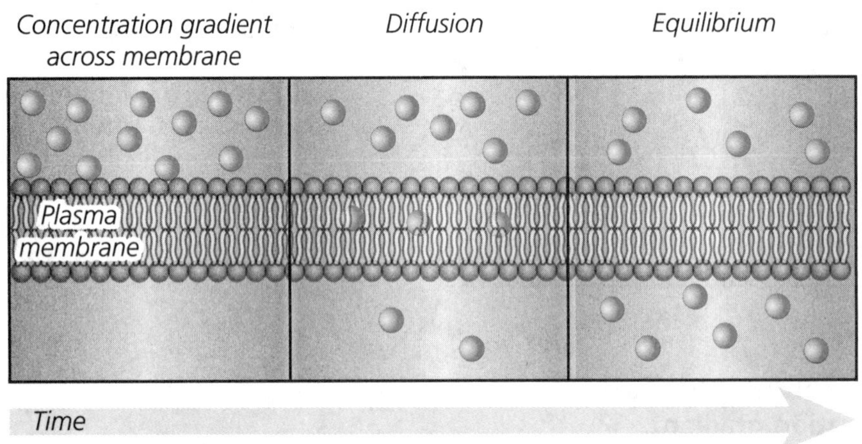

Diffusion *down* a concentration gradient can cause a substance to cross a plasma membrane. Diffusion is a form of passive transport.

However, the plasma membrane is impermeable to certain substances. Recall that large molecules, charged ions, and polar molecules do not readily cross the phospholipid bilayer. In this case, membrane **transport proteins** can provide a way for the substance to enter or exit the cell. This type of transport is called **facilitated diffusion** because it is facilitated, or helped, by proteins. Even though they are helping move molecules that normally would not be able to move across the cellular membrane, they are still using no ATP (energy). Therefore, facilitated diffusion is a form of passive transport.

Passive transport is the movement of a substance across the plasma membrane without any input of energy.

Simple **diffusion** and **facilitated diffusion** are both types of passive transport.

Small, nonpolar molecules, such as oxygen and carbon dioxide, can easily pass between the phospholipids of plasma membranes. Ions and large or polar molecules are repelled by the nonpolar phospholipid tails, and do not cross as easily.

A **transport protein** is a protein built into the plasma membrane that helps certain kinds of molecules or ions pass through.

Facilitated diffusion relies on membrane proteins to help molecules cross a cell membrane.

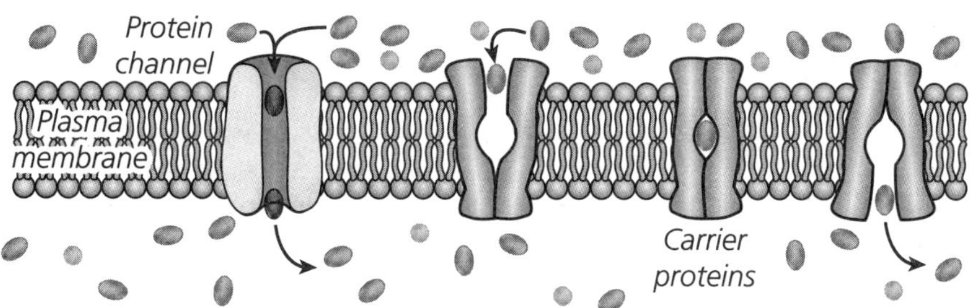

Facilitated diffusion uses transport proteins to move a substance *down* its concentration gradient.

Channel proteins, with their tubelike openings, allow specific substances to enter or exit freely. Aquaporins are protein channels through which water molecules enter and exit the cell. *Carrier proteins* bind to molecules or ions and carry them to the other side of the membrane. Glucose, for example, needs the help of a transport protein to enter cells. Without this transport protein, your cells would not receive enough glucose to power cellular respiration.

Transport proteins include *protein channels* and *carrier proteins.* Many transport proteins are so specific that they help move only a single type of molecule across the membrane.

Which is **not** an example of passive transport?

A Carbon dioxide in a capillary crosses the alveoli membranes of the lungs.

B Oxygen dissolved in the blood crosses the phospholipid portion of the membrane of a red blood cell.

C Glucose molecules are transported by a carrier protein until its concentration on both sides of the membrane is equal.

D Sodium ions move through a protein channel until there is a higher concentration in extracellular fluid than the cytoplasm.

Choices A and B describe simple diffusion through membranes; this is a form of passive transport. Choice C describes facilitated transport, which occurs until equilibrium is reached. Choice D describes the transport of sodium *against* its concentration gradient. This requires energy and is therefore not a form of passive transport.

Osmosis

Diffusion involves the movement of molecules or ions that are dissolved in water. However, the movement of water itself is so important in biology that it is given its own term: osmosis. **Osmosis** refers to the movement of water from areas of higher *water* concentration to areas of lower *water* concentration. The concentration of water is high wherever the concentration of dissolved substances is low. So, the direction of osmosis is usually opposite the direction of diffusion.

Osmosis refers to the movement of water from where dissolved substances are *less* concentrated to where they are *more* concentrated. The identity of the solute does not matter.

Osmosis is a form of passive transport. It requires no energy.

Because a plasma membrane may be impermeable to some solutes, osmosis can change the volume of fluid inside a cell. Consider the semipermeable membrane in the diagram below. Water can move across it, but the solute cannot. Water will move from the side with the *lower solute* concentration to the side with the *higher solute* concentration. This net movement of water down *its own* concentration gradient results in unequal volumes in the two halves of the beaker. Equilibrium is reached when the solute concentration is equal on both sides of the membrane.

A *solute* is a dissolved substance. In osmosis, water "follows" the solute.

Osmosis can result in changes in volume.

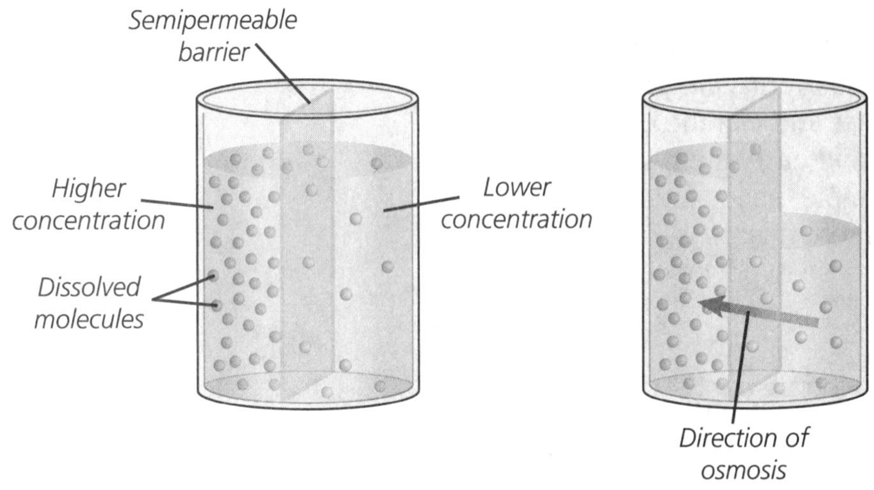

In osmosis, water moves from an area of higher *water* concentration (the right side of the beaker) to an area of *lower* water concentration (the left side of the beaker).

The fluids inside and outside of a cell can be compared in terms of solute concentration. The terms *hypotonic, isotonic,* and *hypertonic* refer to extracellular fluid that is less, equal, and more concentrated than the cell's interior (cytoplasm). For example, fresh water is hypotonic to cells' cytoplasm, while the extremely salty water of Utah's Great Salt Lake is hypertonic to most cells. Due to osmosis, hypotonic and hypertonic fluids can result in changes to a cell's volume.

A *hypotonic* fluid has a lower concentration of dissolved substances than a cell's interior. An *isotonic* fluid has an equal concentration. A *hypertonic* fluid has a greater concentration.

The cell walls of plant cells allow them to survive in a hypotonic freshwater environment.

Microbes that live in the Great Salt Lake maintain water balance by maintaining high solute concentrations in the cytoplasm.

The diagram shows changes to red blood cells placed in solutions of varying concentrations. Identify the solutions as hypotonic, isotonic, or hypertonic to the cells. Explain your responses.

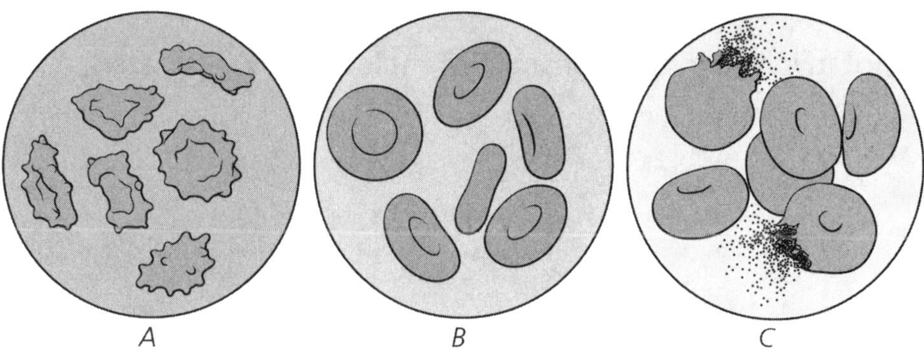

The cells in image A are in a hypertonic solution. Water moves where the solute concentration is higher, that is, out of the cytoplasm and into the extracellular fluid. The cells in image B are in an isotonic solution. They are healthy red blood cells because the solute is equal inside and outside the cell. The cells in image C are in a hypotonic solution. Water moves where the solute concentration is higher, from the extracellular fluid and into the cytoplasm. This causes some of the cells to burst.

IT'S YOUR TURN

Please read each question carefully. For a multiple-choice question, circle the letter of the correct response. For a constructed-response question, write your answers on the lines.

1 Which of the following is **not** involved in the transport of molecules by facilitated diffusion?

A ATP

B phospholipids

C protein channels

D concentration gradient

2 What is one way that facilitated diffusion differs from simple diffusion?

A Facilitated diffusion requires energy input.

B Facilitated diffusion requires membrane proteins.

C Facilitated diffusion requires a concentration gradient.

D Facilitated diffusion requires small, nonpolar molecules.

3 A pipe carries excess rainwater into a lake. The rainwater has picked up dissolved nitrates from surrounding lawns. Which of the following is a consequence of simple diffusion of the nitrates in the lake?

A A concentration gradient of nitrates is created and maintained.

B The total amount of dissolved nitrate in the lake water decreases.

C Nitrate concentration decreases in some places and increases in others.

D Energy is required to move the nitrates from one end of the lake to the other.

Use the image below to answer question 4.

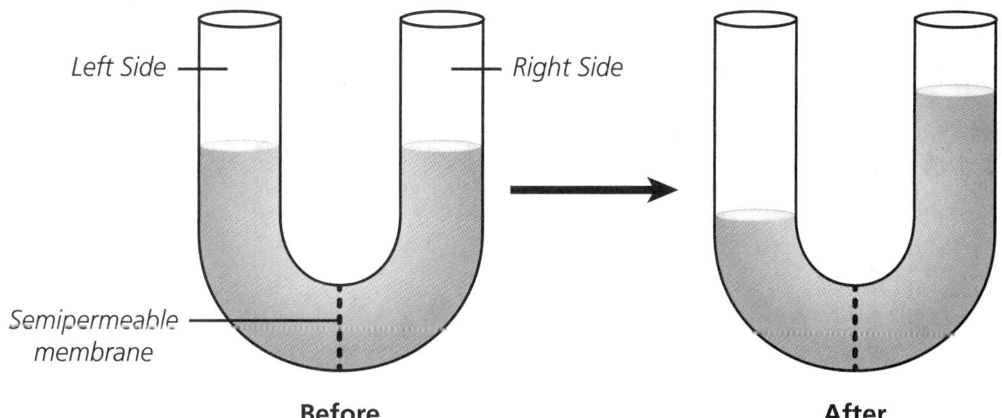

4 The image shows a U-shaped tube with a semipermeable membrane separating the right and left sides. Each side is filled with equal volumes of water and different concentrations of solute. Which statement explains the change in water volume?

A Water moved to the right side, where solute concentration was originally lower.

B Water moved to the right side, where solute concentration was originally higher.

C Water and solute moved to the right side, where solute concentration was originally lower.

D Water and solute moved to the right side, where solute concentration was originally higher.

Use the images below to answer question 5.

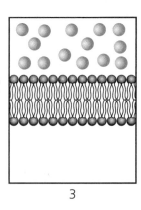

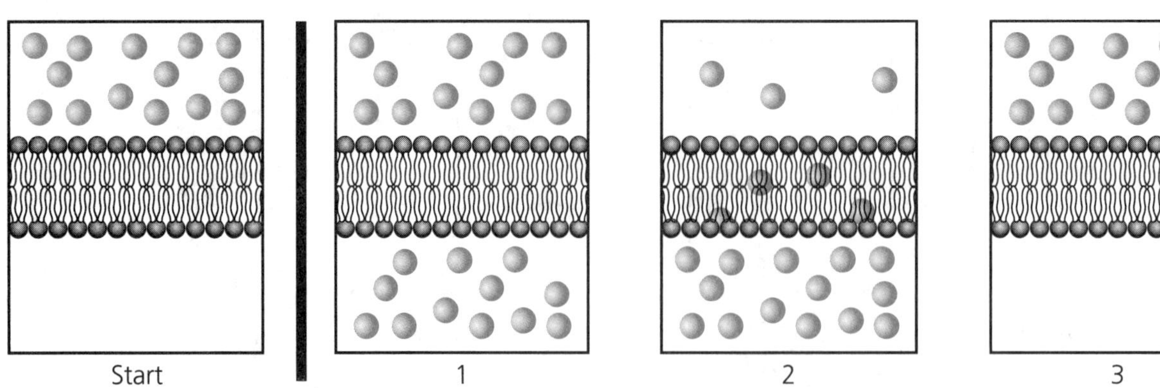

5 The diagram labeled *Start* shows the distribution of a dissolved material near a plasma membrane at a point in time. The concentration is high in the extracellular fluid and the only available method of transport is passive transport. The diagrams numbered 1, 2, and 3 depict possible outcomes after some time has passed.

A Does diagram 1 show a possible outcome of the original situation? Explain your reasoning.

____

____

____

____

B Does diagram 2 show a possible outcome of the original situation? Explain your reasoning.

____

____

____

____

C Does diagram 3 show a possible outcome of the original situation? Explain your reasoning.

____

____

____

____

LESSON 3

Active Transport

BIO.A.4.1.2

Passive transport moves material down its concentration gradient. It requires no energy input and stops once equilibrium is reached. However, some cells require a concentration gradient to be created and maintained. Other cells must take in or expel materials too large to fit through a membrane protein. When passive transport will not get the job done, cells resort to **active transport,** which requires energy in the form of ATP.

Active transport is the movement of particles from an area of low concentration across a membrane to an area of high concentration. It uses ATP as an energy source. Cells use active transport to build up a concentration gradient.

Ion and Molecular Pumps

A variety of active transport mechanisms move materials into and out of the cell. A common type of active transport uses membrane proteins called *ion pumps* and *molecular pumps*. These proteins use energy in the form of ATP to move substances in one direction or another, depending on the needs of the cell.

Ion pumps and *molecular pumps* are mechanisms of active transport. They use ATP to move material *against* a concentration gradient. Ion pumps move ions, or charged atoms. Molecular pumps move uncharged molecules.

For example, a nerve cell requires a very high concentration of sodium ions in the extracellular fluid and a similarly high concentration of potassium ions in the cytoplasm. The cell cannot achieve this state through passive transport. Once the concentration of an ion inside the cell equals that outside the cell, equilibrium is reached and passive transport ceases. To create a concentration gradient, active transport is required.

Remember that at equilibrium, the concentration of a solute is equal throughout. Once equilibrium is reached, passive transport cannot occur.

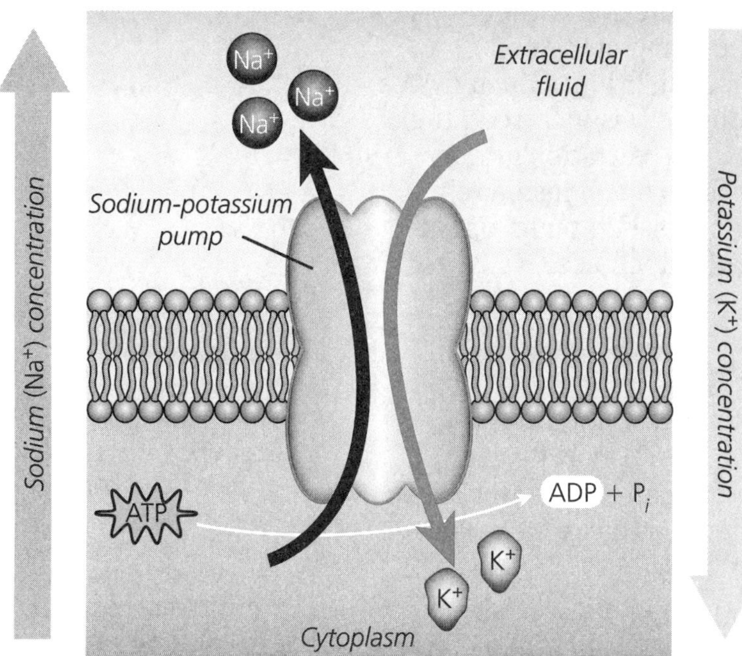

The sodium-potassium pump moves these ions against their concentration gradients with the energy from ATP.

The sodium-potassium pump moves sodium and potassium ions across the cell membrane, even if they are in equilibrium or if the concentration gradient is in the opposite direction of transport. Moving ions *against* a concentration gradient requires energy. ATP powers the pump, allowing it to create and maintain concentration gradients of these ions.

Cells of the small intestine must absorb glucose from digested food. Two types of membrane proteins work together to help glucose cross into these cells. Glucose-sodium cotransport proteins facilitate the absorption of glucose. They allow sodium ions to enter the cell. Each pair of sodium ions that enter take a glucose molecule along with them. Sodium-potassium pumps move sodium ions from inside the cell, into the small intestine.

Which statement compares the sodium-potassium pump and the glucose-sodium cotransporter?

A Both proteins require ATP to transport material.

B Both proteins require a concentration gradient to transport material.

C The glucose-sodium cotransporter relies on a concentration gradient, while the sodium-glucose pump requires ATP.

D The glucose-sodium cotransporter produces a concentration gradient, while the sodium-potassium pump creates an equilibrium.

Choice A is incorrect; the sodium-potassium pump requires ATP to actively transport ions across the cell membrane, while the glucose-sodium cotransporter facilitates diffusion without the need for ATP. Choice B is incorrect; the pump creates a concentration gradient, rather than an equilibrium, which drives diffusion through the cotransporter. Choice D is incorrect; the cotransporter relies on the sodium ion concentration gradient to allow transport of sodium and glucose. This diffusion produces an equilibrium. The sodium-potassium pump uses ATP to produce this concentration gradient; choice C is correct.

Endocytosis and Exocytosis

Macromolecules are often too large to fit through the cell membrane or membrane proteins. Cells can transport these molecules by packaging them in vesicles. Recall that a *vesicle* is a membrane sac found in the cytoplasm. Vesicles carry material between different parts of the cell.

Vesicles also transport material in and out of the cell. In **exocytosis,** a vesicle moves toward the plasma membrane and fuses with it. The phospholipid bilayer that makes up the vesicle joins the plasma membrane, and the material in the vesicle is released into the extracellular space.

Vesicles are small membrane sacs that transport material throughout the cytoplasm. The Golgi apparatus and ER produce vesicles to export proteins and other molecules.

Exocytosis releases substances from the cell. It is used to secrete hormones and neurotransmitters.

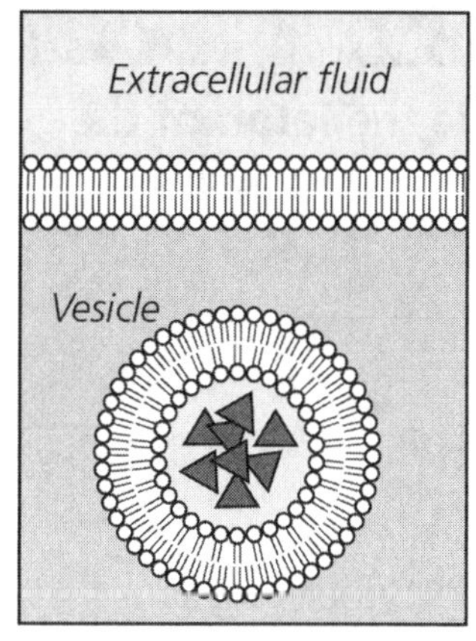

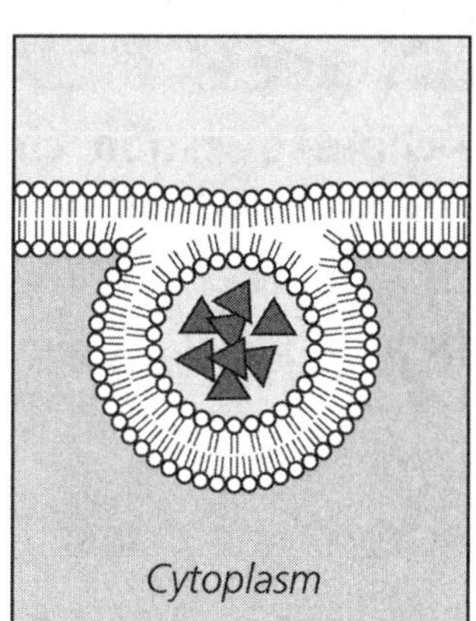

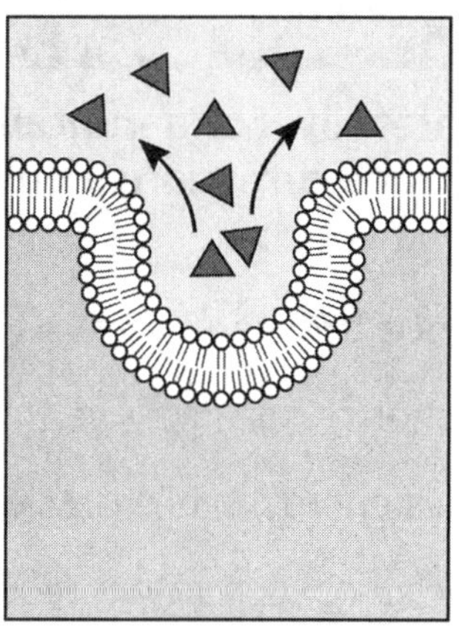

In exocytosis, a vesicle moves toward the membrane, fuses with it, and then releases the contained material to the extracellular fluid.

In **endocytosis,** the reverse occurs. The plasma membrane pinches inward around material located outside of the cell. It "swallows" the material, forming a vesicle around it that separates from the plasma membrane and travels into the cytoplasm. Both endocytosis and exocytosis require energy in the form of ATP. They are forms of active transport.

Endocytosis takes extracellular material into the cell by forming a membrane vesicle around it. The vesicle may then fuse with another vesicle containing digestive enzymes that break down the material.

In some cases, receptor proteins in the cell membrane help to carry out endocytosis.

Both endocytosis and exocytosis require energy in the form of ATP. They are forms of active transport.

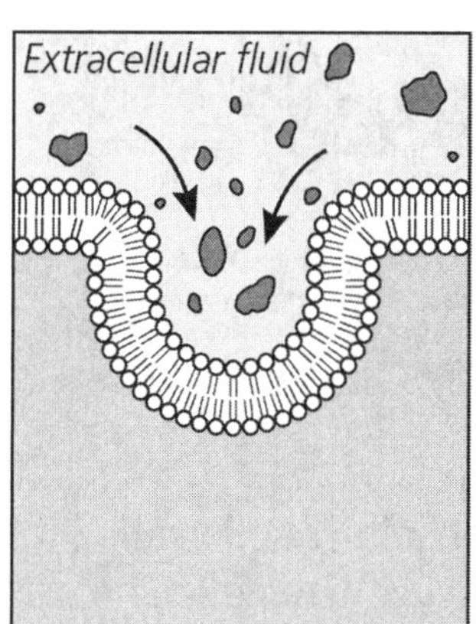

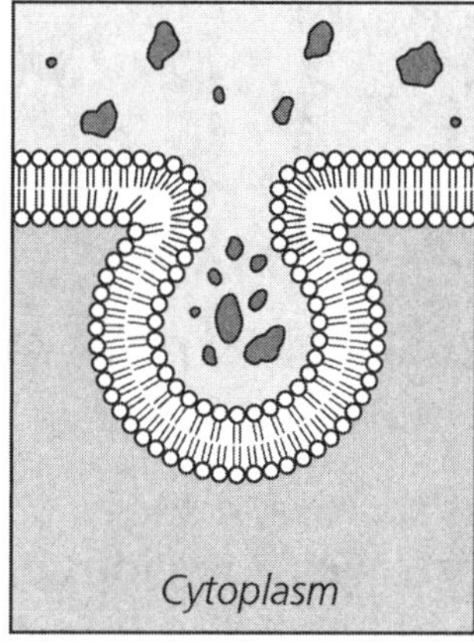

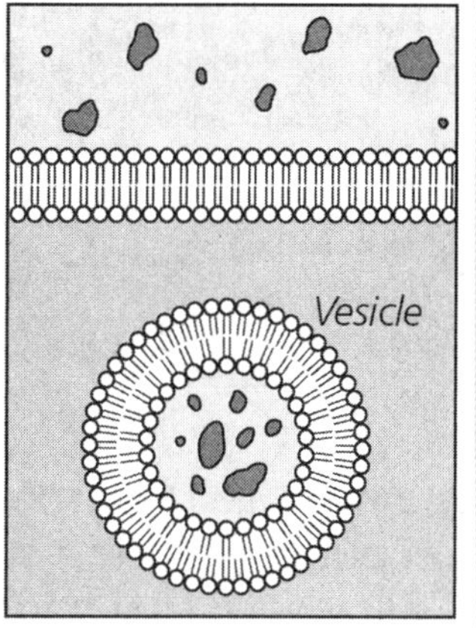

In endocytosis, the membrane engulfs material outside the cell and then transports and releases it in the cytoplasm.

A vesicle forms from the Golgi apparatus. The vesicle membrane holds a protein on the surface that faces the cytoplasm. When the vesicle fuses with the plasma membrane, will the protein face the cytoplasm or the extracellular fluid?

The protein will face the cytoplasm. This example describes exocytosis. When a vesicle fuses with the membrane, as shown in the image of exocytosis, its inner surface becomes the outer surface of the cell. A protein on the outer surface of the vesicle will be located on the inner surface of the plasma membrane, facing the cytoplasm of the cell.

IT'S YOUR TURN

Please read each question carefully. For a multiple-choice question, circle the letter of the correct response. For a constructed-response question, write your answers on the lines.

1 What is a major difference between active and passive transport?

A Active transport moves ions, while passive transport does not.

B Active transport requires energy, while passive transport does not.

C Active transport involves a concentration gradient, while passive transport does not.

D Active transport uses membrane proteins, while passive transport does not.

Use the diagram below to answer question 2.

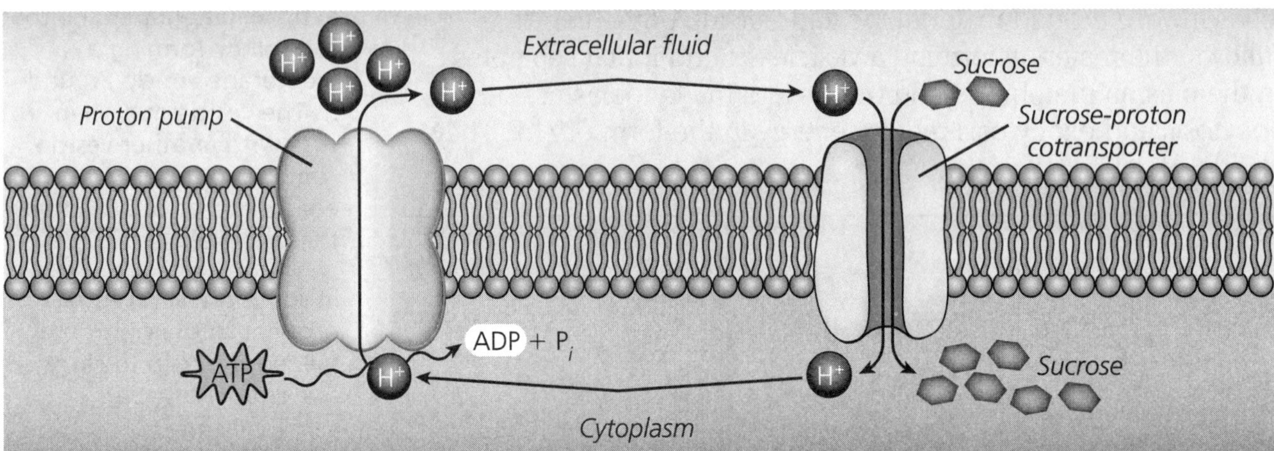

2 The diagram shows how a plant cell transports sucrose, a sugar. (The plant cell wall is not shown.) The proton pump (left) transports hydrogen ions outside the cell. The transport protein (right) allows hydrogen ions to move into the cell, but it must move a sucrose molecule along with each ion. Which statement **best** describes the transport of sucrose across the plasma membrane of the plant cell?

A Active transport of sucrose provides the energy to transport hydrogen ions.

B Facilitated transport of sucrose provides the energy to transport hydrogen ions.

C Active transport of hydrogen ions creates a concentration gradient of sucrose.

D Facilitated transport of hydrogen ions creates a concentration gradient of sucrose.

3 Cholesterol does not dissolve in blood and other water-based body fluids. To be transported throughout the body, it must be encased in lipoproteins, macromolecules that are water-soluble. How can a cell take in lipoproteins from its extracellular fluid?

A exocytosis

B endocytosis

C molecular pump

D facilitated diffusion

Use the diagram below to answer question 4.

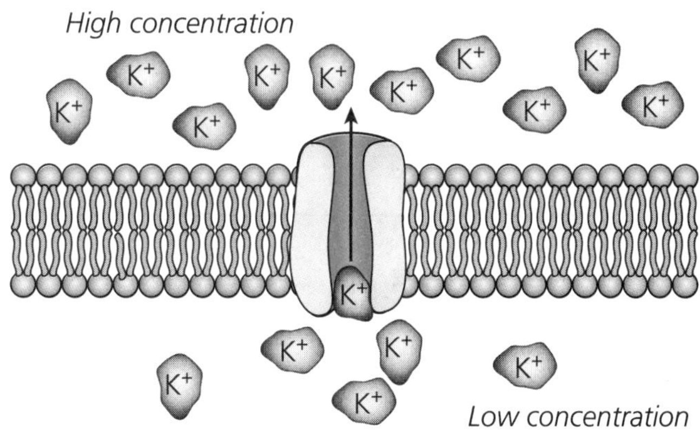

4 The diagram shows the movement of a substance across a plasma membrane. What is true about this process?

A It requires no energy.

B It is called exocytosis.

C It creates a concentration gradient.

D It stops when equilibrium is reached.

5 Materials in cells may be transported by passive or active processes, both of which may involve concentration gradients, the phospholipid bilayer, and membrane proteins.

A Compare the role of concentration gradients in passive and active transport.

B Compare the role of the phospholipid bilayer in passive and active transport.

C Compare the role of membrane proteins in passive and active transport.

Homeostasis

BIO.A.4.2.1

Every cell or complex organism is a **system**—a set of components that interact to produce something greater than the sum of its parts. Living systems work to maintain consistent internal states because changes in temperature or pH can affect their ability to function. All living things perform a balancing act in which internal conditions—including temperature, water, glucose, and oxygen—are regulated and maintained within specific ranges. This process is called **homeostasis.**

Thermoregulation

To maintain homeostasis, the body may rely on a cycle of monitoring and responding to internal conditions, called a *negative feedback loop*. This **homeostatic mechanism** is similar to the central heating and cooling system in a home. The home's thermostat is set to the desired temperature (say, 70°F). It detects the actual temperature of the air and, if it is lower or higher than desired, the thermostat affects the furnace or air conditioning. For example, if the detected air temperature is 74°F, the thermostat causes the air conditioning unit to turn on and cool the air. By continually sensing the air temperature, the thermostat ensures that the temperature remains around the set point.

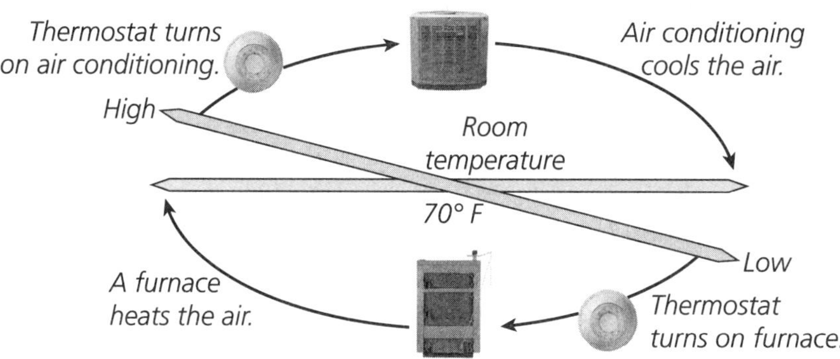

Thermostat turns on air conditioning.
Air conditioning cools the air.
High
Room temperature
70° F
Low
A furnace heats the air.
Thermostat turns on furnace.

A thermostat controls the heating and cooling systems, returning the home's temperature to a set point.

Negative feedback loops also regulate the body's internal states. Normal human body temperature is 37.0°C (98.6°F), and when it strays too far from this point, changes take place throughout the body to bring it back to normal. The hypothalamus of the brain senses the temperature of the blood passing through it. If temperature is too high or low, the hypothalamus sends signals to various parts of the body that cause it to release or retain heat. The mechanisms by which the body regulates temperature include shivering, perspiration, and the dilation (widening) or constriction (tightening) of the tiny blood vessels in the skin.

Homeostasis refers to the maintenance of a constant internal state. Glucose, water, temperature, and pH levels in the blood are maintained at constant levels.

The processes by which an organism monitors and maintains a constant state, such as temperature, is a **homeostatic mechanism.**

Internal conditions are not perfectly constant. Instead, they vary slightly as the body returns them to set points, a process called *dynamic equilibrium.*

A *negative feedback loop* is so called because any change to a system causes the system to return to its original state.

In contrast, a *positive feedback loop* amplifies a change to the system, causing it to move farther and farther from its original state. Contractions of the uterus during childbirth are controlled by a positive feedback loop. They grow stronger and more frequent until childbirth is achieved.

The *hypothalamus* is an area deep within the brain that senses and regulates many of the body's internal states. It acts as the body's thermostat.

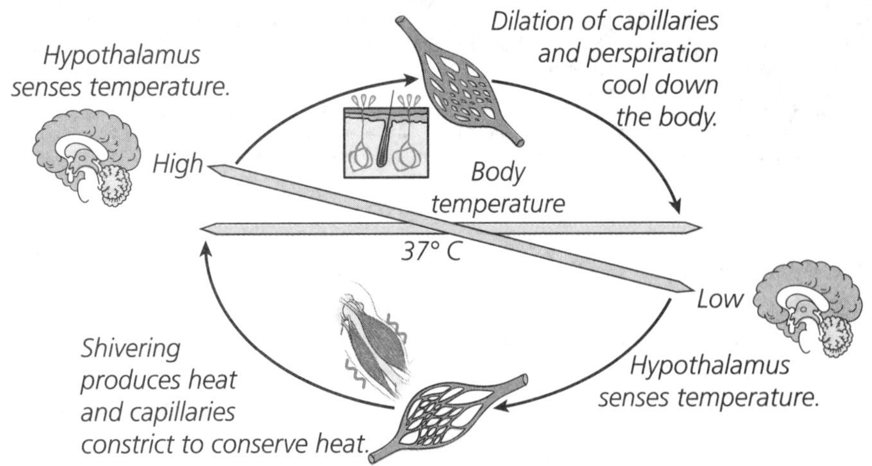

The hypothalamus of the brain detects changes in body temperature and instructs the body to conserve or release heat.

The human body maintains a constant internal temperature of 98.6°F. Which changes occur when the hypothalamus detects a temperature of 100.1°F?

A Muscle tissue shivers and skin capillaries dilate.

B Perspiration increases and skin capillaries dilate.

C Muscle tissue shivers and skin capillaries constrict.

D Perspiration increases and skin capillaries constrict.

The brain regulates body temperature by causing changes to other organ systems when temperature falls too low or rises too high. In the case of high body temperature, the hypothalamus causes the sweat glands (part of the endocrine system) to release more sweat, which cools the skin when it evaporates. The hypothalamus also causes the capillaries in the skin to dilate (widen), allowing more blood through. Because it is near the body's surface, the blood can transfer some of its heat to the environment. Choice B is correct.

Osmoregulation

Water is a critical component of life. Organisms must carefully regulate the balance of water and solutes (dissolved molecules and ions) in their bodies, a process called *osmoregulation*. The challenges of osmoregulation vary, depending on the organism's environment.

The fresh water of lakes and rivers is *hypotonic* to the cells of living things. Organisms that live in freshwater environments are faced with excess water entering the body and the loss of solutes. Freshwater fish, for example, excrete very dilute urine to eliminate excess water.

Thermoregulation is the regulation of body temperature.

Mammals are considered *endothermic* because our body temperature is independent of the external environment.

Reptiles and amphibians are considered *ectotherms* because they rely on the environment to regulate body temperature.

Perspiration cools the body through *evaporative cooling:* as sweat evaporates, it absorbs heat from the skin.

When a person is cold, tiny muscles in the skin lift the hair follicles, causing "goose bumps." Humans' lack of fur makes this a poor mechanism for keeping warm.

A freshwater environment is *hypotonic* to most organism's cells.

The saltwater marine environment is *isotonic* to most animals, such as fish. However, the solutes in seawater differ from those in the animals' bodies.

Organisms that inhabit saltwater oceans and seas are *isotonic* to their environment. However, they must find ways to retain the solutes they need and eliminate the excess sodium and chloride ions in seawater. Marine fish have specialized gill cells that excrete excess chloride ions.

The challenge for land animals is to conserve water. To achieve this, their urine is much more concentrated than their blood, containing a high ratio of solutes to water. This allows them to excrete excess solutes while conserving water. In the kidneys, the blood is first filtered into an intermediate fluid. Then, the kidneys reabsorb water and useful solutes from this fluid. By controlling reabsorption, the body can control how much water is lost in urine.

Another mechanism for maintaining water balance is the sensation of thirst. The brain sends signals to the mouth and throat that produce a feeling of dryness. This creates a drive (motivation) to drink fresh water, replacing the water that the body has lost.

Some prokaryotic organisms are adapted to the extremely salty, *hypertonic* environments of the Great Salt Lake and the Dead Sea.

The feeling of thirst, which motivates you to drink, is the body's way of maintaining water balance. A loss of as little as 1% of the body's water can produce this sensation.

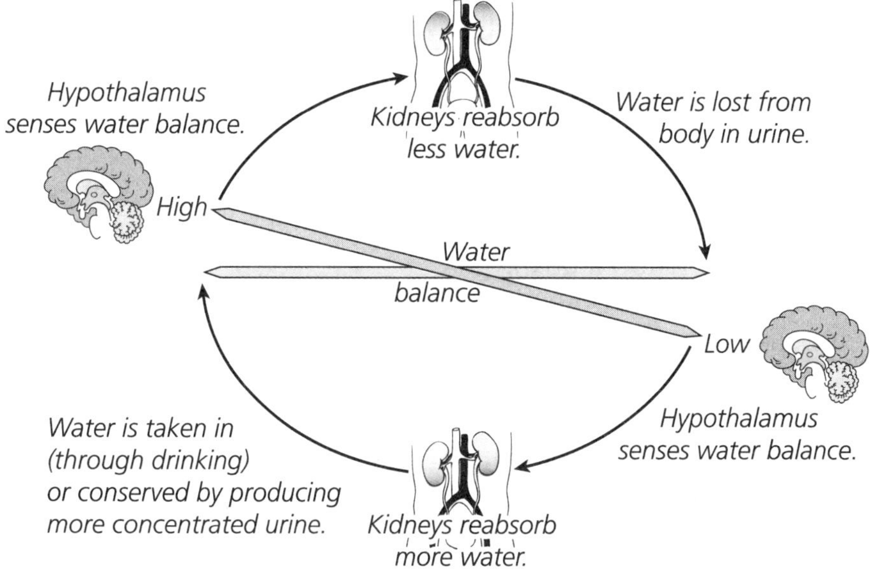

Blood vessels and the hypothalamus of the brain detect water balance in the body. The brain produces the sensation of thirst and hormones regulate water loss in the kidneys.

The body senses both the volume of water outside the cells (such as blood) and the concentration of solutes inside the cells.

Land animals constantly lose water through evaporation, perspiration, and urination. Water balance must be maintained to prevent dehydration. In mammals, the hypothalamus of the brain senses the concentration of solutes in cells. Nerve signals from special blood vessels sense the amount of fluid in the blood. These signals tell the hypothalamus whether the body needs to take in and conserve water, or whether excess water should be excreted. The brain produces hormonal signals that affect the amount of water the kidneys reabsorb.

Dehydration is dangerous because it changes the concentration of solutes in the body. The water lost in perspiration and urine must be replaced by drinking and eating.

A paramecium is a single-celled protist. Its contractile vacuole is an organelle that pumps water out of the cell. What can you conclude about the paramecium's environment?

The contractile vacuole removes excess water from the paramecium. The paramecium must therefore inhabit an environment that is hypotonic to the cell. It most likely lives in a freshwater environment, such as a pond or lake.

Gas Exchange

The body's cells require oxygen to carry out respiration, which produces carbon dioxide. The levels of dissolved oxygen and carbon dioxide in the blood must be regulated to allow respiration to take place.

Fish perform gas exchange through the gills. Water flows over the capillaries in the gills, which contain a higher concentration of carbon dioxide and a lower concentration of oxygen than the surrounding water. These differences cause carbon dioxide to move into the water and oxygen to move into the bloodstream, through passive transport.

Mammals perform gas exchange through passive transport within the lungs. Capillaries, tiny blood vessels, surround each of the microscopic air sacs in the lungs called *alveoli*. The blood flowing to the alveoli contains too much carbon dioxide and too little oxygen. Carbon dioxide in the capillaries crosses the surface of the alveoli and enters the air inside. Oxygen in the alveoli crosses in the other direction, into the capillary blood.

When cells use up oxygen more quickly, such as during strenuous exercise, the body compensates by moving air into and out of the lungs faster. This increases the rate of gas exchange and helps to maintain the levels of oxygen and carbon dioxide in the bloodstream.

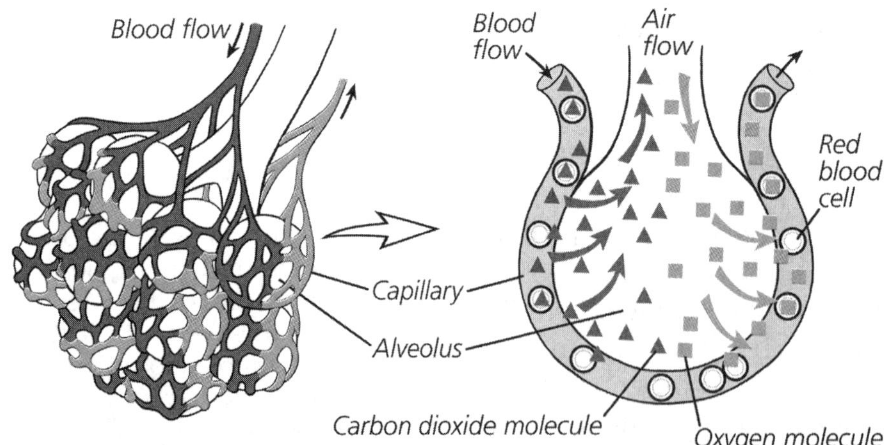

In mammals, the microscopic alveoli of the lungs are surrounded by capillaries. Gases are exchanged between the air inside the alveoli and the blood flowing through the capillaries.

The elimination of carbon dioxide and the intake of oxygen is called *gas exchange.*

Fish gills use a *counter-current exchange system* in which capillary blood moves opposite to the flow of water. This makes gas exchange more efficient.

Carbon dioxide dissolves to form a weak acid. If too much carbon dioxide is present, the pH level of the blood can fall dangerously low.

Gas exchange in gills and the alveoli of lungs takes place through passive transport. Gases move from where they are more concentrated to where they are less concentrated.

The hemoglobin protein in red blood cells helps to bind oxygen molecules.

Air pressure helps to push oxygen into the capillaries. At higher altitudes, air pressure is lower. What is the effect of moving to higher altitudes on the human body? How can the body compensate, in the short and long term, to maintain homeostasis?

At higher altitudes, less oxygen will enter the bloodstream and the cells of the body will receive less oxygen. The body can temporarily compensate by increasing breathing rate. After some time, the body increases the number of red blood cells in the blood, which helps it to take in more oxygen from the alveoli.

Regulation of Blood Glucose

The human body requires a blood glucose level of around 90 mg/100mL. If it falls too low or rises too high, homeostatic mechanisms bring it back into range. The control of glucose is achieved through a negative feedback loop, as shown in the diagram. The organ that senses blood glucose levels is the pancreas.

When the pancreas detects high glucose levels, it releases the *hormone* insulin. Insulin causes the cells of the muscles, liver, and other tissues to allow more glucose to cross the plasma membrane. The liver converts this glucose to glycogen. As a result, blood glucose falls back to normal.

When blood glucose is lower than 90 mg/100mL, the pancreas secretes another hormone, glucagon. Glucagon has the opposite effect on the liver, causing it to break down stored glycogen and release the glucose into the bloodstream. These changes bring about homeostasis.

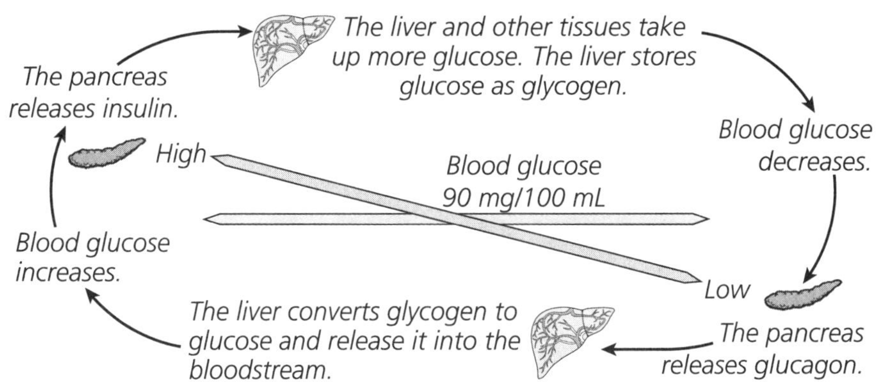

The liver and other tissues take up more glucose. The liver stores glucose as glycogen.
The pancreas releases insulin.
High
Blood glucose 90 mg/100 mL
Blood glucose decreases.
Blood glucose increases.
Low
The liver converts glycogen to glucose and release it into the bloodstream.
The pancreas releases glucagon.

A negative feedback loop regulates blood glucose levels. Hormones produced by the pancreas drive this process.

After skipping a meal and exercising, a body's blood glucose falls to 85 mg/100 mL. What changes will occur in the body?

The pancreas responds by secreting the hormone glucagon. This causes the liver to break down glycogen to its monomer, glucose, and release the glucose into the bloodstream.

A *hormone* is a chemical signal that is released into the blood by endocrine organs. Hormones reach all tissues, but affect only those tissues with specific receptor proteins on their surfaces.

Glucose is the simple sugar that cells break down for energy. Glycogen is the macromolecule that animals form as a way to store glucose. The liver stores glycogen and releases it as glucose when needed.

Diabetes is a disorder of blood glucose homeostasis. In type I diabetes, the pancreas does not produce enough insulin. In type II diabetes, the tissues do not respond to the insulin in the blood.

IT'S YOUR TURN

Please read each question carefully. For a multiple-choice question, circle the letter of the correct response. For a constructed-response question, write your answers on the lines.

1 Which of the following would **best** help to maintain homeostasis when a person's internal body temperature reaches 97.5°F?

A shivering

B perspiring

C dilation of capillaries

D formation of goose bumps

2 Some animals excrete nitrogen-containing wastes as urea in urine. Others excrete uric acid in the form of a thick paste. In which type of environment does the excretion of uric acid provide the greatest advantage?

A a desert ecosystem

B a rainforest ecosystem

C a freshwater pond ecosystem

D a saltwater marine ecosystem

3 Which is **not** an example of an organism maintaining homeostasis?

A A jogger stops to drink at a water fountain.

B A turtle spends hours sitting on a sunny rock.

C A deer seeks out salty foods to add to its diet.

D A rabbit hides among grasses to avoid a hawk.

Use the graph below to answer question 4.

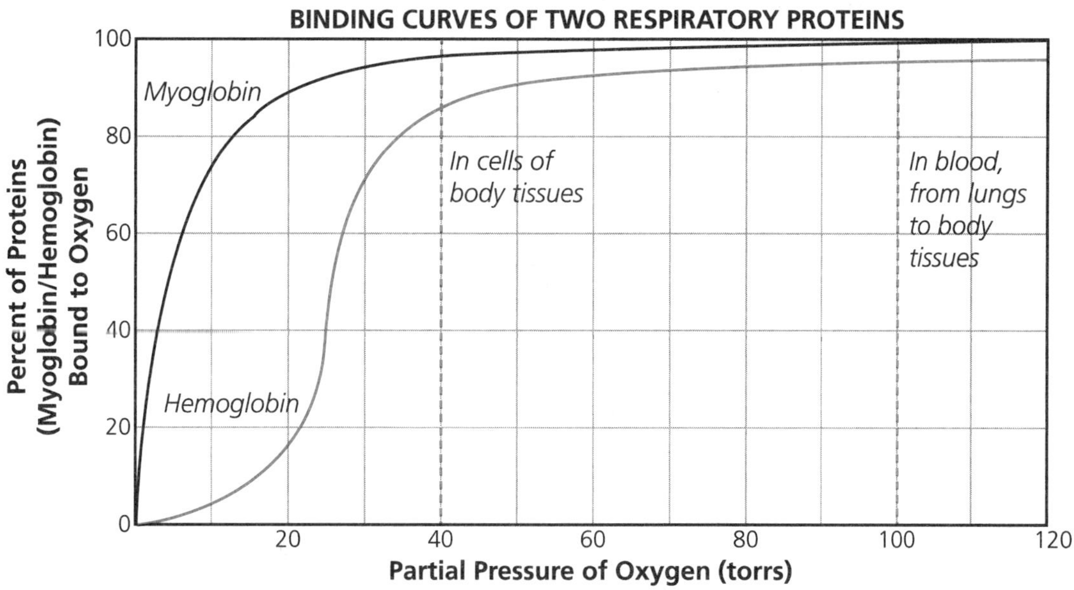

4 Myoglobin and hemoglobin are two proteins that bind to oxygen. Hemoglobin is present in red blood cells. Myoglobin, a similar protein, is present in muscle cells. The amount of oxygen dissolved in body fluids is measured as partial pressure. The graph above shows the percent of each protein that is bound to oxygen at different partial pressures. How does the binding of oxygen by myoglobin affect oxygen homeostasis?

A It reduces the amount of oxygen in the cells of body tissues.

B It increases the amount of oxygen in the alveoli of the lungs.

C It reduces the amount of oxygen in the blood returning to the lungs.

D It increases the amount of oxygen in the blood leaving the body tissues.

5 The digestive system breaks down food to basic components, such as glucose. These molecules are then absorbed into the body.

A person consumes a large meal.

A Explain how the consumption of the meal will affect blood glucose, which is normally maintained at 90 mg/mL.

____

____

____

____

B Explain how the body of a healthy person will respond to this change.

____

____

____

____

C In type II diabetes, the body tissues become less sensitive to insulin. Explain how the response of a person with type II diabetes will differ from that of a healthy person.

____

____

____

____

____

____

Module A Review
Cells and Cell Processes

Please read each question carefully. For a multiple-choice question, circle the letter of the correct response. For a constructed-response question, write your answers on the lines.

1 Which characteristic is shared by **all** prokaryotes and eukaryotes?

A a nucleus to control cell activities

B DNA to transmit genetic information

C photosynthesis to produce chemical energy

D organelles to transport proteins throughout the cell

2 Of the elements commonly found in biological molecules, which is capable of forming the greatest number of covalent bonds?

A carbon

B hydrogen

C nitrogen

D oxygen

3 Which of the following does **not** occur due to passive transport?

A A substance moves to an area of lower concentration.

B The concentration of a solution approaches equilibrium.

C The volume of a solution changes due to the movement of water.

D A concentration gradient of a dissolved substance in a solution is created.

Use the diagram below to answer question 4.

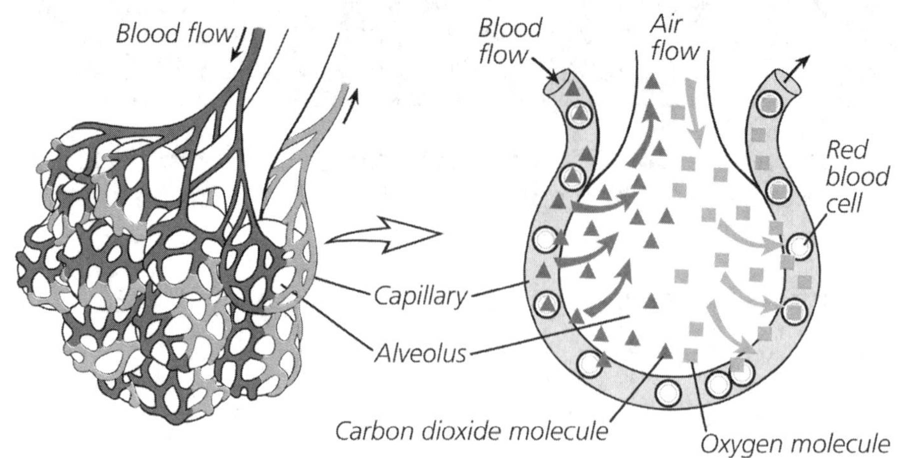

4 Inside the lungs are a large number of tiny sacs called alveoli, as shown in the diagram. A network of capillaries, or tiny blood vessels, surrounds each alveolus.

A Identify the function of alveoli and describe how their structure helps them to carry out this function.

____

____

____

____

B Identify the process that occurs in cells, and the organelle(s) responsible for it, that requires the function of the alveoli. Explain your response.

____

____

____

____

C At certain times, the blood builds up high levels of carbon dioxide and has low levels of oxygen. Explain how one or more of the body's organ systems can affect the alveoli to maintain homeostasis.

____

____

____

____

5 **Which statement correctly describes the location of DNA in prokaryotic and eukaryotic cells?**

A Prokaryotic cells have DNA in the nucleus; eukaryotic cells have DNA in the cytoplasm.

B Prokaryotic cells have DNA in the cytoplasm; eukaryotic cells have DNA in the nucleus.

C Prokaryotic cells have DNA in the ribosomes; eukaryotic cells have DNA in the nucleus.

D Prokaryotic cells have DNA in the cytoplasm; eukaryotic cells have DNA in the ribosomes.

6 **After a light rain, beads of water form on the waxy surfaces of leaves. Which statement correctly identifies the physical property of water that causes beads of water to form?**

A capillarity due to high specific heat of water

B cohesion due to the polarity of water molecules

C surface tension due to solubility of substances in water

D adhesion due to hydrogen bonding with the waxy surfaces

7 **Olive oil is a lipid. Wheat starch is a carbohydrate. Which describes how olive oil differs from wheat starch?**

A Wheat starch is a polymer, but olive oil is not.

B Wheat starch is an organic compound, but olive oil is not.

C Wheat starch contains nitrogen atoms, but olive oil does not.

D Wheat starch contains carbon, hydrogen, and oxygen, but olive oil does not.

Use the graph below to answer question 8.

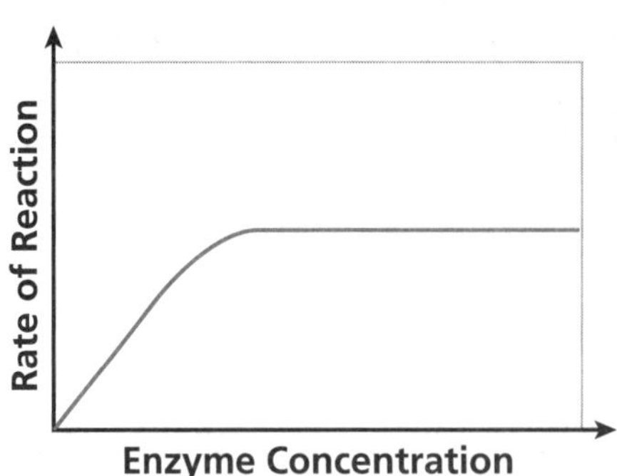

8 In an experiment, test tubes are filled with equal substrate concentrations and different enzyme concentrations. The graph shows the effect of enzyme concentration on the reaction rate.

A Describe how the quantities of enzyme, substrate, and product in a single test tube change over time.

____

____

____

____

B Describe how the quantities in the test tube can be changed to obtain a faster reaction rate than is shown in the graph.

____

____

____

____

C Describe one change that could be made to the test tube solution, other than changing the concentrations of substrate or enzyme, that would change the reaction rate. Explain.

____

____

____

____

9 Which of the following processes take place in the chloroplasts of a cell?

A Glucose is broken down into smaller molecules.

B Oxygen combines with hydrogen to form water.

C Lactic acid is released as a metabolic by-product.

D Carbon dioxide reacts to form organic compounds.

10 The cells of some organisms contain chlorophyll, which gives the organisms a characteristic appearance. Which statement **best** describes the role of chlorophyll in the cell?

A It stores energy for later use by the cell.

B It absorbs energy directly from sunlight.

C It releases energy when it is broken down chemically.

D It provides energy to chemical reactions throughout the cell.

11 The fumarase enzyme catalyzes the chemical conversion of fumarate to malate in the cell. This biochemical reaction is required for aerobic respiration. Which statement describes the reaction without the enzyme?

A It occurs but at a significantly slower rate.

B It cannot occur because there is no reactant.

C It occurs but at a faster, poorly regulated rate.

D It cannot occur because it lacks an energy source.

12 Epithelial cells have a large number of aquaporins compared to other cell types. Aquaporins are protein channels that allow water, but not other molecules, across the plasma membrane. Aquaporins aid in the transport processes of osmosis and facilitated diffusion.

A Describe one similarity shared by osmosis and facilitated diffusion.

____

____

____

____

B Describe one difference between osmosis and facilitated diffusion.

____

____

____

____

C Compared to other cell types, how will epithelial cells behave when placed in a hypotonic solution? Explain.

____

____

____

____

Use the graph below to answer question 13.

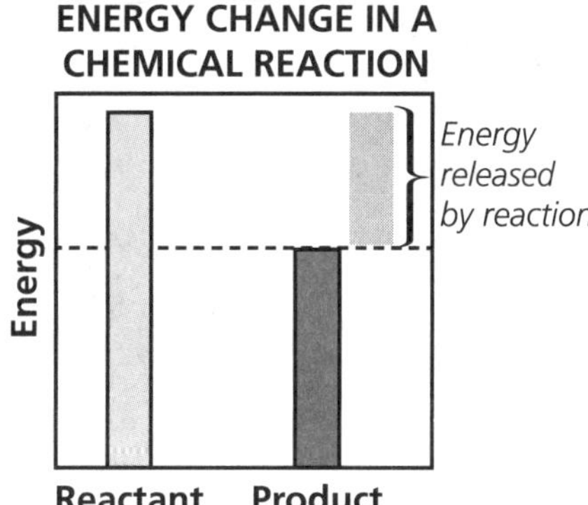

13 The graph above describes the energy change that results from a chemical reaction. To what is that energy change due?

A a reaction that requires ATP

B a reaction that requires ADP

C the breakdown of ATP to ADP and phosphate

D the synthesis of ATP from ADP and phosphate

14 The phospholipid bilayer of the plasma membrane is **least** permeable to which substances?

A starch molecules, due to their size

B oxygen molecules, due to their solubility

C cholesterol molecules, due to their polarity

D carbon dioxide molecules, due to their charge

15 Which statement correctly describes a reaction that forms a biological macromolecule?

A The hydrolysis of nucleotides forms DNA.

B The dehydration synthesis of amino acids forms RNA.

C The hydrolysis of a fatty acid and glycerol forms a lipid.

D The dehydration synthesis of monosaccharides forms glycogen.

Use the diagram below to answer question 16.

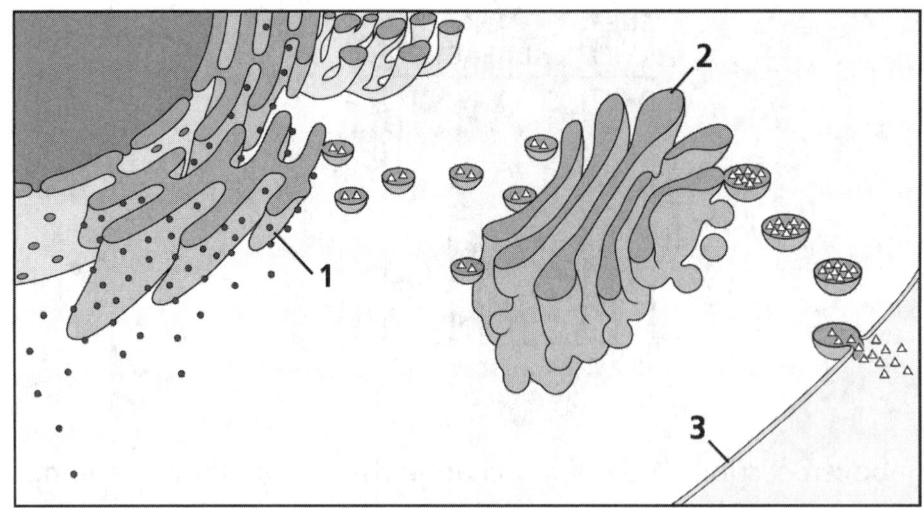

16 Three structures are labeled in the image of the animal cell above.

A Describe how material moves from structure 1 to structure 2.

____

____

____

____

B Identify and describe the process that moves material from structure 2 to structure 3 and the exterior of the cell.

____

____

____

____

C Classify the processes that transport materials from structure 1 to structure 2 to structure 3 to the outside of the cell as passive or active transport. Justify your response.

____

____

____

____

Module B

Continuity and Unity of Life

Unit 5

Cell Growth and Reproduction

To grow and reproduce, cells follow specific processes. This unit will help you review the processes of mitosis and meiosis as a cell goes through the cell cycle.

1 Genes and Protein Synthesis DNA serves as a blueprint for the synthesis of proteins and the transmission of genetic information. In this lesson, you will review the process of protein synthesis through transcription and translation, and the roles of particular organelles in the production of specific proteins. You will also review the basic structure of DNA and its relationship to genes.

2 The Cell Cycle, DNA Replication, and Mitosis The process that cells undergo to grow and reproduce is called the cell cycle. In this lesson, you will review the specific events that occur during the cell cycle: interphase, nuclear division in mitosis, and cytokinesis. You will also review how the process of DNA replication results in the transmission and/or conservation of genetic information.

3 Genes, Alleles, and Meiosis Meiosis is a second kind of cell division that occurs in organisms that reproduce sexually. In this lesson, you will review the processes and outcomes of meiotic nuclear division and compare them to mitosis. You will also review the functional relationships between DNA, genes, alleles, and chromosomes.

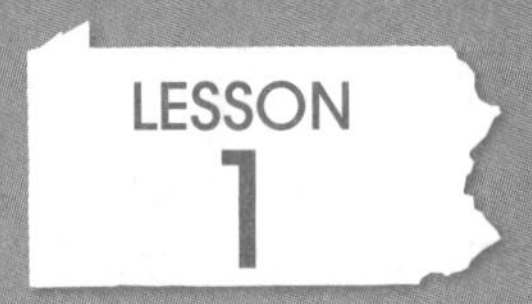

LESSON 1 Genes and Protein Synthesis

BIO.B.1.2.2, BIO.B.2.2.1, BIO.B.2.2.2

Proteins are vital to the functioning of cells. Nearly all cellular processes require proteins. Proteins are also important structural components of cells, and they play a role in cellular communication. To build proteins, the cell uses instructions contained in molecules of **deoxyribonucleic acid,** or **DNA.** Just as the blueprint for a building describes how to build the building, DNA is a blueprint that describes how to "build" a protein.

Deoxyribonucleic acid, or **DNA,** is the molecule that stores genetic information in living things.

DNA, Genes, and Chromosomes

A DNA molecule is a long polymer chain made up of *nucleotides.* Each nucleotide contains one of four nitrogen bases: adenine (A), cytosine (C), guanine (G), and thymine (T). DNA is usually found in the form of a double strand, made up of two molecules joined by bonds between the bases. The DNA bases can bond only in specific ways: adenine bonds only with thymine, and cytosine bonds only with guanine. These bonding rules are called *complementary base pairing rules.*

Nucleotides are the subunits that make up DNA. Each nucleotide consists of a sugar, a phosphate group, and a nitrogen base that varies among nucleotides.

The *complementary base pairing rules* state that base A pairs with T and C pairs with G.

Hydrogen bonds between nitrogen bases hold two DNA strands together as a double strand.

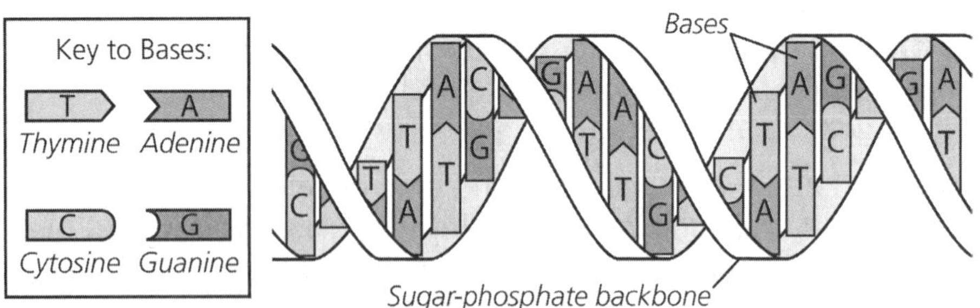

The two strands of DNA are joined by complementary base pairing.

The sequence of bases in DNA can be compared to the sequence of letters in this paragraph. Each group of three nucleotides, called a *codon,* stands for a particular amino acid. A string of nucleotides specifies the protein that will be built from the DNA instructions. A region of DNA that codes for a protein is a **gene,** and the rules for translating a DNA sequence to an amino acid sequence are known as the *genetic code.* The process by which genetic information is used to make a protein is called **gene expression.**

A *codon* is a sequence of three nucleotide bases that codes for a specific amino acid.

A **gene** is a stretch of DNA that contains the information needed to make a protein.

Although species differ in many of their genes, the *genetic code* is the same for nearly all the organisms on Earth. This is evidence for a common origin for all life.

Genes are found on **chromosomes.** In eukaryotes, these structures are confined to the nucleus. They are made up of DNA wound around proteins called *histones,* which can coil and condense further. Prokaryotic chromosomes are simple, circular DNA structures located in the cytoplasm.

A **chromosome** is a single piece of DNA, made up of genes.

One strand of DNA contains the base sequence ACGGTATCG. What base sequence does the complementary strand contain?

A CTAAGCGTA

B ACGGTATCG

C TGCCATAGC

D GCTATGGCA

Adenine (A) can bond only to thymine (T), and cytosine (C) can bond only to guanine (G). Therefore, to determine the base sequence on the complementary strand, replace each A with a T, each C with a G, each T with an A, and each G with a C. These replacements yield the sequence TGCCATAGC, so the correct choice is C.

Transcription: From DNA to RNA

In eukaryotes, DNA is located inside the nuclei of cells, but proteins are assembled in the cytoplasm outside the nucleus. Although DNA carries the instructions for making proteins, it does not leave the nucleus. Instead, the information contained in DNA is copied, and a "transcript" of the information moves out into the cytoplasm. This transcript is a molecule of *ribonucleic acid,* or *RNA.*

Ribonucleic acid, or *RNA,* is a single-stranded nucleic acid and contains a uracil base (U) in place of the thymine (T) found in DNA.

RNA is similar in structure to DNA; it is also made up of nucleotides. An RNA molecule, however, is made up of only one strand of nucleotides. A second difference between DNA and RNA is that RNA does not contain the base thymine. Instead, it contains uracil (U). Like thymine, uracil bonds only to adenine.

There are three main types of RNA: messenger RNA (mRNA), transfer RNA (tRNA), and ribosomal RNA (rRNA). Messenger RNA (mRNA) copies the information in the DNA molecule in the nucleus. The process in which information in DNA is copied is called **transcription.**

Transcription is the process in which genetic information from DNA is copied to mRNA.

Sequences of "junk DNA" may be snipped out of an mRNA transcript by enzymes in the nucleus.

Before transcription begins, specific proteins separate the two strands of the DNA molecule. The bonds between the bases break, but the backbone of the DNA molecule remains intact.

Only one DNA strand will be transcribed into mRNA. This DNA strand is called the *transcribed strand.* Within the nucleus, special proteins called *RNA polymerases* match individual mRNA nucleotides with complementary DNA nucleotides on the transcribed strand. The polymerases bond each mRNA nucleotide to the previous one, building up a strand of mRNA.

In eukaryotes, once an mRNA strand has been transcribed, it is further processed before it exits the nucleus for the cytoplasm.

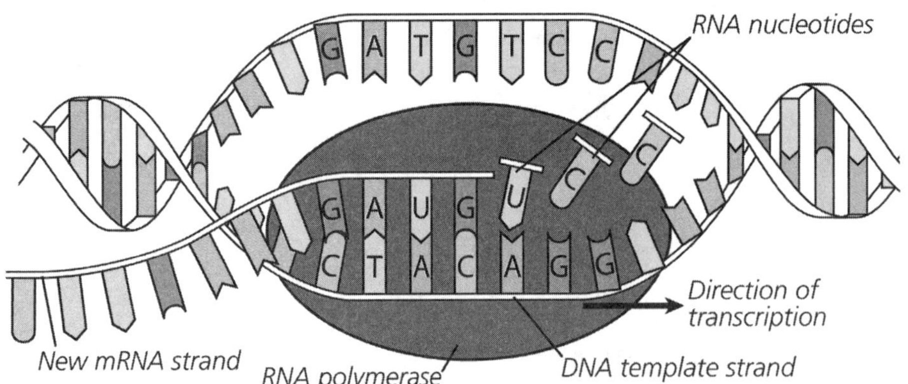

RNA polymerases transcribe DNA into mRNA.

Describe two roles for proteins in the transcription process.

Before an mRNA strand can be constructed, the two strands of a DNA molecule must be separated. Proteins separate the DNA strands. Once the strands are separated, RNA polymerases (which are also proteins) match the mRNA nucleotides to the DNA strand and build the mRNA strand.

Translation: From RNA to Protein

Proteins consist of chains of amino acids, and most proteins contain hundreds of these building blocks. There are about 20 different amino acids that make up proteins. The order of amino acids in a protein determines the protein's three-dimensional structure and its function. In turn, the sequence of bases in a strand of mRNA specifies the sequence of amino acids in the protein. The process of synthesizing proteins from mRNA sequences is called **translation,** as the language of genes is transformed into the language of proteins.

Proteins are synthesized in the cytoplasm of the cell. Translation is carried out by the **ribosomes,** small structures made of rRNA and protein that are found in all cell types. An mRNA strand will bind to a ribosome, which directs the assembly of the amino acid chain.

Ribosomes translate mRNA with the help of another type of RNA called tRNA. The two ends of a tRNA molecule have special functions. One end binds to a free amino acid in the cytoplasm. Each of the 20 different types of amino acids in a cell can be bound by one or more specific tRNA molecules.

The opposite end of a tRNA molecule is a special region called the *anticodon.* Recall that the genetic information in mRNA is read as triplets called *codons.* The anticodon of tRNA is complementary

A protein consists of one or more long chains of amino acids. The chains fold to give it a three-dimensional structure.

Translation is the process in which the base sequence in a strand of mRNA is converted, or "translated," into the amino acid sequence of a protein.

The **ribosomes** of eukaryotic cells may be found free in the cytoplasm or bound to the rough endoplasmic reticulum. rRNA and protein make up each ribosome.

tRNA stands for *transfer RNA,* because it transfers free amino acids to the growing peptide chain on the ribosome.

to a codon on the mRNA transcript. For example, the base sequence UGG is the codon for the amino acid tryptophan. A tRNA molecule that binds to tryptophan has the complementary anticodon sequence ACC. When it bonds with the codon on mRNA, it brings the correct amino acid along with it.

A ribosome, mRNA strand, and tRNA molecules work together to assemble a protein. The mRNA strand attaches to a specific site on the ribosome, where the first or "start" codon is exposed. A tRNA molecules with a complementary anticodon binds to the start codon, bringing the first amino acid along with it.

Then, the ribosome moves along the mRNA strand and exposes the next codon, allowing the appropriate tRNA molecule to bring its amino acid into place. As each amino acid is carried to the ribosome, it is bound to the previous amino acid, making the polypeptide chain longer. The tRNA molecule is detached and released into the cytoplasm, the ribosome shifts to the next codon, and the process is repeated.

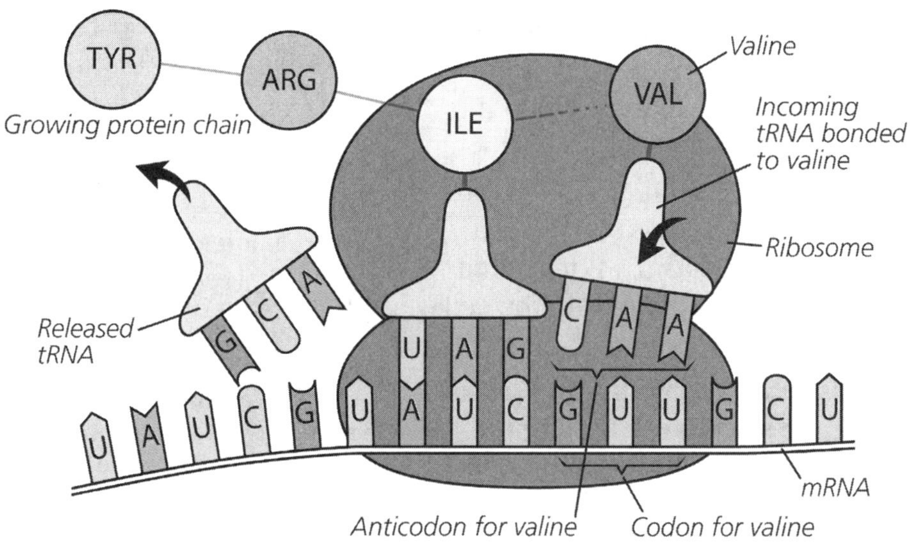

The ribosome and amino-acid–carrying tRNA translate the mRNA sequence into a protein.

The table below identifies several amino acids and their associated tRNA anticodons.

Amino Acid	Anticodon
Serine	AGA
Valine	CAA
Leucine	GAU

A protein contains the following sequence of amino acids: leucine, serine, leucine, valine. What DNA sequence was used as a template for the mRNA coding for this sequence of amino acids? Explain your answer.

An *anticodon* is a sequence of three tRNA bases that binds to a complementary mRNA codon.

tRNA and rRNA are also transcribed from genes in the nucleus.

Some amino acids are coded for by more than one codon. For example, histidine is coded for by both CAU and CAC.

A polypeptide is a chain of amino acids, i.e., a protein.

The order of amino acids in a protein is only one of the factors that determine the protein's properties. Once the chain has formed, it folds in a specific way, giving it a particular three-dimensional shape. The shape of the protein is very important in allowing it to function properly. Disruption to the shape of a protein can change the protein's function or make it completely nonfunctional.

Special "start" and "stop" codons on mRNA tell the ribosome where translation should begin and end.

The anticodon sequence was GAU-AGA-GAU-CAA. The anticodons are complementary to the mRNA codons. Therefore, the mRNA strand that coded for this sequence must have had the codon sequence CUA-UCU-CUA-GUU. The DNA strand was complementary to that mRNA strand, so it must have had the sequence GAT-AGA-GAT-CAA. Notice that this DNA sequence is the same as the tRNA sequence, except that all the uracil (U) has been replaced by thymine (T).

Protein Synthesis in the Cell

The process of transcription of DNA to RNA, followed by the translation of mRNA into protein, is called the *central dogma of biology.* It occurs in all living cells, both prokaryotic and eukaryotic. All cells have polymerase enzymes that transcribe DNA to mRNA and ribosomes that translate the information in mRNA to a sequence of amino acids.

In eukaryotic cells, a number of organelles are also involved in these processes. Chromosomes cannot leave the nucleus, which is where transcription of mRNA occurs. The mRNA strand exits to the cytoplasm through a pore in the nuclear membrane.

In the cytoplasm, ribosomes may be free or bound to the rough endoplasmic reticulum (ER). Proteins that will be used by the cell are translated by the free ribosomes in the cytoplasm. Proteins that are destined for the plasma membrane or for secretion from the cell are assembled by the ribosomes of the rough ER.

The rough ER modifies the newly assembled proteins and packs them into vesicles. These small membrane sacs travel through the cytoplasm to the Golgi apparatus. There, they are further modified so that they reach their intended destinations. From the Golgi apparatus, protein-containing vesicles head toward the plasma membrane of the cell. The flowchart on the next page summarizes the process of protein synthesis in a eukaryotic cell.

The *central dogma of molecular biology* states that information in DNA is transcribed to RNA, which is then translated to protein.

In prokaryotic cells, which lack nuclei, transcription and translation both take place in the cytoplasm.

In eukaryotes, ribosomes may be found either free in the cytoplasm or bound to the rough endoplasmic reticulum (ER).

There are two kinds of ER, rough and smooth. Smooth ER is involved in the production of fatty acids and lipids. No ribosomes are attached to smooth ER.

A vesicle is a small membrane sac inside the cell, which may contain material for transport. Proteins are transported in vesicles from the ER to the Golgi apparatus, and then to the plasma membrane.

The Golgi apparatus is an organelle made up of many stacks or folds of membrane. It accepts proteins from the ER, modifies the proteins, packages them into vesicles, and releases the vesicles on the side nearest the plasma membrane.

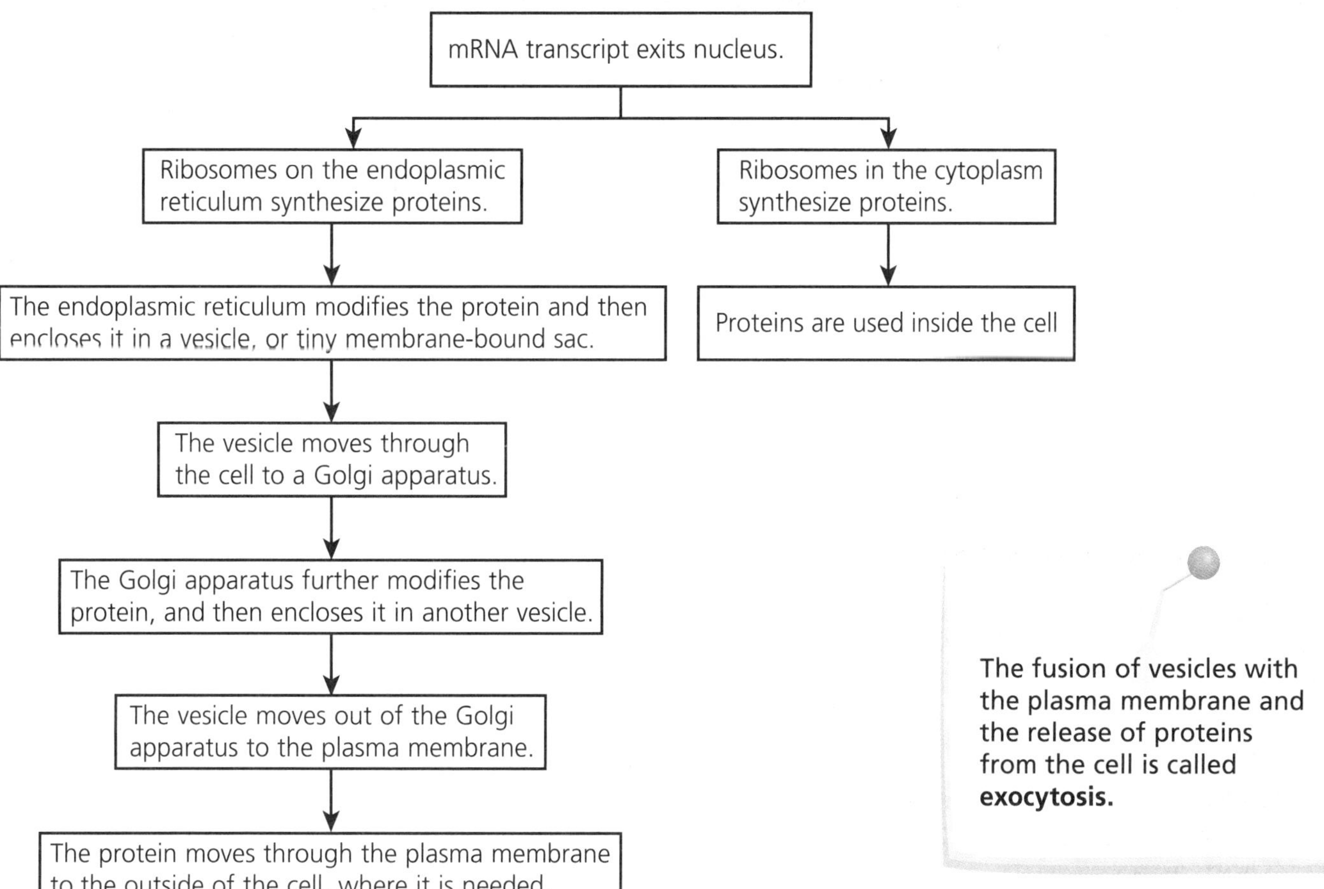

PROTEIN SYNTHESIS IN EUKARYOTIC CELLS
mRNA transcript exits nucleus.
Ribosomes on the endoplasmic reticulum synthesize proteins.
Ribosomes in the cytoplasm synthesize proteins.
The endoplasmic reticulum modifies the protein and then encloses it in a vesicle, or tiny membrane-bound sac.
Proteins are used inside the cell
The vesicle moves through the cell to a Golgi apparatus.
The Golgi apparatus further modifies the protein, and then encloses it in another vesicle.
The vesicle moves out of the Golgi apparatus to the plasma membrane.
The protein moves through the plasma membrane to the outside of the cell, where it is needed.

The fusion of vesicles with the plasma membrane and the release of proteins from the cell is called **exocytosis.**

Which organelle is **not** involved in the synthesis and secretion of a protein from the cell?

A ribosome

B smooth ER

C Golgi apparatus

D plasma membrane

Proteins are synthesized by ribosomes of the rough ER and sent to the Golgi apparatus for further modification, so choices A and C are incorrect. From there, the proteins are packaged in vesicles that fuse with the plasma membrane to exit the cell by exocytosis, so choice D is incorrect. The smooth ER, which lacks ribosomes, synthesizes lipids and hormones rather than proteins. Choice B is correct.

IT'S YOUR TURN

Please read each question carefully. For a multiple-choice question, circle the letter of the correct response. For a constructed-response question, write your answers on the lines.

1 Which pair consists of terms that represent equivalent units of information?

A codon : DNA

B gene : polypeptide

C chromosome : protein

D nucleotide : amino acid

Use the table below to answer questions 2 and 3.

mRNA CODONS FOR SEVERAL AMINO ACIDS

Amino Acid	Codons	Amino Acid	Codons
Asparagine	AAU, AAC	Lysine	AAA, AAG
Cysteine	UGU, UGC	Tyrosine	UAU, UAC

2 An mRNA strand codes for the amino acid sequence cysteine-tyrosine-lysine-cysteine-asparagine. Which of the following DNA sequences is used as the template for this mRNA?

A ACA-ATG-TTT-ACG-TTG

B TGT-TAC-AAA-TGC-AAC

C UGU-UAC-AAA-UGC-AAC

D ACA-AUG-UUU-ACG-UUG

3 A tRNA molecule with which of the following anticodons would be able to bind to a molecule of lysine?

A TTT

B TTC

C AAA

D UUC

4 Suppose all of the ribosomes in a cell were destroyed. How would this **most likely** affect the process of gene expression?

A The DNA double strand would be unable to separate.

B The cell would be unable to form mRNA strands.

C The amino acids could not be joined to form a protein.

D The tRNA molecules would bind to the wrong amino acids.

5 A gene specifies a protein that is to be secreted by the cell. Which sequence traces the path of the protein through the cell?

A Golgi apparatus → vesicle → rough ER → vesicle

B rough ER → vesicle → Golgi apparatus → vesicle

C smooth ER → rough ER → vesicle → Golgi apparatus

D unbound ribosome → rough ER → vesicle → Golgi apparatus

6 Consider the process of gene expression in a eukaryotic cell.

A Describe two similarities between transcription and translation.

____

____

____

____

____

____

B Describe two differences between transcription and translation.

____

____

____

____

C Identify one difference between the synthesis of proteins used within the cell and the synthesis of proteins that will be secreted from the cell.

____

____

____

____

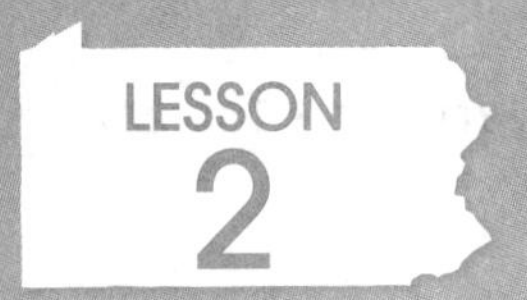

LESSON 2 The Cell Cycle, DNA Replication, and Mitosis

BIO.B.1.1.1, BIO.B.1.2.1

Every multicellular organism begins as a single cell. That cell divides into two cells, which then divide to make four cells, then eight, and so on, until a body with trillions of cells is formed. Cell division continues throughout life, helping to repair tissues and replace damaged cells. A cell does not spend all its time dividing, however. It undergoes distinct changes at each step of the **cell cycle.**

Although nearly every cell in your body has the same DNA, different genes are expressed in different cells.

The **cell cycle** describes the stages of a single cell's life.

The Cell Cycle

A cell passes through three main stages in its lifetime: interphase, nuclear division, and cytokinesis. The longest of these is **interphase,** which is itself divided into three stages, as shown in the diagram. During interphase, the cell grows and prepares for cell division. An important stage of interphase is the S phase. S stands for *synthesis,* because this is when a cell synthesizes a copy of its DNA.

Interphase is the longest phase of the cell cycle. In interphase, the cell grows during the G1 stage, replicates its DNA during the S stage, and prepares to divide during the G2 stage.

S phase is when the genetic material in a cell doubles.

Cell division (mitosis and cytokinesis) is sometimes called the *M phase.*

For simplicity, this cell cycle diagram shows only a single chromosome in the cell nucleus. In reality, a cell has many more chromosomes undergoing these phases at the same time.

THE CELL CYCLE

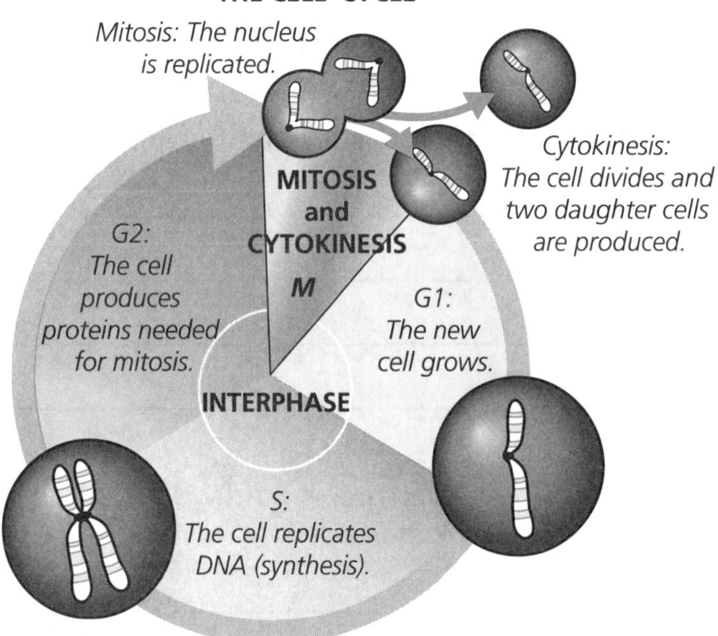
Mitosis: The nucleus is replicated.
Cytokinesis: The cell divides and two daughter cells are produced.
MITOSIS and CYTOKINESIS
M
G2: The cell produces proteins needed for mitosis.
G1: The new cell grows.
INTERPHASE
S: The cell replicates DNA (synthesis).

Notice how most of the cell cycle is spent in preparation for nuclear and cell division. By preparing early, the cell is able to undergo the next stage as soon as new cells are needed. The form of nuclear division that produces most cells of the body is **mitosis,** which produces an exact replica of the nucleus and all its chromosomes. The final stage of the cell cycle is **cytokinesis,** in which the original *parent cell* splits into two *daughter cells.*

In **mitosis,** chromosome number remains the same in the two daughter cells that form.

Cytokinesis is the final phase of the cell cycle during which the cytoplasm divides in two.

Every species has a characteristic number of chromosomes in its body cells. For humans, that number is 46. Egg and sperm cells, or gametes, have 23 chromosomes each. Can mitosis produce gametes? Explain.

Mitosis cannot produce gametes because it keeps the number of chromosomes in the daughter cell the same as in the parent cell.

Chromosome Number

For a cell to form two genetically identical daughter cells, it must first duplicate its nucleus. If the parent cell has 46 chromosomes, each daughter cell must also have 46 chromosomes. This requires first making a copy of the DNA in each chromosome. Before **DNA replication,** each chromosome consists of two DNA "arms" with a centromere in the center. Replication produces an identical copy of each chromosome "arm," but the copies are still joined at the centromere. They are called sister chromatids, and they will remain joined until nuclear division.

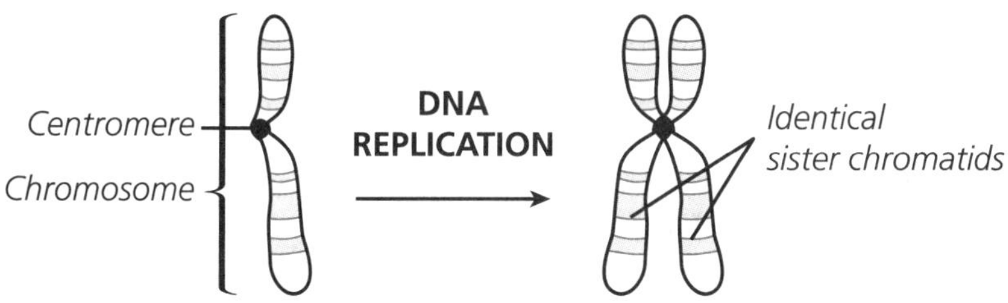

An unreplicated chromosome (left) and replicated chromosome (right).

Every species has a characteristic *chromosome number,* which is the number of chromosomes in its body cells. This is sometimes called the *diploid* number of chromosomes.

DNA replication produces an exact copy of the genetic material in a chromosome. The identical *sister chromatids* are joined at the *centromere.*

To determine the number of chromosomes, count the number of centromeres.

Mitosis keeps the number of chromosomes in a cell the same. Examine the diagram of the cell cycle on page 114. When does the cell have twice the normal number of chromosomes?

A during the S phase only

B during the M phase only

C during the G2 and S phases

D during the G2 and M phases

Choices A and C are incorrect because chromosome number does not double in S phase. Although DNA is replicated and each chromosome consists of a pair of identical sister chromatids, the number of centromeres is the same. Choice D is incorrect because sister chromatids do not separate in the G2 phase. Sister chromatids separate during mitosis, the M phase, and for a brief period of time, the cell contains twice the normal chromosome number. Choice B is correct.

DNA Replication

DNA replication is carried out by enzymes. At the beginning of DNA replication, an enzyme, *DNA helicase,* binds to a site on the double-stranded DNA and begins to separate the two strands. Then, the enzyme *DNA polymerase* moves along each strand, pairing free nucleotides to the nucleotides in the strand.

Hydrogen bonds join the two strands of a DNA double strand. These temporary bonds are easily broken and reformed.

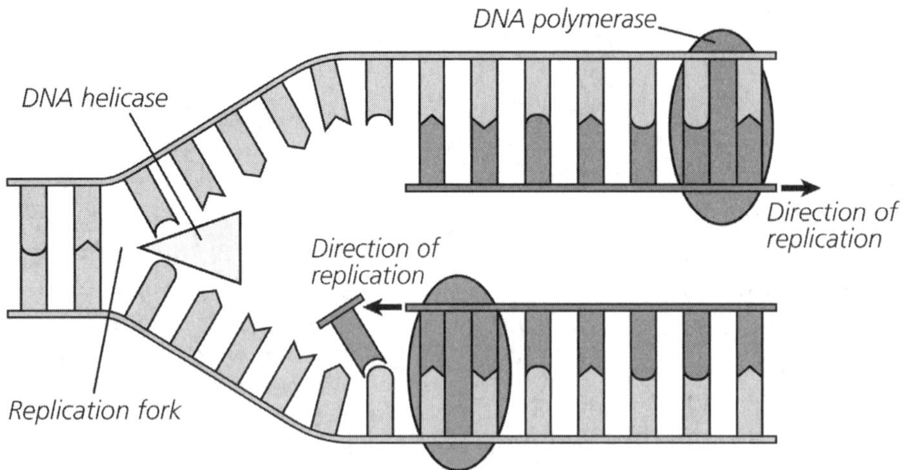

The DNA double strand separates at specific sites, and DNA polymerase assembles a new, complementary strand on each original strand.

Enzymes are often named for their function. The DNA polymerase enzyme helps to assemble a DNA polymer.

The pairing of new nucleotides follows complementary base pairing rules (A pairs with T and C pairs with G). This complementary pairing ensures that a complete copy of the DNA can be produced from either strand of the original DNA. Each single strand from the original DNA serves as a template for a new complementary strand. As a result, each "new" double strand contains one strand that came from the original DNA and one newly synthesized strand. For this reason, DNA replication is called **semiconservative.**

Complementary base pairing rules (A with T and C with G) ensure that new strands are identical to old strands.

Semiconservative replication means that each "new" double strand consists of one original strand and one newly assembled strand.

The image below represents the DNA of a cell that is just entering the S phase of interphase. The darker DNA strands are composed of "old" nucleotides.

DNA before S phase of interphase

In the answer options, the lighter strands are composed of "new" nucleotides joined during DNA replication. Which image represents the DNA strands found in the cell **after** S phase?

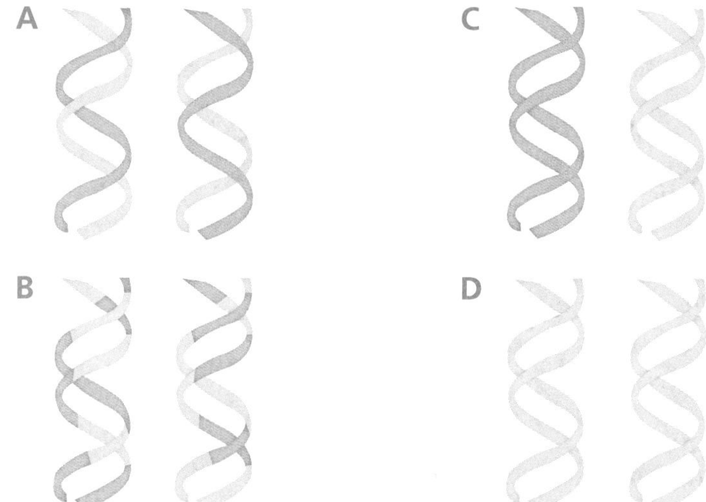

During DNA replication, each new DNA strand forms as the complementary strand of an existing DNA strand. Because the "old" strands remain, choice D is incorrect. Because each replicated double strand consists of one old and one new strand, choices B and C are incorrect. Choice A shows that the newly assembled strands are each paired with one existing strand.

Mitosis and Cytokinesis

After a eukaryotic cell's DNA has been replicated in the S phase, and the required proteins have been synthesized in the G2 phase, the cell is ready to undergo mitosis. **Mitosis** is the duplication of the nucleus. It is divided into four main phases: *prophase, metaphase, anaphase,* and *telophase.*

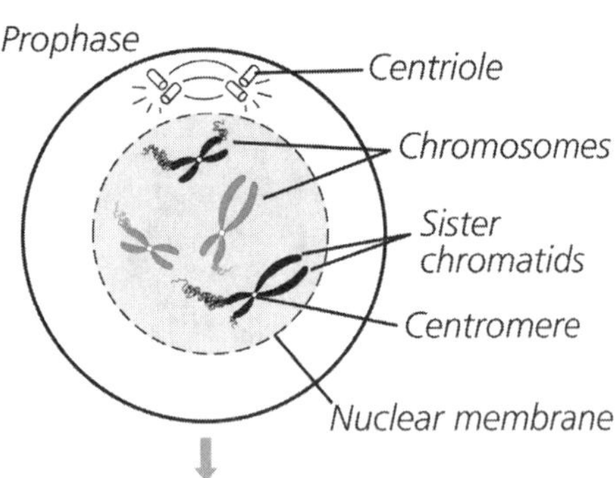

During prophase, the nuclear membrane begins to break down. The DNA molecules coil up, making the chromosomes much smaller. Tiny structures called *centrioles* begin to move toward the poles of the cell.

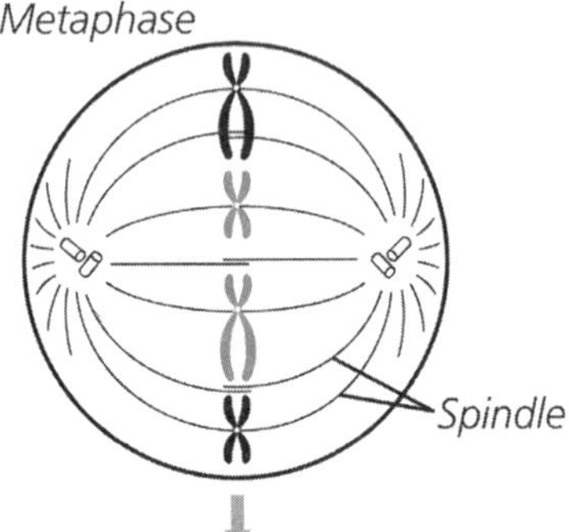

During metaphase, the centrioles produce structures called *spindles.* The spindles attach to the centromeres on the sister chromatids. The chromatids line up along the center of the cell.

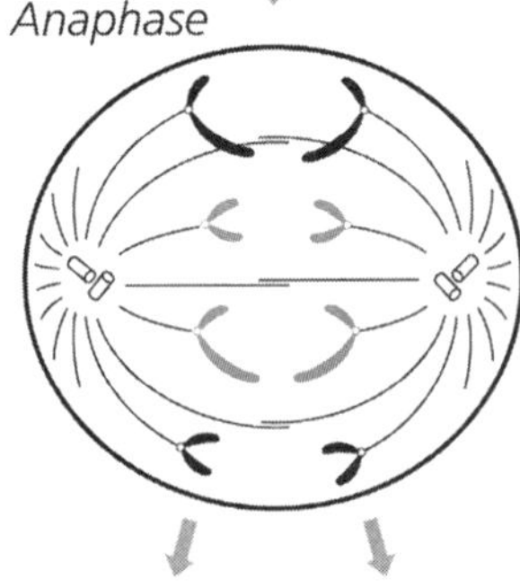

During anaphase, the spindles shorten. As they shorten, they pull the sister chromatids apart. The chromatids from each pair move to opposite poles of the cell.

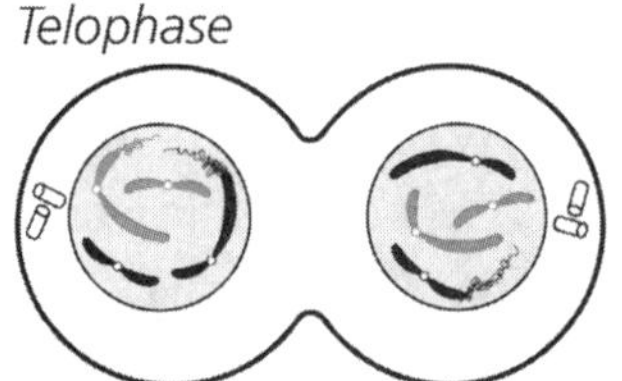

During telophase, new nuclear membranes form around the newly separated chromosomes. The chromosomes unwind, becoming longer and thinner.

At the end of mitosis, two new nuclei have formed. The cell is now ready to divide into two daughter cells, a process called **cytokinesis.** Cytokinesis may begin even as the last stage of mitosis is still underway. The cell membrane "pinches in" at the center, cleaving the cell into two equal halves. Imagine an invisible string tied around the cell, tightening around the center and eventually separating the two halves completely. The daughter cells that result from mitosis are genetically identical to each other, and to the original parent cell.

Mitosis is the process of duplicating the nucleus of a eukaryotic cell.

The phases of mitosis are *prophase, metaphase, anaphase,* and *telophase.*

Normally, the chromosomes are very loose strands instead of the compact X-shaped structure shown here. During prophase, chromosomes condense, their DNA and proteins coiling tightly, to produce this familiar shape.

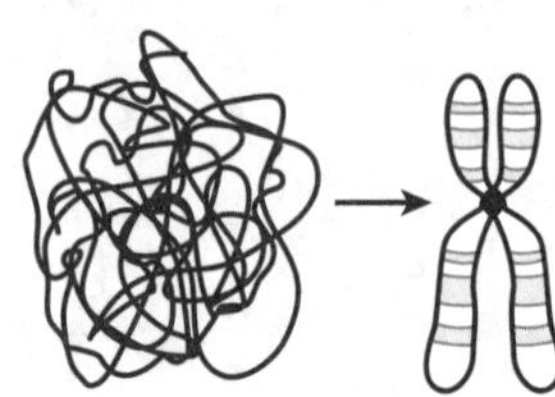

Although you may read about the phases of mitosis, you should keep in mind that mitosis is a continuous process. The cell does not "jump" from one phase to the next. The transitions between phases are smooth and continuous.

Cytokinesis is the process in which the cytoplasm, organelles, and plasma membrane of a cell divide to form two daughter cells.

Plant cells, which have cell walls, must form a new cell wall plate between the two nuclei during cytokinesis.

Explain how mitosis ensures that daughter cells have the correct number and types of chromosomes.

At the beginning of mitosis, each chromosome has replicated its DNA. The two identical sister chromatids are joined at the centromere. During metaphase, spindle fibers attach to the centromeres. The fibers are anchored to centrioles at opposite ends of the cell. When the chromatids separate, each one is joined to one centromere. The chromatids are pulled to opposite sides of the cell, and each one becomes part of one new nucleus. In this way, mitosis ensures that each nucleus contains one copy of each chromosome.

IT'S YOUR TURN

Please read each question carefully. For a multiple-choice question, circle the letter of the correct response. For a constructed-response question, write your answers on the lines.

Use the diagram below to answer question 1.

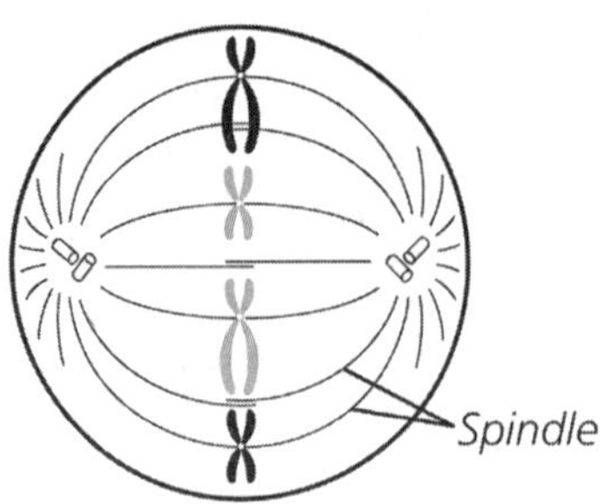

1 Which statement **best** describes the stage of mitosis shown in the illustration?

A The cell is in telophase because the chromosomes are unpaired.

B The cell is in anaphase because the chromosomes have replicated.

C The cell is in prophase because the chromosomes have condensed.

D The cell is in metaphase because the chromosomes are aligned in the center.

2 Which is one difference between a parent cell and a daughter cell that results from mitosis?

A The daughter cell has sister chromatids, while the parent cell does not.

B The daughter cell has half the number of chromosomes as the parent cell.

C The daughter cell has paired chromosomes, while the parent cell does not.

D The daughter cell has half the amount of genetic material as the parent cell.

3 Which sentence lists events in the cell cycle in correct order, from earlier to later?

A The chromosomes replicate; the nuclear membrane dissolves.

B The sister chromatids are separated; the chromosomes condense.

C The nuclear membrane reforms; the chromosomes align in the middle of the cell.

D The chromosomes become longer and thinner; spindle fibers attach to the centromeres.

Use the DNA sequence to answer question 4.

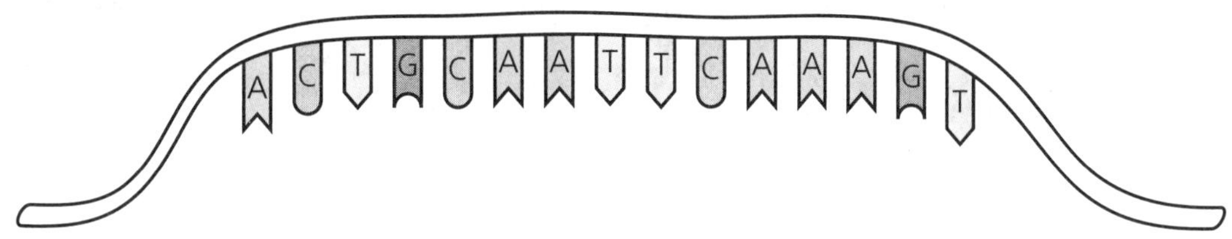

4 The DNA sequence above is found on a chromosome in a eukaryotic cell. The cell is allowed to undergo DNA replication and mitosis in a solution containing radio labeled free nucleotides. These nucleotides are similar to normal free nucleotides found in the cell, but contain a radioactive atom.

A What is the sequence of the new strand formed by DNA polymerase?

____

B Which parts of the resulting sister chromatids will be radioactive? Explain.

____

____

____

____

____

____

C Which of the resulting daughter cells will be radioactive? Explain.

____

____

____

____

LESSON 3 Genes, Alleles, and Meiosis

BIO.B.1.1.2, BIO.B.1.2.2

Mitosis is the main process by which the body grows and repairs itself. It produces genetically identical cells with the same number of chromosomes. A second type of cell division, called **meiosis,** also occurs in organisms that reproduce sexually. Meiosis produces the **gametes,** or sperm and eggs cells.

Meiosis is a type of cell division that produces **gametes,** or cells used in sexual reproduction.

Genes, Alleles, and Chromosomes

Every species of organism has a characteristic *chromosome number,* meaning that all members of that species have that many chromosomes in their normal body cells. For humans, this number is 46. The chromosomes are found in *homologous pairs*. Each member of a pair is inherited from one parent, either the mother or the father. So a human cell contains two copies of each of 23 different chromosomes for a total of 46 chromosomes.

Each species has a characteristic *chromosome number,* sometimes called the *diploid* number. Gametes have half this number of chromosomes; they are *haploid.*

Homologous chromosomes appear very similar in overall structure and have nearly the same DNA sequences. Although they contain the same genes, homologous chromosomes may have different alleles. An **allele** is a version or "flavor" of a gene. Usually, the base sequence will be slightly different, or one allele may contain slightly more or fewer bases than the other. Because every normal body cell contains homologous pairs of chromosomes, it holds two alleles of each gene.

Normally, chromosomes occur in *homologous pairs,* which have the same genes but may have different alleles.

An **allele** is a version of a gene. For example, redheads may have one version of the *MC1R* gene, while blonds may have a different version.

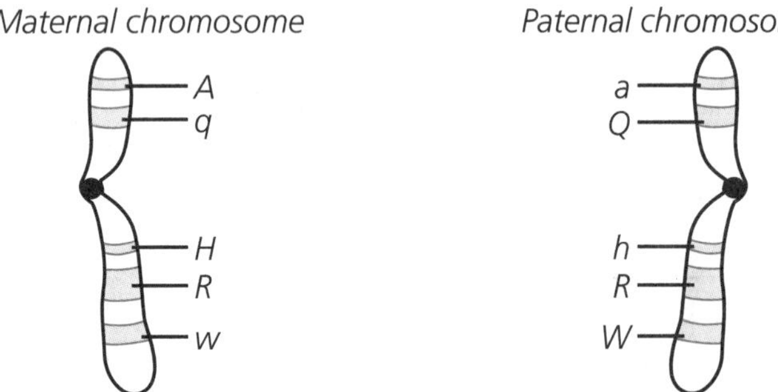

In a homologous pair of chromosomes, some alleles may differ, but the same genes occur in the same locations on each chromosome.

Gametes, however, are different. Each sperm or egg cell contains half the normal number of chromosomes. Each gamete holds one chromosome from each pair, and therefore only one allele of each gene. This is essential for sexually reproducing organisms. When a sperm and an egg join, the offspring inherits one chromosome for each homologous pair from each parent. It gains the normal number of chromosomes for its species. Gametes are produced by meiosis.

In mammals, sex is determined by a pair of sex chromosomes, called X and Y. These are not completely homologous. The Y chromosome is much smaller than the X. However, they do share a small homologous region of DNA.

A carp, a type of fish, has 52 homologous pairs of chromosomes in its brain cells. How many chromosomes are contained in one of its gametes?

A 13

B 26

C 52

D 104

The brain cell of a carp contains 52 chromosome pairs, or 104 chromosomes. A gamete contains only one chromosome per pair, or 52 chromosomes. Choice C is correct.

Sperm and eggs cells each contribute half of the genetic material to offspring.

An Overview of Meiosis and Crossing-over

Meiosis produces gametes through two stages or rounds of cell division. Meiosis starts with a cell that has the normal number of chromosomes. Because the cell has completed the S (*synthesis*) phase of the cell cycle, the DNA in its chromosomes has replicated.

In *meiosis I*, the first stage of meiosis, pairs of homologous chromosomes are separated, with each daughter cell keeping one chromosome from each pair. The chromosome number is halved in this stage.

Remember that a chromosome with replicated DNA is still a single chromosome. It has only one *centromere,* where the chromatids are joined.

Identical sister chromatids result from DNA replication. Centromere

Meiosis I is when the number of chromosomes is halved. Homologous pairs of chromosomes are separated in this stage.

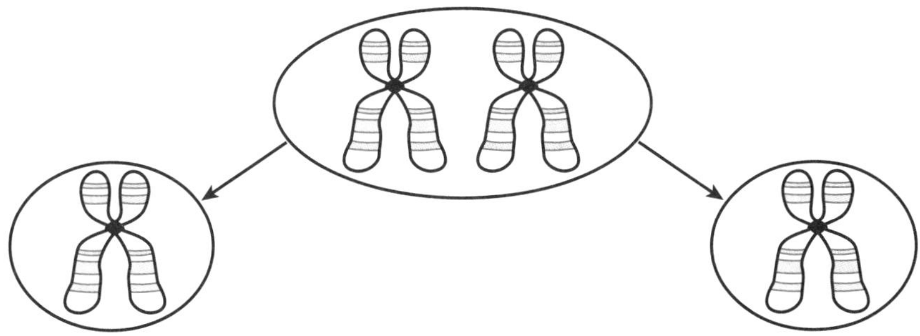

In meiosis I, each daughter cell gains half the normal chromosome number.

The second stage, *meiosis II,* is similar to mitosis. Each replicated chromosome is separated into two chromosomes. The daughter cells still have half the normal number of chromosomes, but now the chromosomes are unreplicated.

Meiosis II is when the *sister chromatids* that make up a chromosome separate.

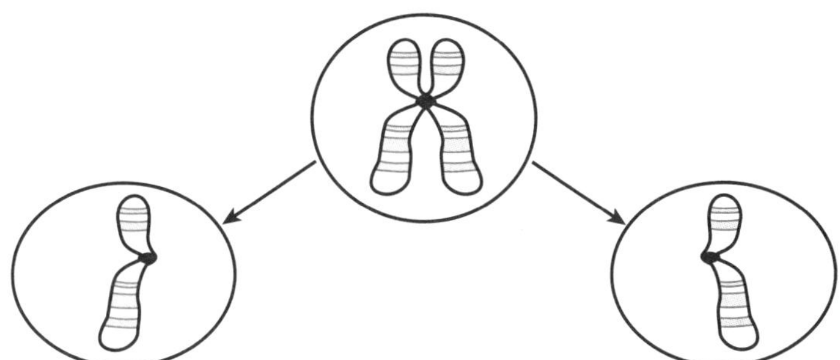

In meiosis II, the sister chromatids of each chromosome are separated.

It may seem as if a sperm or egg cell should contain either one or the other chromosome from a homologous pair. However, it is not so simple. Early in the first stage of meiosis, homologous chromosomes pair up and **crossing-over** occurs. DNA strands from one chromosome join with the other, breaking off and piecing themselves back together. The end result of this process is that each chromosome contains pieces of DNA from its homolog.

Crossing-over is the exchange of genetic material between homologous chromosomes. It occurs early in meiosis I.

Homologous chromosomes are also called *homologs.*

Crossing-over makes each sister chromatid different and unique. It increases the genetic variation in a species.

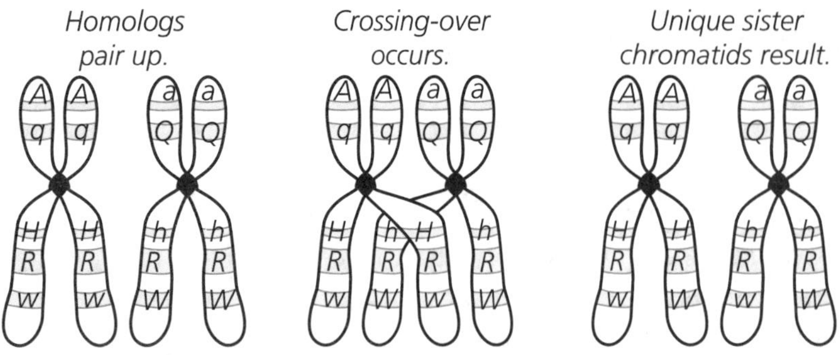
Homologs pair up.
Crossing-over occurs.
Unique sister chromatids result.

Crossing-over between homologous chromosomes swaps some of the genetic material between them. It results in new combinations of alleles.

What is the result of crossing-over? Recall that each homolog has a slightly different set of alleles. Crossing-over "shuffles" the genetic material so that each sister chromatid has a different combination of alleles. Instead of just the two original allele combinations, there are now four. Crossing-over makes it possible for offspring to inherit unique combinations of alleles. It increases the genetic variation in the gene pool of a species.

A parent has the alleles *C, f, r,* and *J,* in that order, along one copy of chromosome 11, and the alleles *c, F, R,* and *j* on the other copy of chromosome 11. The parent passes the alleles *C, F, r,* and *J* on to its offspring. Where did crossing-over **most likely** occur on chromosomes 11?

A between gene *C/c* and gene *F/f,* only

B between gene *R/r* and gene *J/j,* only

C between gene *C/c* and gene *F/f,* and between gene *R/r* and gene *J/j*

D between gene *C/c* and gene *F/f,* and between gene *F/f* and gene *R/r*

For allele *C* to occur with allele *F,* crossing-over must have occurred at a location between these two genes. For allele *F* to occur with allele *r,* crossing-over must have occurred between these two genes. Because the alleles *r* and *J* occur together on the same parental chromosome, no crossing-over event is required between them. Choice D is correct.

The Phases of Meiosis

In meiosis, two cell divisions take place. For this reason, meiosis is divided into stages I and II. During each stage, the cell undergoes the same phases as mitosis: *prophase*, *metaphase*, *anaphase*, and *telophase*.

As in mitosis, the chromosomes condense and the nuclear membrane breaks down. Then, spindle fibers (protein chains) from each centriole extend and connect to the chromosomes. Chromosomes line up in the center, separate, and are pulled by the spindle fibers to opposite sides of the cell. The nuclear envelope reforms and the cytokinesis produces two daughter cells.

However, the events during each phase differ slightly from those of mitosis. Most importantly, in meiosis I, it is homologous pairs of chromosomes that line up and are separated.

Each stage of meiosis (I and II) contains the same phases as mitosis: *prophase, metaphase, anaphase,* and *telophase.*

Prophase I

Pair of homologous chromosomes

Sister chromatids

Crossing-over

Nuclear membrane

During prophase I, the nuclear membrane breaks down. Homologous chromosomes pair up. Similar sections of homologous chromosomes are exchanged in a process called *crossing-over.*

In prophase I, crossing-over increases the genetic variation of the gametes. It holds the homologous pairs together until they are separated by the spindle fibers in anaphase I.

Metaphase I

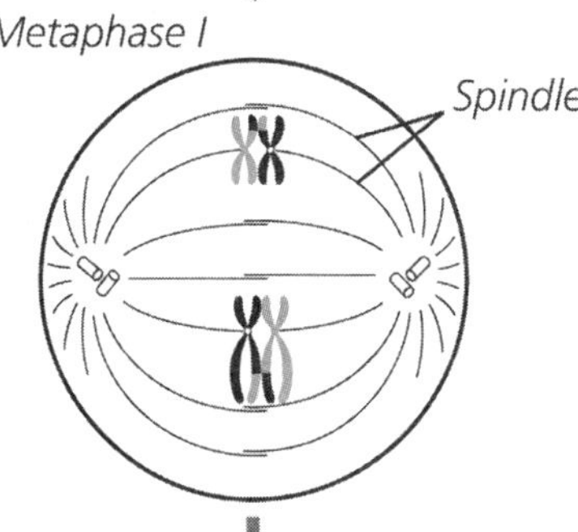
Spindle

During metaphase I, the spindles attach to the centromeres of the sister chromatids. The chromatids line up along the center of the cell.

Anaphase I

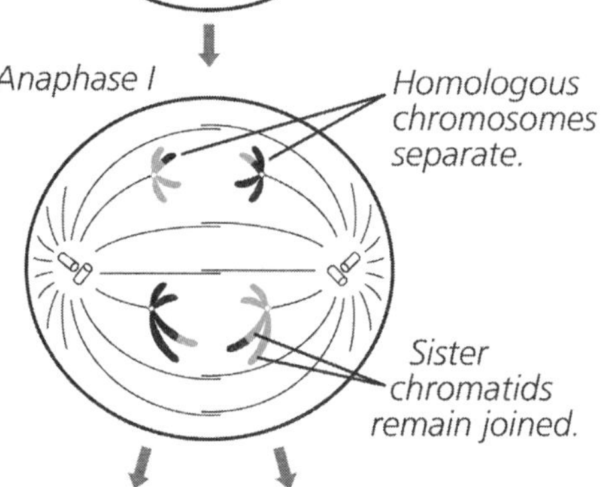
Homologous chromosomes separate.
Sister chromatids remain joined.

During anaphase I, the spindles shorten. The pairs of homologous chromosomes separate. Unlike anaphase in mitosis, during anaphase I the sister chromatids remain joined.

Telophase I

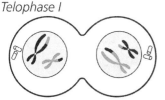

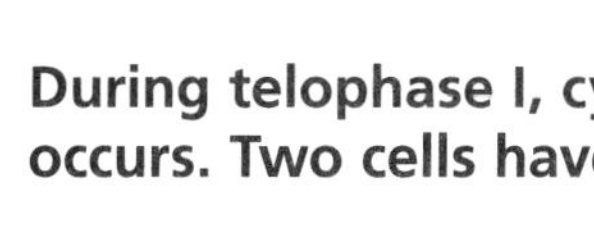

During telophase I, cytokinesis occurs. Two cells have formed.

As meiosis I ends, there are two daughter cells with half the normal chromosome number.

At the end of telophase I, the two daughter cells have half the normal chromosome number. The cells then enter meiosis II, which is similar in many ways to mitosis. In meiosis II, sister chromatids separate to different daughter cells.

Prophase II

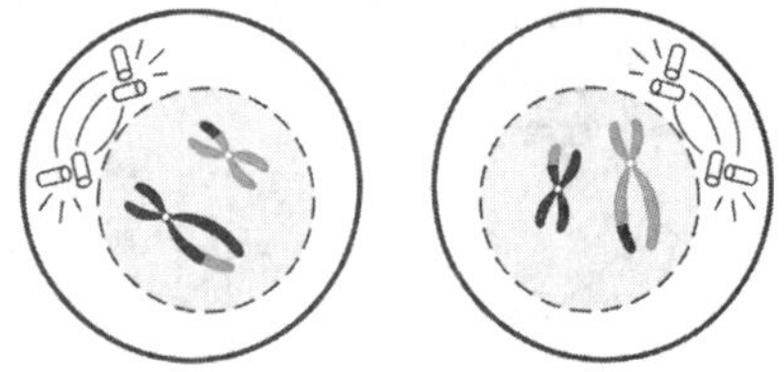

During prophase II, the chromosomes condense again. New spindles form.

Metaphase II

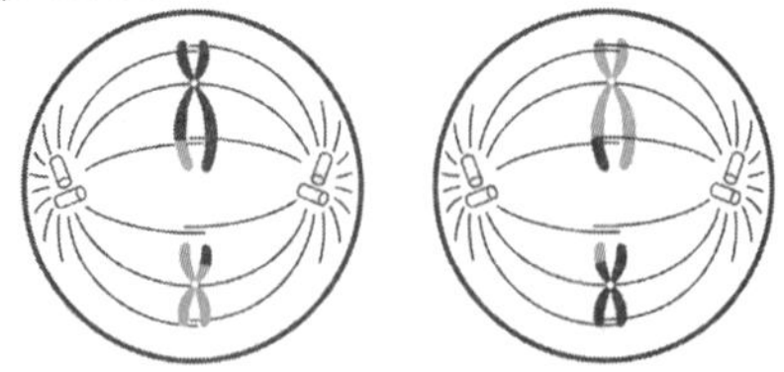

During metaphase II, the spindles attach to the centromeres of the sister chromatids. The chromatids line up along the center of the cell.

Anaphase II

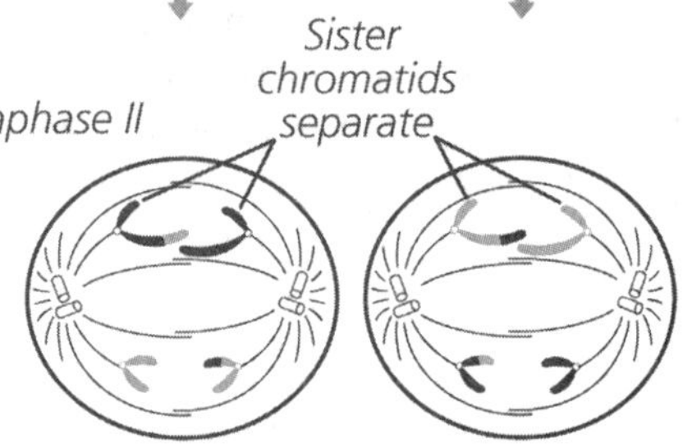

Sister chromatids separate

During anaphase II, the spindles shorten. The sister chromatids separate.

Telophase II

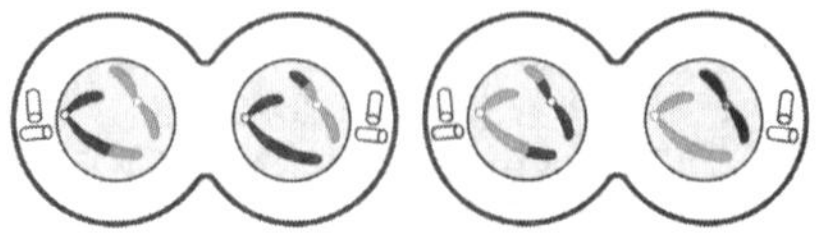

During telophase II, the chromosomes begin to elongate. New nuclear membranes form around the chromosomes in the four daughter cells.

In many female organisms, only one of the four daughter cell resulting from meiosis becomes a viable egg. The rest are discarded. In males, all four daughter cells become gametes. An egg cell contributes its cytoplasm and organelles to the offspring, while a sperm cell contributes only its chromosomes.

Fill in the table to compare the processes of mitosis, meiosis I, and meiosis II.

	Mitosis	Meiosis I	Meiosis II
Number of daughter cells			
Chromosome number			
Crossing-over occurs			
Sister chromatids separate			
Daughter cells genetically identical to parent cell			
Daughter cells genetically identical to each other			

Mitosis and meiosis I produce 2 daughter cells, while meiosis II produces 4. The chromosome number after mitosis is normal (diploid), while it is halved (haploid) after meiosis I and meiosis II. Crossing-over occurs in meiosis I only. Sister chromatids separate in mitosis and meiosis II. Only mitosis produces daughter cells identical both to the parent cell and to each other.

IT'S YOUR TURN

Please read each question carefully. For a multiple-choice question, circle the letter of the correct response. For a constructed-response question, write your answers on the lines.

Use the diagram below to answer questions 1 and 2.

The diagram represents a cell undergoing meiosis. The cell is from an organism with 60 chromosomes in its normal body cells.

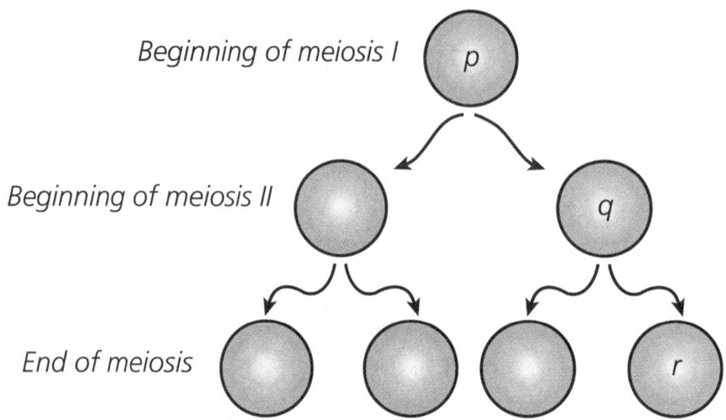

1 Which option correctly identifies the number of chromosomes in the cells at each point?

A Cell *p* contains 30 chromosomes, cell *q* contains 30, and cell *r* contains 15.

B Cell *p* contains 60 chromosomes, cell *q* contains 30, and cell *r* contains 15.

C Cell *p* contains 60 chromosomes, cell *q* contains 30, and cell *r* contains 30.

D Cell *p* contains 60 chromosomes, cell *q* contains 60, and cell *r* contains 30.

2 How many alleles of each gene are present in the nucleus of cell *p?*

A 1

B 2

C 4

D 8

3 A cell in the process of cell division contains the normal chromosome number. Each chromosome consists of two identical sister chromatids. During which stages and processes can such a cell exist?

A telophase of mitosis, but no stage of meiosis

B metaphase of mitosis, but no stage of meiosis

C anaphase I of meiosis and anaphase of mitosis

D prophase I of meiosis and prophase of mitosis

4 Which statement correctly describes the alleles for **any** gene in a female cat's body cell?

A They have the same DNA sequence, but are located on separate chromosomes.

B They have different DNA sequences, but are located on the same chromosome.

C They may have the same or different DNA sequences, but are located on the same chromosome.

D They may have the same or different DNA sequences, but are located on separate chromosomes.

5 A cell undergoes several rounds of mitosis before finally undergoing meiosis.

A Describe two processes that occur in both meiosis and mitosis.

B Describe two processes that occur in meiosis, but do not occur in mitosis.

C Identify two differences between the daughter cells produced by meiosis and those resulting from mitosis.

Module B
Continuity and Unity of Life

Unit 6
Genetics

Genetic information passes on the instructions for building and operating an organism from one generation to the next. This unit will help you review how genes are inherited, how they may be altered or mutated to increase variability, and how they are engineered through human intervention.

1 Genes and Inheritance Genetic information is inherited according to particular patterns. In this lesson, you will review the patterns of inheritance, including dominant, recessive, co-dominant, incomplete dominant, sex-linked, polygenic, and multiple alleles. You will also review the functional relationships between DNA, genes, alleles, and chromosomes and their roles in inheritance.

2 Mutations and Chromosome Abnormalities Genetic information may be altered in various ways. In this lesson, you will review processes that alter genetic information, including crossing-over, nondisjunction, duplication, translocation, deletion, insertion, and inversion. You will also review ways that genetic mutations alter the DNA sequence and may result in genotypic and phenotypic variations within a population.

3 Genetic Engineering Genetic engineering is the control of genetic variability through technology and human intervention. In this lesson, you will review the impacts of selective breeding, gene splicing, cloning, genetically modified organisms, and gene therapy on such diverse fields as medicine, forensics, and agriculture.

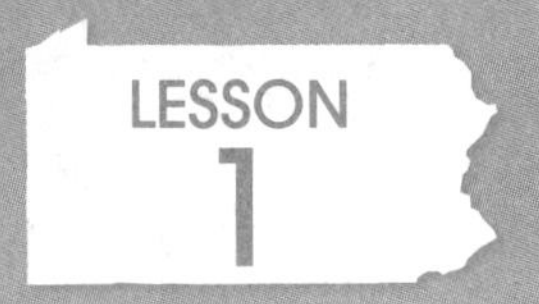

LESSON 1 Genes and Inheritance

BIO.B.1.2.2, BIO.B.2.1.1

Remember that a gene is a region of DNA that codes for a specific protein. Genes come in different versions, called **alleles.** An organism's alleles, along with its environment, determine that organism's traits. In most cases, traits are **polygenic,** meaning that they are determined by a number of different genes located on different chromosomes. More rarely, a single gene will determine a single trait. In the 1800s, Gregor Mendel discovered the basic rules of inheritance by studying single-gene traits in pea plants.

A **gene** is a DNA sequence that specifies a protein. An **allele** is a version of a gene. Each sexually reproducing organism inherits two alleles of each gene.

A **polygenic trait** is determined by many different genes.

In the 1800s, Gregor Mendel founded the field of genetics with his studies on pea plants. The traits Mendel studied are determined by single genes.

Dominant and Recessive Alleles

Just as there are different versions of a trait—for example, tall and short pea plants—there are different versions, or alleles, of the genes that determine those traits. The gene that determines height in pea plants has two different alleles—one causing a tall **phenotype** and one causing a short phenotype.

The body cells of most sexually reproducing organisms contain two alleles of each gene. An organism may have inherited two identical alleles or two different alleles for a gene. The combination of alleles in an organism's cells is its **genotype.** If a pea plant inherits two **dominant** alleles (*TT*), it expresses the dominant phenotype. If it inherits two **recessive** alleles (*tt*), it expresses the recessive phenotype. Genotypes with two matching alleles are described as *homozygous.*

A **genotype** is the combination of alleles of a particular gene. A **phenotype** is the appearance of a trait.

Dominant alleles are often represented by capital letters and recessive alleles by lowercase letters.

Genotype		Phenotype
TT	homozygous dominant	tall
Tt	heterozygous	tall
tt	homozygous recessive	short

A **dominant** allele is expressed if the individual inherits just a single copy of the allele.

A **recessive** allele is expressed only if the individual inherits two copies of the allele.

A *heterozygous* organism inherits one of each allele. Because a dominant allele masks the effects of the recessive allele, this organism will show the dominant phenotype. The table describes the effects of genotype for a gene with alleles *T* and *t* on phenotype.

Homozygous means "same alleles" and *heterozygous* means "different alleles."

Remember that a gamete contains only one chromosome of each pair. Therefore, it contains one of the two alleles making up the organism's genotype. A homozygous pea plant (*TT* or *tt*) can produce gametes with only one allele. Half of the gametes produced by a heterozygote (*Tt*) have the *T* allele, and half have the *t* allele.

If a gamete contains an allele, that allele must also be present in the organism's body cells.

In fruit flies, the allele for normal-sized wings (*W*) is dominant to the allele for small wings (*w*). A fly that has normal wings breeds with a fly that has small wings. Several offspring have small wings, and others have normal wings. Identify the genotype of each of the parent flies.

The small-wing phenotype is expressed only in individuals that have two *w* alleles. Therefore, the small-wing parent must have the *ww* genotype. The small-wing offspring must have inherited one *w* allele from each parent. Therefore, each parent must have at least one *w* allele. The normal-wing parent must have one *W* allele, because it has normal wings. The normal-wing parent must therefore be heterozygous, or *Ww*.

Predicting Inheritance

Scientists use *Punnett squares* to show the possible allele combinations and phenotypes of the offspring of a given set of parents. Punnett squares also show the probability that each offspring will have a given genotype. The diagram below shows an example for a human trait: the genetic disease cystic fibrosis. The alleles for this trait are the dominant *F* (no cystic fibrosis) allele and the recessive *f* (cystic fibrosis) allele.

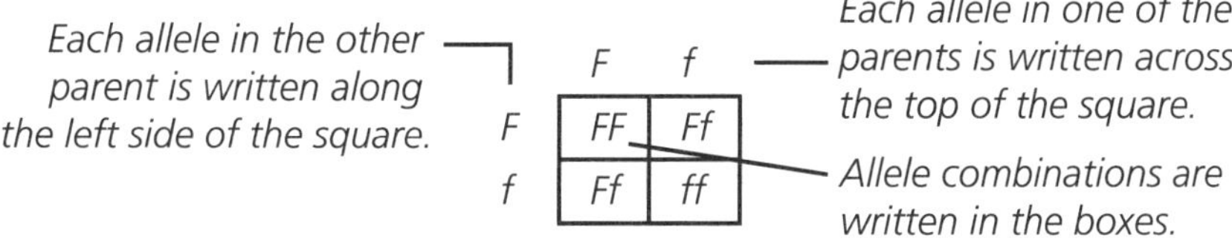

Each allele in the other parent is written along the left side of the square.
F
f
F
f
FF
Ff
Ff
ff
Each allele in one of the parents is written across the top of the square.
Allele combinations are written in the boxes.

Cystic fibrosis is an example of a genetic disease that is caused by a mutation in a single gene. This gene codes for a specific cell protein, which is involved in the transport of chloride ions across the cell membrane. The mutation produces a faulty protein.

Not all traits are governed by a single gene. Some traits, such as height in humans, are affected by multiple genes. In addition, some genes produce proteins that affect multiple traits.

In this example, the probability that an offspring will be heterozygous is 50%. The probability that an offspring will be homozygous recessive is 25%, and the probability that an offspring will be homozygous dominant is 25%. Therefore, the probability that each child of these parents will have cystic fibrosis is 25%. Note that a Punnett square cannot be used to predict the genotype or phenotype of a specific offspring.

A *pedigree* chart can be used to trace inheritance of a trait through multiple generations of related individuals. In a pedigree, males are typically represented by squares and females are represented by circles. Shaded shapes indicate that the individual has the trait in question. Half-shaded shapes indicate the individual is a *carrier* of the trait but does not express the trait. A horizontal bar directly connecting two individuals represents a set of parents. A horizontal bar joining short vertical branches represents all the offspring of a set of parents.

In a pedigree, the *carrier* of a recessive disease may be represented by a half-shaded shape. Carriers are heterozygous.

INHERITANCE OF A TRAIT OVER THREE GENERATIONS

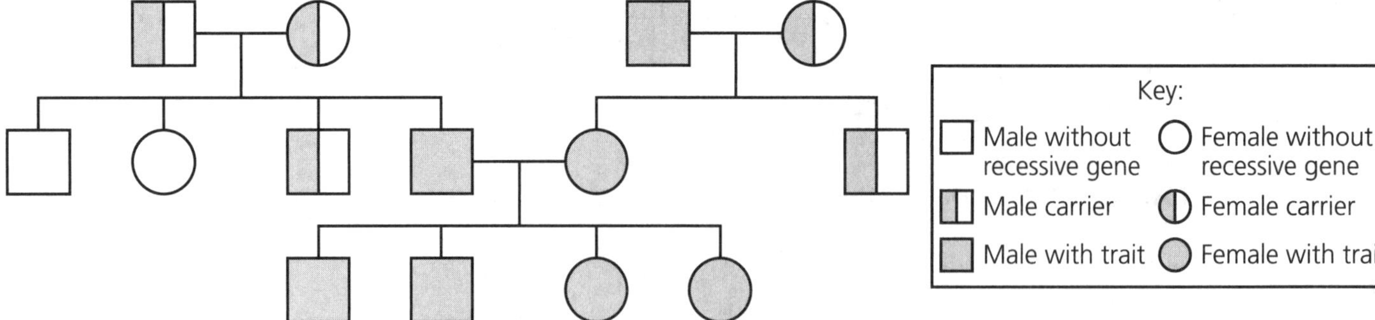

Look at the pedigree chart above. Complete the Punnett square below for the first (left) couple in the top row of the chart. Determine the probability of inheriting each genotype and phenotype. Do the results of the Punnett square differ from the pedigree for the four children of this couple? Explain.

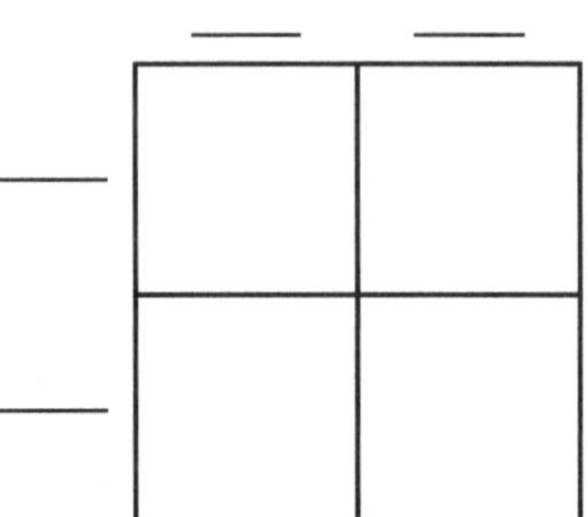

As carriers, each parent is heterozygous, and the completed Punnett square looks like this:

	A	*a*
A	*AA*	*Aa*
a	*Aa*	*aa*

The genotypes (and phenotypes) are, *AA* (normal), *Aa* (carrier), *aa* (disease), and *Aa* (carrier). The actual genotypes and phenotypes observed in this couple's offspring are, from left to right in the pedigree chart: *AA* (normal), *AA* (normal), *Aa* (carrier), and *aa* (disease). Although there was a 50% chance of being a carrier, only one of the four offspring is a carrier. Despite only a 25% chance of having the *AA* genotype, two offspring have this genotype. The results differ because a Punnett square allows you to predict the chances of inheriting a genotype, and can tell you which genotypes are impossible, but it cannot specify exactly which alleles an individual will inherit.

All multicellular organisms are eukaryotes, so all multicellular organisms have cells with nuclei and membrane-bound organelles.

Predictions from Punnett squares are accurate for very large numbers of offspring, such as the hundreds produced in fruit fly crosses.

Incomplete Dominance, Co-Dominance, and Multiple Alleles

Not all genes have one dominant and one recessive allele. Some alleles may show **incomplete dominance,** meaning that a heterozygous individual has a phenotype that differs from those with either homozygous genotype. The inheritance of flower color in snapdragons is an example of incomplete dominance. The allele *R* results in the red flower phenotype and the allele *r* results in white flowers. However, heterozygous flowers are pink. This phenotype is "in between" the dominant and recessive phenotypes.

In **incomplete dominance,** the heterozygous phenotype is "in between" the homozygous phenotypes.

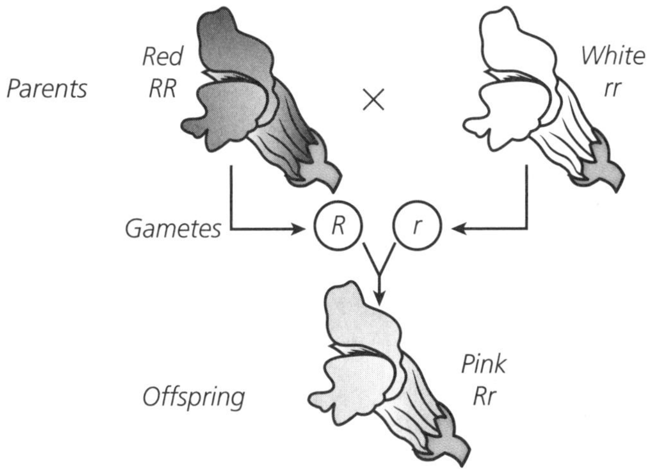

Snapdragon flower color shows incomplete dominance. The pink color of the offspring is "in between" the colors of the parents.

Alleles may also show **co-dominance,** meaning that heterozygotes express *both* the dominant and recessive phenotypes, rather than a blend of the two. For example, some cattle have a *roan* coat, which is made up of white and colored hairs. Roan cattle have one allele for white hair and another for reddish-brown hair. Roan cattle have one of each allele, and both types of hair. Notice that the heterozygous phenotype is not tan or light red hair. Rather, both phenotypes are expressed completely.

An organism heterozygous for **co-dominant alleles** expresses *both* of the homozygous phenotypes.

Some genes have more than two possible alleles. ABO blood type in humans is one example of a **multiple-allele** trait. Within the human population, there are three blood type alleles: I^A, I^B, and i. Each person has only two of the possible three alleles. Instead of three possible genotypes, multiple alleles produce a larger number of genotypes.

A gene may have **multiple alleles** in the population, even though each individual still carries only two alleles.

The ABO blood type gene is also an example of co-dominance. Blood type is determined by the presence of a carbohydrate group attached to a protein on the surface of red blood cells. Different carbohydrate groups result from the I^A and I^B alleles. If both alleles are present, the individual has type AB blood. These alleles are both dominant to the i allele, which results in a surface protein with *no* attached carbohydrate and type O blood.

ABO type is just one of many different ways to classify blood types. People can also be Rh factor positive or negative. ABO and Rh blood types are important in medicine.

This table summarizes the phenotypes associated with each of the six possible human blood-type genotypes.

Genotype	Phenotype
I^AI^A	type A blood
I^BI^B	type B blood
I^AI^B	type AB blood

Genotype	Phenotype
I^Ai	type A blood
I^Bi	type B blood
ii	type O blood

A child has type O blood. If the child's mother has type A blood, what are all the possible genotypes and phenotypes of the father?

A ii only

B ii and I^Ai

C ii, I^Ai, and I^Bi

D ii, I^Ai, I^AI^A, and I^Bi

Choice D is incorrect; the father cannot have type AB blood (I^AI^B), because he would then have to pass on one dominant allele to his child. We know that the type O child has no dominant alleles (ii). Choice A is incorrect because the father needs only one i allele to pass on to his child. Choice B is incorrect because genotype I^Bi is also possible, as it includes at least one i allele. Choice C is correct; the father may have genotypes ii (type O), I^Ai (type A), or I^Bi (type B).

Other genes may also result in type O blood. For example, a gene may prevent the carbohydrate group from being made at all. In rare cases, two AB parents may have a type O child.

Sex-Linked Traits

In humans and many other animals, a single pair of chromosomes, called the *sex chromosomes,* determines an individual's sex. The human sex chromosomes are the X chromosome and the Y chromosome. An XX individual is female, while an XY individual is male.

The X chromosome is much larger, and contains many more genes, than the Y. Most genes on the X chromosome determine traits that have nothing to do with being male or female. Males, who have only one X chromosome, therefore have only one allele of each of these genes. Traits governed by the genes on a sex chromosome are called **sex-linked traits.**

Hemophilia, a blood-clotting disorder, is determined by a single gene on the X chromosome. The allele for the disorder is recessive. A female will have hemophilia only if both of her X chromosomes have the recessive alleles. In contrast, a male needs only one recessive allele to have hemophilia. He has only one X chromosome, and there is no other allele to possibly mask the disorder.

A father with hemophilia will pass the recessive allele to all of his daughters. Assuming that the mother is homozygous dominant, the daughters will be carriers of (heterozygous for) the disorder. However, they may pass the recessive allele to male children.

A **sex-linked trait** is determined by genes on either the X or Y chromosome.

Non-sex chromosomes are called *autosomes.*

Recessive sex-linked traits governed by genes on the X chromosome are observed more often in males than in females.

A man with hemophilia and a woman who has no history of the disease in her family plan to have a child. The parents' genotypes are X^hY and X^HX^H.

A Complete the Punnett square to show the possible genotypes of offspring.

B Determine the probability of a child inheriting hemophilia.

C How would this probability differ if the mother had hemophilia instead of the father?

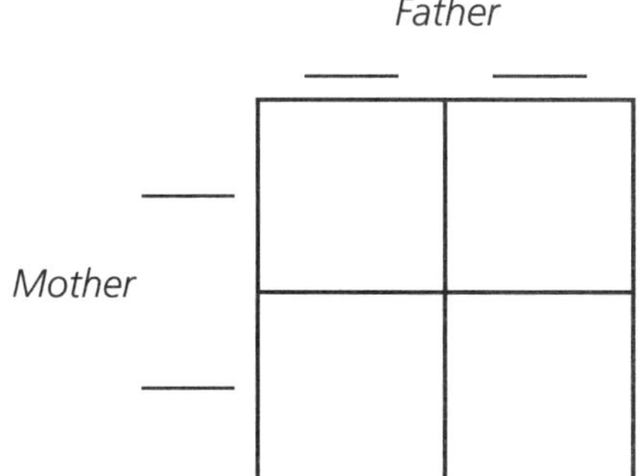

For part A, write each of the parents' chromosomes on the outside of the Punnett square and fill in the boxes with the genotypes. The completed square should look like this:

	X^h	Y
X^H	X^HX^h	X^HY
X^H	X^HX^h	X^HY

For part B, the probability of a child having hemophilia is zero. The boys will inherit the male Y chromosome, which does not carry the recessive hemophilia allele. However, because each daughter *must* inherit the father's X chromosome with its recessive *h* allele, all of the daughters will be heterozygous, or carriers. For part C, if the mother had hemophilia instead of the father, her genotype would be X^hX^h. Any male child of the couple would have hemophilia and any daughter would be a carrier.

IT'S YOUR TURN

Please read each question carefully. For a multiple-choice question, circle the letter of the correct response. For a constructed-response question, write your answers on the lines.

1 The gene for seed shape in pea plants has two alleles, resulting in either smooth or wrinkled peas. A pea plant with one *smooth* allele and one *wrinkled* allele produces only smooth peas. Based on this information, which conclusion can be drawn?

A Both alleles are co-dominant.

B One allele is incompletely dominant.

C The allele for smooth seeds is recessive.

D The allele for wrinkled seeds is recessive.

Complete the Punnett square below to help you answer questions 2 and 3.

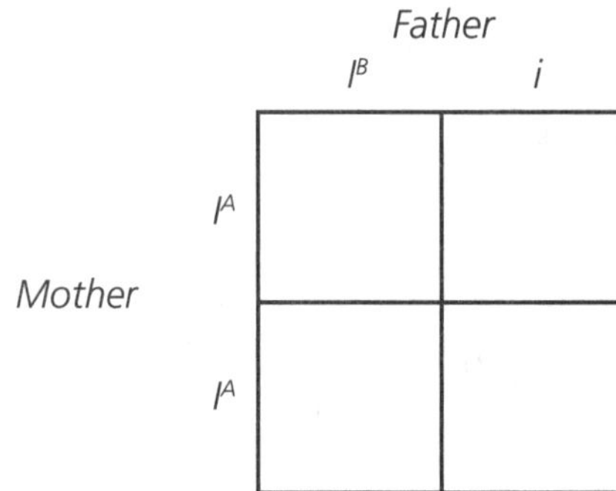

2 Which of the following describes the parents' phenotypes?

A The father has type O blood, and the mother has type B blood.

B The father has type B blood, and the mother has type A blood.

C The father has type O blood, and the mother has type A blood.

D The father has type B blood, and the mother has type AB blood.

3 Which of the following correctly predicts their child's chance of inheriting a blood type?

A The child has a 0% chance of inheriting the B blood type.

B The child has a 25% chance of inheriting the A blood type.

C The child has a 50% chance of inheriting the O blood type.

D The child has a 75% chance of inheriting the AB blood type.

Use the pedigree chart below to answer question 4.

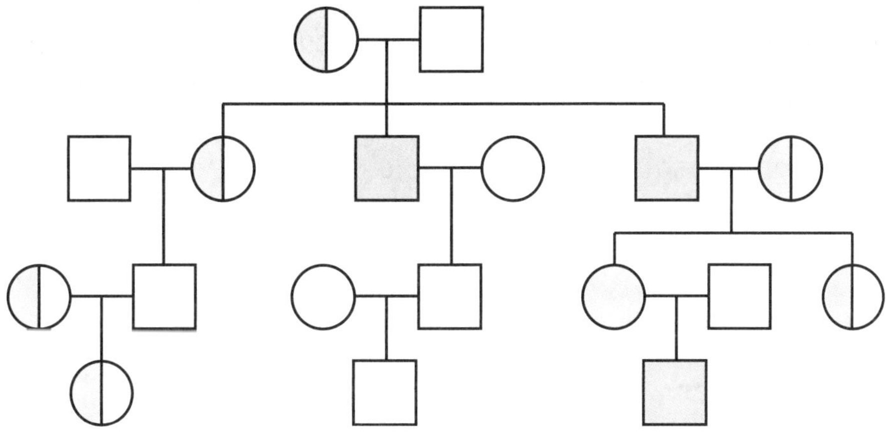

4 What is the **most likely** pattern of inheritance for the trait indicated by the shaded figures?

A simple recessive

B simple dominant

C X-linked recessive

D X-linked dominant

5 Fruit flies normally have red eyes. A recessive allele causes some fruit flies to have purple eyes. Which statement describes the purple-eyed offspring of a red-eyed parent and a purple-eyed parent?

A The offspring has two recessive alleles located on the same chromosome.

B The offspring has two chromosomes with a recessive allele present on each.

C The offspring has one dominant and one recessive allele located on the same chromosome.

D The offspring has one chromosome with a dominant allele and one chromosome with a recessive allele.

6 Red-green color blindness is the inability to distinguish the colors red and green. The gene for this trait is located on the X chromosome. The allele for normal color vision (X^B) is dominant and the allele for color blindness (X^b) is recessive. A color-blind woman and a man with normal color vision plan to have their first child.

A Complete the Punnett square for the couple.

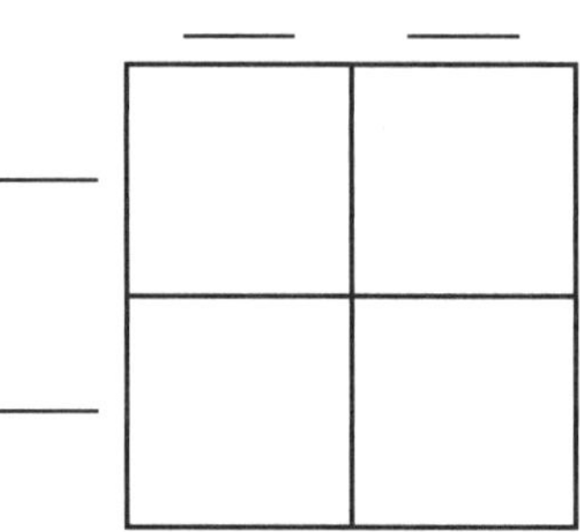

B Identify the phenotypes represented in the Punnett square and percentage probability for each phenotype.

C The woman has an ultrasound and determines that the child is male. Has the probability of having a color-blind child changed? Explain.

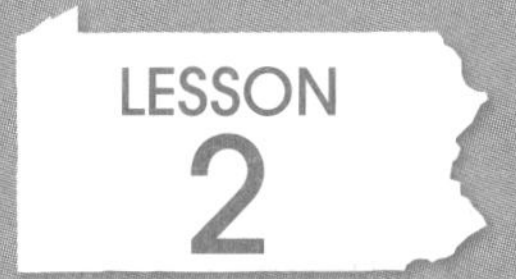

Mutations and Chromosome Abnormalities

BIO.B.2.1.2, BIO.B.2.3.1, BIO.B.3.1.3

For most genes, there exist at least two alleles in a population's "gene pool." Alleles that are not passed on to offspring can be lost from a population. New alleles result from mutations in genes and chromosomes. A **mutation** is a permanent change in genetic material that may be passed from parents to offspring. Mutations are the source of genetic variety within populations and species.

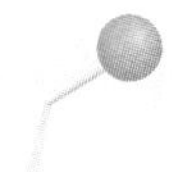

A **mutation** is a change in a DNA sequence. Mutations are the source of the different alleles found in a species or population.

Mutations can occur in any cell of the body. However, only mutations in the cells that give rise to gametes may be passed on to offspring.

Mutations in Genes

DNA encodes genetic information that specifies how proteins should be assembled. The sequence of bases (A, C, G, and T) in a gene spells out the order of amino acids in the protein. A mutation in the DNA sequence of a gene can result in a different protein being made, or even no protein at all. The type and severity of the change in the protein depends on the type of mutation that has occurred.

Recall that amino acids are represented by triplets of bases called *codons*. Sometimes, a single amino acid may be represented by more than one codon. For example, the codons TTA and TTG both code for the amino acid leucine (LEU). What would happen if the base G in the sequence below mutated to an A? The gene sequence would be different, but the same protein would be made. Because this type of mutation does not cause a change in the protein, it is called a *silent mutation*.

A codon is a set of three nucleotide bases that specify an amino acid.

A *silent mutation* in DNA does not change the resulting protein.

Original protein sequence: ARG — **LEU** — HIS — MET — TYR
Original DNA sequence: CGA — TT**G** — CAC — ATG — TAT
↓
New DNA sequence: CGA — TT**A** — CAC — ATG — TAT
New protein sequence: ARG — **LEU** — HIS — MET — TYR

What if the second base in the same codon were changed to a C? The new codon specifies a different amino acid. When the protein is assembled, the amino acid serine will be substituted for leucine. This may have a positive, negative, or neutral effect on phenotype. Because the "meaning" of the codon changes, this type of mutation is called a *missense mutation*.

A *missense mutation* changes one amino acid in the resulting protein.

Original protein sequence: ARG — **LEU** — HIS — MET — TYR
Original DNA sequence: CGA — TTG — CAC — ATG — TAT
↓
New DNA sequence: CGA — T**C**G — CAC — ATG — TAT
New protein sequence: ARG — **SER** — HIS — MET — TYR

Stop codons tell the ribosome that it has reached the end of the gene sequence on the mRNA strand. A *nonsense mutation* is one that changes a codon into a *stop* codon. This ends translation before the entire protein is assembled, resulting in a shortened protein.

A *nonsense mutation* inserts a *stop* codon and shortens the resulting protein.

Original protein sequence: ARG — **LEU** — HIS — MET — TYR
Original DNA sequence: CGA — T**T**G — CAC — ATG — TAT
↓
New DNA sequence: CGA — T**A**G — CAC — ATG — TAT
New protein sequence: ARG — ***stop*** —

Some mutations insert or delete nucleotides in a gene. If three (or a multiple of three) bases are added or removed, the number of codons changes slightly. However, if the number of inserted or deleted bases is *not* a multiple of three, this changes how the bases are grouped into codons. This is called a **frame-shift mutation,** and it results in changes to the amino acids assembled after the mutation.

A **frame-shift mutation** changes how bases are grouped into codons, or the *reading frame* of the gene.

Original protein sequence: ARG — **LEU** — HIS — MET — TYR
Original DNA sequence: CGA — T**X**G — CAC — ATG — TAT
↓
New DNA sequence: CGA — TGC — ACA — TGT — ATC
New protein sequence: ARG — **CYS** — **THR** — **CYS** — **ILE**

A mutation causes six nucleotides to be inserted at one location into the DNA that encodes a protein. How may the resulting protein be affected?

A It may gain two amino acids or it may lose two amino acids.

B It will have different amino acids starting at the mutation site.

C It may gain two amino acids or it may be shortened at the mutation site.

D It will have two different amino acids but the same number of total amino acids.

The insertion of six nucleotides adds two codons to the DNA sequence. The protein can lose two amino acids only if bases are removed rather than added; choice A is incorrect. The protein has different amino acids starting at the mutation site only if a frame-shift occurs. However, because six is a multiple of three, the remaining bases will be grouped as they were originally and the remaining protein will be the same; choice B is incorrect. Only missense mutations, in which bases are changed rather than added, can alter two amino acids while conserving the total number of amino acids; choice D is incorrect. Choice C is correct; if the codons specify amino acids, two amino acids will be added, but none will be lost. If one of the codons is a stop codon, the protein will be shortened at the mutation site.

Chromosomal Mutations and Rearrangements

Just as the bases making up a gene may be altered, so can entire chromosomes. Pieces of a chromosome may be deleted, duplicated, inverted, or swapped among different chromosomes.

A chromosomal *deletion* occurs when a segment of chromosome is lost, removing tens or hundreds of genes. In contrast, a *duplication* occurs when a part of the chromosome is repeated. These genes occur twice on the chromosome. In an *inversion*, a chromosome segment is flipped in the reverse direction.

A chromosomal *deletion* removes a large segment of genetic material.

A chromosomal *duplication* causes genes to be repeated on the same chromosome.

A chromosomal *inversion* flips the order of genes on a chromosome.

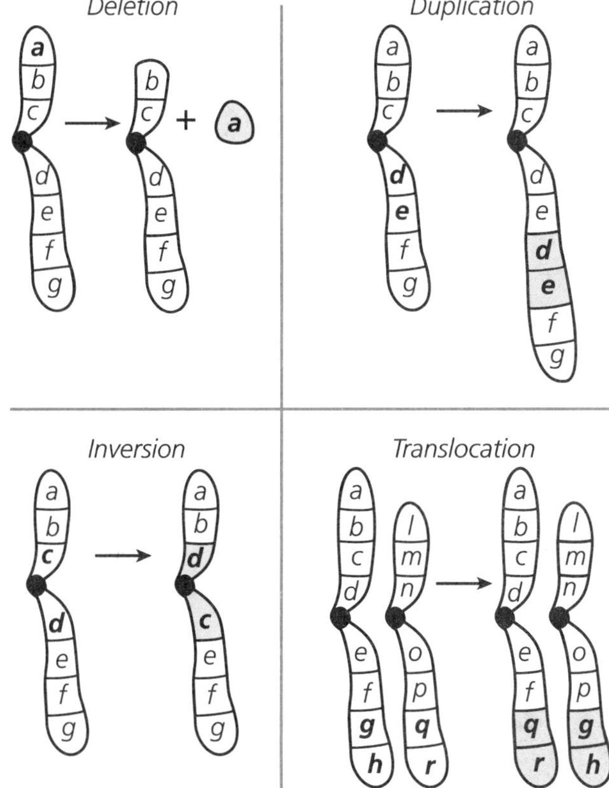

Chromosomes as well as genes can undergo mutation in several ways.

Sometimes, a segment of one chromosome may move to join another chromosome. This is called a **translocation.** A translocation may involve a single segment moving to a new location, or two segments of different chromosomes may trade places.

A chromosomal **translocation** moves segments from one chromosome to another, sometimes exchanging genetic material between two chromosomes.

Chromosomal mutations that occur in normal body cells may disrupt the cell cycle and lead to cancer.

Which types of chromosomal mutations are likely to have more severe effects, and which are likely to have less severe effects, on the health of the individual? Explain.

Deletions and duplications are likely to have more severe health consequences, while inversions and translocations are likely to have less severe effects. A deletion or duplication changes the number of alleles present for the genes involved. An inversion or translocation simply moves alleles without deleting them, keeping their numbers the same.

Changes in Chromosome Number

Every species has a characteristic number of chromosomes. A missing or extra chromosome alters this number and causes medical conditions ranging from moderate to severe. Abnormal chromosome numbers result from errors that may occur during either stage of meiosis.

In meiosis I, pairs of homologous chromosomes exchange genetic material (cross-over) and then segregate into different daughter cells. If the chromosomes in a pair fail to separate properly, each daughter cell ends up with one more or fewer chromosomes than normal. The failure of chromosomes to properly separate is called **nondisjunction.**

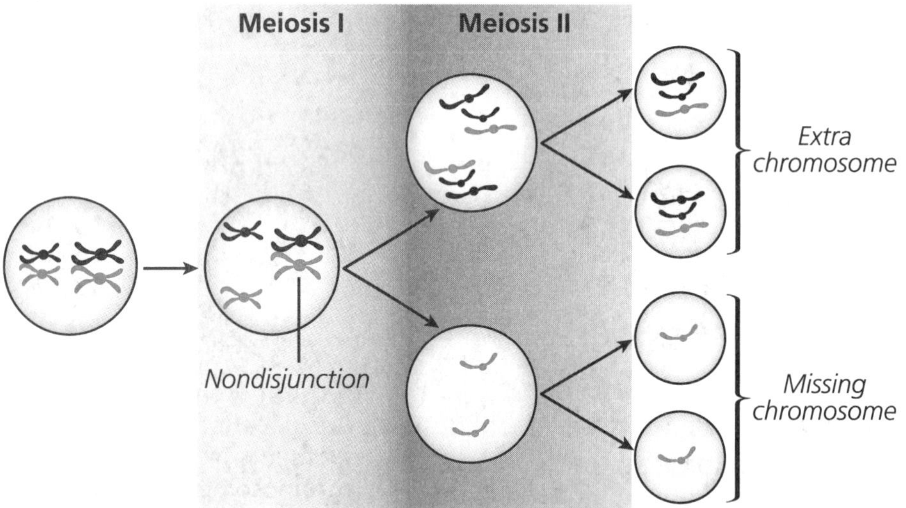

If disjunction occurs during meiosis I, the daughter cells have either an extra chromosome or a missing chromosome.

Meiosis is the cell division process that produces gametes (egg and sperm cells). In meiosis, the pairs of homologous chromosomes separate and each daughter cell has half the normal number of chromosomes.

Nondisjunction is the failure of chromosomes or chromatids to separate during meiosis or mitosis.

Chromosome number abnormalities are usually so severe that the embryo is miscarried. One exception is Down syndrome, caused by an extra copy of chromosome 21.

In meiosis II, pairs of sister chromatids separate into different daughter cells. Here, too, nondisjunction can occur if sister chromatids remain together.

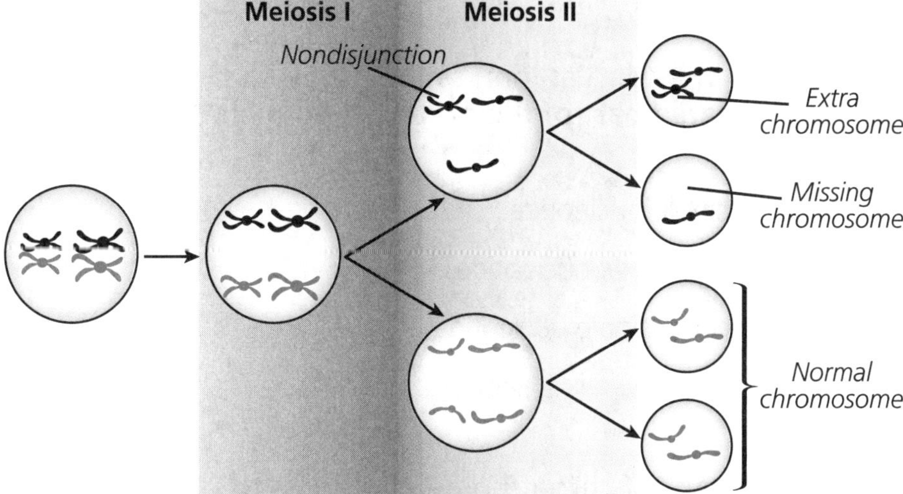

If disjunction occurs during meiosis II, the daughter cells may have an extra chromosome, a missing chromosome, or the normal number.

During the formation of a human gamete, the homologs of chromosome 18 pair up and crossing-over occurs between them. However, they fail to separate when the cell divides. How will this affect the gametes that form?

When a nondisjunction event occurs in meiosis I, one of the daughter cells gains both homologs and the other lacks any. All of the gametes that form have either one extra chromosome or one missing chromosome.

IT'S YOUR TURN

Please read each question carefully. For a multiple-choice question, circle the letter of the correct response. For a constructed-response question, write your answers on the lines.

1 A mutation results in a protein that is one-third as long as the normal protein. However, the amino acid sequence for the translated part of the protein is normal. Which best describes the mutation that occurred?

A It was a silent mutation that altered a single nucleotide.

B It was a missense mutation that inserted several nucleotides.

C It was a nonsense mutation that replaced a single nucleotide.

D It was a frame-shift mutation that deleted several nucleotides.

2 Alagille syndrome results when a segment of chromosome 2 attaches to chromosome 20, and a segment of chromosome 20 attaches to chromosome 2. What type of chromosomal mutation causes this disorder?

A deletion

B duplication

C inversion

D translocation

Use the diagram to answer question 3.

PARTIAL KARYOTYPE FROM INFANT BODY CELL

3 A full karyotype is an image of all the chromosomes present in a cell, while a partial karyotype shows only some of the chromosomes. The partial karyotype shown above is from an infant born with a rare disorder. Only chromosomes 10, 11, 17, and 18 are shown. Which event caused the disorder?

A nondisjunction

B chromosome duplication

C separation of sister chromatids

D segregation of homologous chromosomes

Use the table and diagram below to answer question 4.

DNA CODONS FOR SEVERAL AMINO ACIDS

Amino Acid	Codons
Arginine (ARG)	CGA, CGC, CGG, CGT, AGA, AGG
Asparagine (ASP)	GAC, GAT
Glycine (GLY)	GGA, GGC, GGG, GGT
Glutamic acid (GLU)	GAA, GAG
Isoleucine (ILE)	ATA, ATC, ATT
Proline (PRO)	CCA, CCC, CCG, CCT
Tyrosine (TYR)	TAC, TAT

MUTATION IN A GENE SEQUENCE

Original DNA sequence: TAT — ATC — CCG — GAC — GAA

↓

New DNA sequence: TAT — ATC — CCC — GGA — CGA

4 The mutation shown occurs in a skin cell of a coyote belonging to a population in the Northeastern United States. The mutation has a neutral effect on the cell.

A Identify the type of mutation and describe how it affects the protein that is produced in the skin cell.

____

____

____

____

B Will the mutation be passed on to the coyote's offspring? Explain.

____

____

____

____

C If the mutation were passed on to offspring, how would it affect the gene pool of the coyote population?

____

____

____

____

LESSON 3 Genetic Engineering

BIO.B.2.4.1

Only recently have people discovered the ability to manipulate the *genomes* of other organisms by taking genes from one species and placing them in other species. This activity is so new that we are still debating whether it is safe and ethical to do so. However, humans have less directly changed organisms' genomes since prehistoric times, giving us our familiar crops, livestock, and pets.

Technology now allows us to sequence entire genomes. A *genome* refers to all the genetic information contained in the chromosomes of a species.

Selective Breeding vs. Genetic Engineering

Since the dawn of civilization, humans have altered the genes of plant and animal species. By choosing and breeding organisms with useful traits, people transformed wild species into the livestock and crops that we still use today. For example, teosinte, a wild grass with small, tough seeds, was bred to produce ears of larger, tender kernels familiar to us as corn. By planting only the most desirable teosinte seeds, farmers selected for traits that differed from those of the rest of the species. Over time, the plant grown by the farmers was transformed into a genetically distinct species that we know as corn. This type of transformation is called **selective breeding.**

In **selective breeding,** people choose only organisms with desirable traits to reproduce, making the alleles for these traits more common. Selective breeding is also called *artificial selection.*

A *hybrid* is a cross between two breeds or two closely related species. Crossing two varieties of wheat, for example, may result in a better wheat variety.

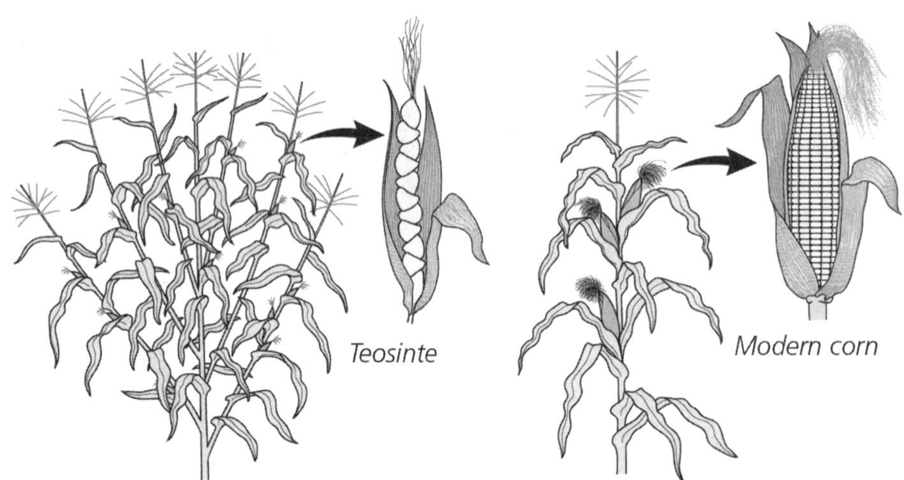

Wild teosinte is the ancestor of domestic corn.

While selective breeding takes many generations and requires only simple tools, technological advances have allowed scientists to manipulate organisms' genes directly. Scientists have tools that allow them to remove a gene from one species and insert it into the genome of another, combine parts of genes in new ways, and use genes to improve medicine and agriculture. The use of technology to manipulate and change genes is called **genetic engineering.**

Genetic engineering involves directly inserting, removing, or altering an organism's DNA.

One use of genetic engineering is to make corn crops resistant to pests. The European corn borer is an insect that lays eggs on corn plants. The larvae then feed on the corn leaves, damaging the crop and causing it to produce poorer-quality ears of corn. To combat this pest, scientists turned to *Bacillus thuringiensis* (*Bt*), a species of soil bacteria that makes a protein that is deadly to the corn borer. By taking the protein's gene from *Bt* and inserting it into the cells of corn plants, scientists created a **genetically modified organism,** or **GMO.**

A **genetically modified organism (GMO)** contains DNA from other organisms. GMOs are also called *transgenic* organisms because they contain *transgenes,* or genes from other species.

Genetically modified organisms, such as *Bt* corn, raise safety and environmental concerns. Although the transgenic protein in *Bt* corn has been found safe for both humans and wildlife, consumers still want GMO foods to be labeled so that they may decide for themselves whether to consume it.

The impact of GMOs on the environment is also a concern. The *Bt* protein is very specific to European corn borers. Reducing this insect's numbers may increase those of its competitors or have other unintended effects on the ecosystem.

Which is **most likely** an example of a genetically modified organism?

A a blue violet that is grafted to an African violet

B a hybrid dog crossbred from a pug and a beagle

C a bacterium that contains DNA from another bacterium

D a microorganism that develops resistance to an antibiotic

A genetically modified organism contains DNA that has been introduced, using technology, from another source. Grafting two violets does not change their DNA, so choice A is incorrect. Producing a hybrid dog does not involve introducing DNA from another species, so choice B is incorrect. Antibiotic resistance develops from selection on an existing mutation, so choice D is incorrect. Choice C, a bacterium with foreign DNA, is most likely to be a GMO.

Gene Splicing

Genes, which are pieces of DNA, can be moved from place to place using enzymes. Special enzymes are able to digest, or cut, DNA at specific base sequences. For example, the enzyme *Hind*III (hindy-three) recognizes the sequence AAGCTT. If this sequence occurs on both ends of a gene, the enzyme can be used to cut the gene out of the surrounding DNA.

An enzyme is a protein that catalyzes a reaction. Enzymes are used to cut DNA at specific sites and bind pieces of DNA together.

The gene can then be inserted into a *plasmid,* a naturally occurring piece of circular DNA that is exchanged between bacterial cells. Scientists take advantage of plasmids as vehicles for recombinant DNA. Cutting the plasmid with the same enzyme allows the gene to insert itself into the plasmid. Cutting and recombining a gene in this way is known as **gene splicing.**

In **gene splicing,** DNA is cut apart and recombined in different ways. *Recombinant DNA,* combined from several sources, is created in this way.

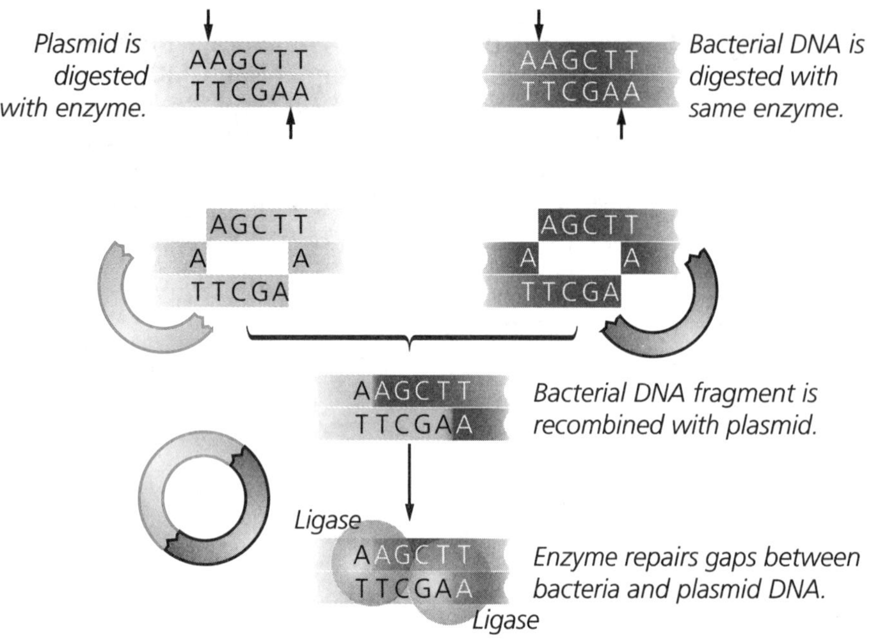
Plasmid is digested with enzyme.
AAGCTT
TTCGAA
Bacterial DNA is digested with same enzyme.
AGCTT
A
A
TTCGA
Bacterial DNA fragment is recombined with plasmid.
AAGCTT
TTCGAA
Ligase
Enzyme repairs gaps between bacteria and plasmid DNA.
Ligase

Gene splicing cuts a gene out of the surrounding DNA and inserts it into a plasmid. Enzymes cut and bond pieces of DNA.

Notice that the sequence recognized by the enzyme is the same on both DNA strands. Although the rest of the DNA is different, the ends have identical single-stranded regions. This allows different pieces of DNA, cut by the same enzyme, to be joined together.

Inserting a gene into a plasmid makes it more useful. The plasmid can be inserted into bacteria or other organisms. To make GMO corn, scientists inserted the plasmid with the *Bt* gene into cultured corn plant cells and allowed the cells to incorporate the DNA into their genomes. Plants grown from these genetically modified cells contain the *Bt* transgene in each of their cells.

The cellular machinery of bacteria is used to do much of the work of genetic engineering. For example, inserting a plasmid into a single bacteria and allowing it to divide results in a population of cells that contain the plasmid. The cells can then be destroyed to remove the plasmid copies.

Scientists can grow plant and animal cells as single cells in nutrient-containing liquid. These are known as *cell cultures.*

Why does using the same enzyme to digest DNA allow the DNA to combine?

The enzyme produces ends that have complementary base pairs, allowing the ends of different pieces of DNA to join together.

Genetic Engineering and Health

Recombinant DNA is useful in making vaccines. Vaccines work by exposing a person's immune system to a *pathogen,* such as a virus or bacterium. Once exposed, the immune system is able to recognize that pathogen and will quickly attack and destroy it should it infect the person again. Vaccines expose a person to a pathogen without actually transmitting the disease. Exposure to

Pathogens are disease-causing organisms. They include viruses and bacteria.

even a small part of the pathogen, such as a single protein, is enough to give a person immunity.

Scientists use recombinant DNA to make vaccines. They isolate the gene for a protein from the virus or bacteria and place the recombinant DNA into another cell, such as a yeast cell. The yeast cell incorporates the recombinant DNA into its own genome and expresses the gene. The protein it produces is used to vaccinate against the pathogen.

Genetic engineering is also used to produce the insulin hormone, which is a protein. The gene for human insulin is cut and spliced into a plasmid, which is then taken up by bacteria cells. The bacteria make the hormone, which is processed and sold as medicine.

More recently, scientists have tried using genetic engineering to treat people with genetic disorders. Cystic fibrosis, for example, is caused by a mutation in the gene for an ion channel protein. This causes mucus to build up in the lungs and other organs. Every cell in a cystic fibrosis patient's body has the nonfunctioning allele, although not every cell needs to produce the protein.

Gene therapy tries to insert functional genes into the cells that need them. Of course, it is difficult to place recombinant DNA into the nuclei of human cells. Scientists must first determine an appropriate *vector* (vehicle) that can deliver the DNA into patients' cells. For cystic fibrosis, scientists have tried using a modified cold virus. By placing a working copy of the gene into the virus, and allowing the virus to enter the lungs, scientists hope that the gene will insert itself into the lung cells' genetic material. An effective gene therapy for cystic fibrosis is still being developed.

Gene therapy changes the DNA of a person with a genetic disease by introducing working genes into cell nuclei.

Which disorder would be the **best** target for gene therapy?

A type II diabetes, which is influenced by diet and genetics

B high blood pressure, which is influenced by multiple genes

C hemophilia, which is caused by a gene on the X chromosome

D Lyme disease, which is caused by bacteria transmitted by ticks

Because gene therapy replaces a nonfunctioning gene, the best target is a disease caused by a single, known gene. Type II diabetes and high blood pressure are influenced by multiple genes and/or unidentified genes, and so would make poor targets for gene therapy. Lyme disease is caused by a pathogen, rather than a gene. Hemophilia, choice C, is the best target for gene therapy because it is caused by a single gene.

DNA Technology in Forensics

One major application of genetic technology is in **forensics,** the investigation of crimes. Both criminals and victims leave DNA evidence at the scene of a crime and, possibly, on each other. Each individual has a sort of DNA "fingerprint."

Forensics is the use of science and technology to investigate and solve crimes.

Amazingly, most of the DNA in the human genome is identical from one person to the next. Only a very small percentage varies. In order to identify individuals on the basis of DNA, scientists need to examine variable regions of the genome. One type of variable region consists of short, repeated DNA sequences (STRs) that are not part of a gene. Each repeat consists of between two and five bases. They are arranged end-to-end and repeat a different number of time in different individuals. For example, the STR sequence GATA may repeat between 6 and 15 times.

Allele 1: GATAGATAGATAGATAGATA
Allele 2: GATAGATAGATAGATAGATAGATAGATAGATAGATAGATA...

Two alleles of the STR GATA show different numbers of repeats.

STRs occur in thirteen different *loci* (places in the genome), providing a good source of measureable variation for forensics. While two people may share the same alleles at one locus, they are less likely to do so at two loci, and even less likely at more loci. Therefore, examining STRs at several different loci allows investigators to distinguish the DNA from different individuals.

To examine STRs, investigators make multiple copies of the DNA at different STR loci. They use *gel electrophoresis* to separate the DNA fragments on the basis of size. By matching individuals' DNA with blood samples, investigators can determine the source of blood, saliva, or hair found at a crime scene.

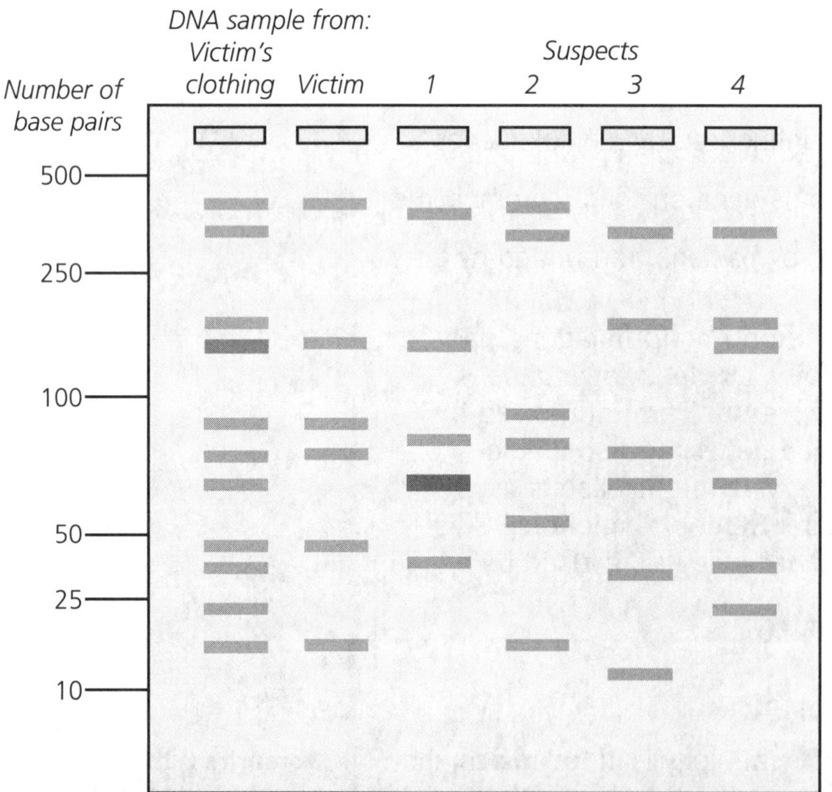

This electrophoresis gel shows DNA from three different STR loci, each represented by two alleles. The DNA on the victim's clothing comes from more than one source.

STR stands for *short tandem repeat.* These nongenetic DNA sequences differ among individuals, making them useful in identification.

CODIS is the FBI database that stores DNA fingerprints. CODIS stores information on alleles at 13 different STR loci for each person on file.

Sometimes, there is little or poor-quality DNA at a crime scene. *Polymerase chain reaction,* or PCR, is a technique that makes multiple copies of even miniscule amounts of DNA. Making multiple copies of DNA fragments allows them to be visualized on an agarose gel.

Gel electrophoresis separates DNA by size. DNA that has been amplified by PCR is loaded into the little "wells" at the top of the electrophoresis gel. An electric current applied to the gel causes the DNA fragments to move toward the other end. Small fragments move more quickly than larger fragments.

DNA fingerprinting is also used to determine paternity (identify the father of an infant).

Examine the electrophoresis gel image on page 152. The victim of this crime wounded the suspect, whose blood stained the victim's clothing. Which suspect is the source of the DNA?

A 1

B 2

C 3

D 4

The DNA on the victim's clothing comes from multiple sources. One source is the victim: Notice how all the DNA fragments from the victim also appear on the clothing. Ignore these fragments, and match the remaining fragments with one of the suspects. The DNA from suspect 4 matches the remaining fragments. Choice D is correct.

Cloning

Normally, a sexually reproducing organism inherits its genes from different parents and is genetically distinct from both of them. In contrast, reproductive **cloning** attempts to create animals that are genetically identical. All of the genes and chromosomes in the clone must be from the original animal.

To clone a mammal, scientists use a nucleus from one of the animal's body cells. They also need an egg cell to accept the nucleus and a host mother to gestate the offspring. The nucleus is removed from the egg cell, and the nucleus from the original animal's cell is inserted into the egg. The egg cell now has a full set of chromosomes. It is allowed to develop into an embryo, which is then inserted into the uterus of the host mother. The resulting offspring is genetically identical to the animal that donated the nucleus.

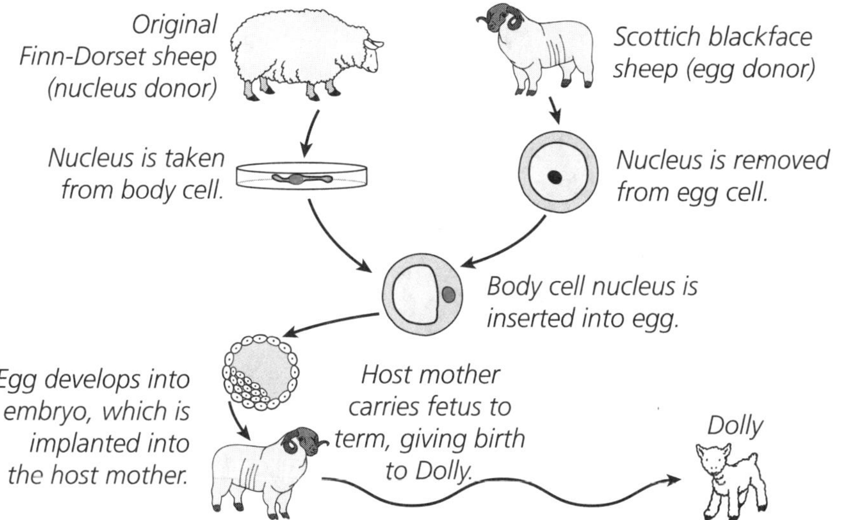
Original Finn-Dorset sheep (nucleus donor)
Scottich blackface sheep (egg donor)
Nucleus is taken from body cell.
Nucleus is removed from egg cell.
Body cell nucleus is inserted into egg.
Egg develops into embryo, which is implanted into the host mother.
Host mother carries fetus to term, giving birth to Dolly.
Dolly

Three different animals were used in the cloning of Dolly.

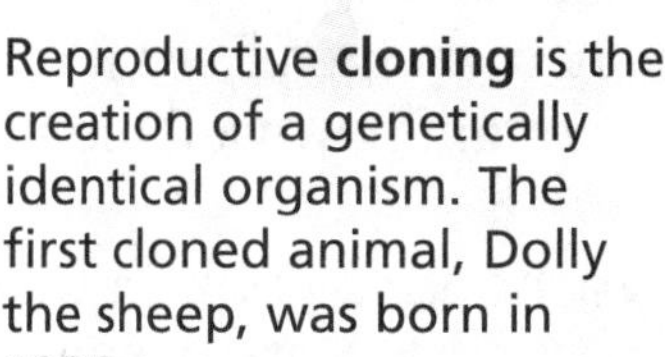

Reproductive **cloning** is the creation of a genetically identical organism. The first cloned animal, Dolly the sheep, was born in 1996.

Dolly the sheep was cloned through *somatic cell nuclear transfer* (SCNT). The somatic (body) cell's nucleus is transferred to an egg cell, and must be specially treated to encourage it to develop. Cloning Dolly required creating several hundred embryos in this way, most of which were not successful.

Cloning animals is still a difficult process and most cloned embryos do not develop successfully. Despite this, there are several reasons why people might want to clone an animal. A farmer might want more of a certain livestock animal with particularly good traits, or a person might want a clone of a favorite pet that has passed away. However, because the environment also influences development, a cloned animal's phenotype will not be identical to the original in every way.

Another reason for cloning has to do with preserving endangered species and bringing back extinct species. Ecologists worry, however, that cloning will discourage people from protecting endangered species' habitats. Habitat destruction is the leading cause of species decline. If animals can simply be cloned, why be concerned with habitat protection? So far, however, cloning has not played a major role in wildlife conservation.

Creating a clone of an extinct species is especially difficult because an intact cell nucleus is needed. The wooly mammoth is one species that scientists have considered cloning. Scientists are trying to isolate viable cells from frozen mammoths. The nucleus of a mammoth cell would need to be transferred to a donor egg from a suitable, closely related species, which would then need to act as the host mother. Even if cloning a mammoth were successful, it is not certain how well the animal would survive outside of captivity.

In 2001, scientists cloned a cowlike animal called a gaur. Gaurs are endangered and the scientists hoped that cloning would help preserve the species. However, the cloned gaur died soon after birth due to unrelated causes.

Mitochondria contain their own DNA. A fertilized egg's mitochondria are contributed by the egg cell, but not the sperm cell. Which two sheep in the diagram on page 153 have identical mitochondrial DNA?

A the egg donor and Dolly

B the host mother and Dolly

C the egg donor and the host mother

D the original Finn-Dorset sheep and Dolly

Dolly inherits mitochondrial DNA from the mitochondria in the egg cell. These mitochondria are identical to those in the egg donor. Choices B and D are incorrect because neither the original sheep nor the host mother contribute an egg cell. Choice C is incorrect because, although these are both Scottish blackface sheep, they do not necessary have the same mitochondria. Choice A is correct.

IT'S YOUR TURN

Please read each question carefully. For a multiple-choice question, circle the letter of the correct response. For a constructed-response question, write your answers on the lines.

1 Which of the following is **not** an example of genetic engineering?

A An agricultural scientist creates a hybrid strain of rice by crossing two rice varieties.

B A biology student inserts plant DNA into bacteria to determine its role in the cell cycle.

C A vaccine manufacturer inserts a plasmid containing a gene from a virus into yeast cells.

D A medical researcher isolates a functional copy of a muscular dystrophy gene for gene therapy.

2 Which is the **most** challenging step in developing effective gene therapy for human diseases?

A determining the DNA sequence for the gene

B delivering the gene into the cells of the body

C splicing the functional gene involved in the disorder

D determining which disorders can be cured by gene therapy

3 A scientist uses enzymes to splice genetic DNA into a plasmid, and then inserts the plasmid into a cell. Which of the following is **most likely** an application of this process?

A producing an exact genetic clone of a prized racehorse

B producing a vaccine against the human papillomavirus

C determining which of several rice varieties should be crossed

D determining whether a suspect's blood was present at a crime scene

Use the diagram below to answer question 4.

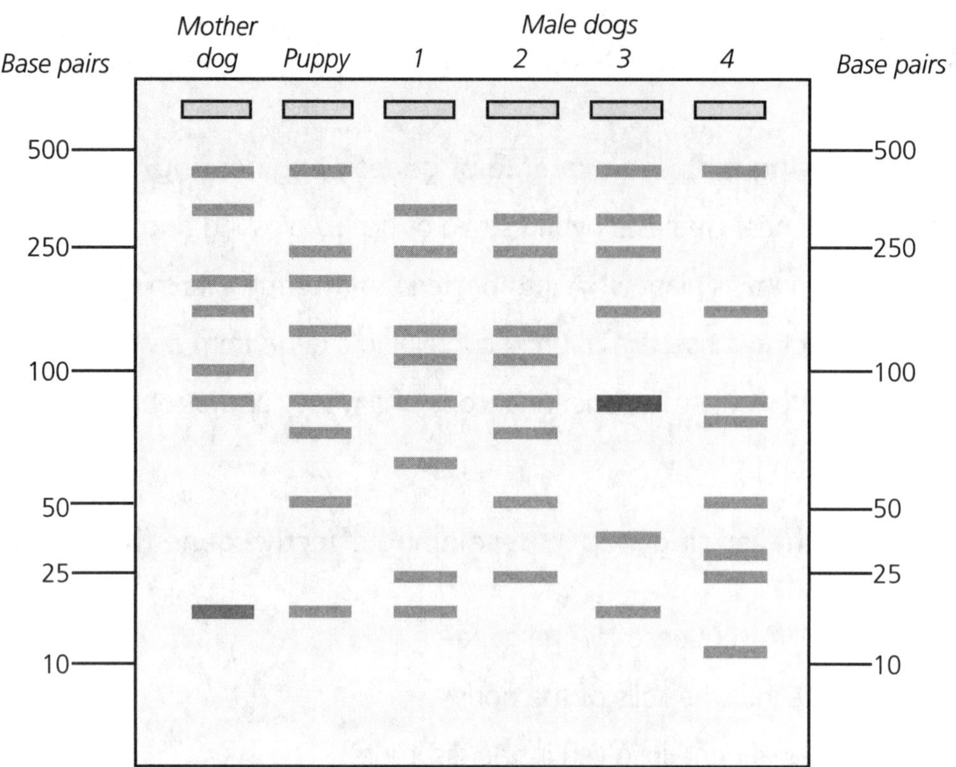

4 A purebred dog has a litter of puppies. The dog's owners are not sure which dog is the father of the puppies. They hire a scientist to identify the father through DNA fingerprinting. The scientist takes blood samples from four dogs and examines STRs at several different loci. She amplifies the amount of DNA at each STR and separates the resulting DNA fragments using gel electrophoresis. The resulting gel, with DNA fragments visible as bands at different locations, is shown above.

A How many STR loci were examined by the scientist? Explain. (Keep in mind that a single STR locus has two alleles.)

B Why are the DNA bands located at different positions in each lane?

C Which male dog is the puppy's father? Explain your choice.

Module B
Continuity and Unity of Life

Unit 7
Theory of Evolution

Evolution is the process by which new species develop from existing species. This unit will help you review the mechanisms by which evolution occurs, the evidence that supports evolution, and the scientific vocabulary used to describe evolution.

1 Mechanisms of Evolution A number of evolutionary mechanisms can contribute to the development of new species. In this lesson, you will review natural selection and genotypic and phenotypic variation within a population. You will also review factors such as isolating mechanisms, genetic drift, founder effect, and migration.

2 The Evidence for Evolution The theory of biological evolution is supported by evidence from a variety of sources. In this lesson, you will review these forms of evidence, including fossil, anatomical, physiological, embryological, and biochemical. You will also review how the universal genetic code supports evolution.

3 Scientific Terminology Precise scientific terminology is among the tools applied to the study of the theory of evolution. In this lesson, you will review the scientific terms *hypothesis, inference, law, theory, principle, fact,* and *observation* and how to distinguish them.

LESSON 1 Mechanisms of Evolution

BIO.B.3.1.1, BIO.B.3.1.2, BIO.B.3.1.3

Species are defined by their genetic characteristics. Each species has a typical number of chromosomes and a particular set of genes. Within a species, however, organisms differ. Because individuals have different alleles (versions of genes), they have different traits. As species evolve over time, some traits (and the alleles that cause them) become more common and others disappear entirely. A precise definition of **evolution** is "the change in allele frequencies over time."

Evolution is the change in allele frequencies over time that results in new species developing from existing species.

The idea that species evolve existed before Charles Darwin published his theory of natural selection in 1859.

Natural Selection and the Peppered Moth

One mechanism that drives evolution is **natural selection,** the process by which certain individuals are more likely to survive and reproduce, leading to changes in the alleles of a population or species. A classic example of natural selection is the change in coloration of the peppered moth, *Biston betularia.* Prior to the 1800s, most peppered moths in the United Kingdom were grey with black speckles. This coloring helped to camouflage the moths against the lichen-covered trees of the moth's environment, helping them to avoid predators.

Natural selection is the process in which alleles for traits that give an advantage in survival and reproduction are more likely to be passed on to offspring. These alleles increase in the population.

Then, coal-burning factories were built near U.K. cities during the Industrial Revolution. Coal burning releases soot that settles on trees, darkening their barks and killing lichens. In 1848, the first black-colored peppered moth was observed and recorded in England. By 1900, most peppered moths in industrial areas were black. (The speckled phenotype still occurred in rural areas.)

The black moth phenotype is an example of an *adaptation,* a behavior or characteristic that helps an individual to survive and reproduce in its environment. When the environment changed, a solid black phenotype helped camouflage the moths against the blackened tree barks. Moths with this phenotype were more likely to survive and produce offspring than moths with the speckled phenotype. As a result, a greater fraction of the next generation inherited the black phenotype. The moth populations in industrial areas successfully adapted to the change in their environment.

An *adaptation* is a behavior or trait that helps an organism to survive and reproduce in its environment.

Natural selection does not make organisms better or superior in any general way. Instead, it makes them more fit to survive in their local environments.

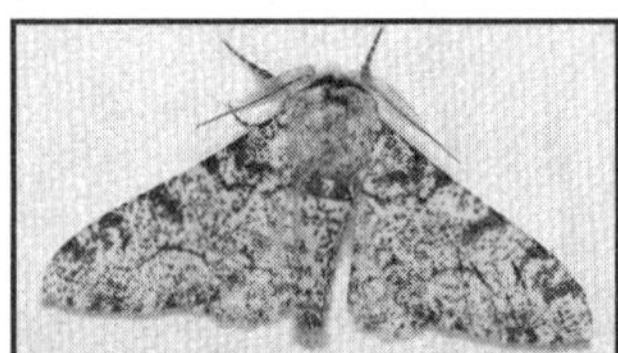

As a result of natural selection, the black phenotype of the moth became more common than the speckled phenotype.

Explain why the change in color of peppered moths is an example of evolution, but the change in the color of tree bark in the same region is not.

Evolution is a change in allele frequencies in a population. That is, evolutionary change occurs at the genetic level across a population as a whole. Because more black moths than gray moths survived to reproduce, the moth population gradually became darker over several generations. The trees changed color because of environmental factors; the color change was not due to a change in the genotypes within the tree populations.

Natural Selection and Alleles

Natural selection includes the following principles and processes:

- Organisms produce more offspring than their environments can support. Not all individuals in a population survive.
- Offspring vary in phenotype. Some offspring are better able to survive in their environment than others.
- Much of this variation in phenotype is caused by differences in the alleles inherited by individuals.
- The inheritance of alleles determines how likely an individual organism is to survive and reproduce.
- The ability of some organisms, with certain alleles, to survive and produce more offspring will lead to a change in **allele frequency** in the population. Over time, more individuals will have the "helpful" alleles.

Remember that an organism's phenotype is influenced by the alleles it inherits from its parents. In most species, each individual has two alleles for each gene, and they may be either the same or different. During reproduction, alleles from parents recombine in offspring, giving the offspring different combinations of alleles—and traits—than either parent.

In the case of the peppered moth, a single gene determines coloration. Assume, for the sake of simplicity, that the gene has two alleles: one for black coloration (*B*) and one for speckled coloration (*b*). For many generations prior to the Industrial Revolution, the speckled phenotype provided better camouflage. Therefore, moths with the *bb* genotype were more likely to survive, reproduce, and pass the *b* allele to the next generation of moths. Because the *b* allele occurred at a very high frequency, almost all moths had the speckled phenotype.

When the environment changed, however, new selection pressures acted on some of the moth populations, leading to changes in allele frequencies. The ability of black moths to blend

An organism's observable phenotype, or traits, is influenced by its genotype, or combination of inherited alleles.

An allele may be beneficial, harmful, or neutral to an organism's survival in a particular environment.

Allele frequency refers to how commonly an allele occurs in a population. An allele with a higher frequency is more common than one with a lower frequency.

into the soot-covered trees gave them an advantage over speckled moths. Each year, black moths survived and reproduced more often than speckled moths, passing on their alleles at a greater frequency. In the generations that followed, a higher percentage of moths had the *BB* or *Bb* genotypes and the black phenotype.

Natural selection acts only on phenotype, but it ultimately affects the genotypes of an entire population. Explain how this is true in terms of the peppered moth example.

The phenotypes of the peppered moths (black vs. speckled coloration) determined how well they survived in the changed environment. It did not matter which alleles, or how many genes, determined the phenotype. Natural selection can "see" phenotype, but not genotype. However, because moth coloration is determined by genotype, selection favoring black moths also favors the alleles that cause this phenotype. By selecting for the black phenotype, the relevant alleles increase throughout the moth population.

Other Mechanisms of Evolution

A **population** is a group of organisms of the same species that share a geographical area and breed with each other. As the peppered moth example shows, natural selection can change the frequencies of alleles in a population. However, there are other ways in which allele frequencies may change. **Genetic drift** refers to changes in allele frequencies that are due to chance events.

For example, consider a bird population that colonizes a cliff side once a year to nest and lay eggs. A landslide may eliminate a portion of the population. If, just by chance, more of the birds in the landslide area have a certain allele, that allele's frequency will decrease. Genetic drift produces changes unrelated to an allele's impact on survival and reproduction. It does not cause any steady, directed increase or decrease over generations, as natural selection does.

The simplest way for an allele's frequency to change is through **migration,** the movement of individuals into or out of a population. These individuals bring their alleles with them. If the population is small, the effect of even a small number of migrating individuals can be great. This is especially true if, by chance, migration removes a rare allele from a population. (In a larger population, migration is less likely to cause large changes in allele frequencies.)

Sometimes, several members of a population may leave a geographical area and found a new population. Their allele frequencies will, by random chance, differ from those of the original population, which still exists. The new population's allele

A **population** of organisms inhabits an area and shares a gene pool.

Genetic drift is a change in allele frequencies that occurs due to chance events rather than differences in fitness.

Migration, the movement of individuals into and out of a population, can change the population's allele frequencies.

If you flip a coin 500 times, it would likely fall on heads close to 250 times. If you were to flip the coin five times, it would not be unusual for it to land on heads all five times, or none. This demonstrates that a small number of events is more likely to differ from expected probabilities than a large number of events.

frequencies will reflect those of the founding population rather than the original population. Uncommon alleles in the larger, original population are less likely to be included in the founding group. The **founder effect** decreases the genetic variation in the new population by reducing the number of different alleles.

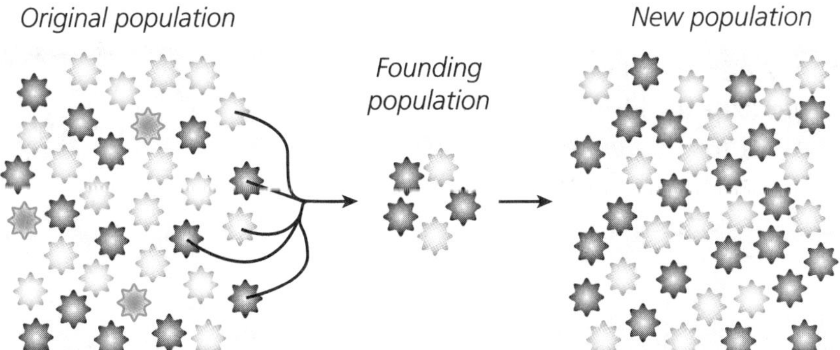

The genetic variation of a small group of founders and of the new population is lower than that of the original population.

Similarly, a *population bottleneck* occurs when an entire population is reduced to just a few individuals, often as a result of some form of disaster such as disease. This smaller population has less genetic variation than the original, larger one. Even when this small population increases in size, its genetic variation will remain low. For example, cheetahs have extremely low genetic variation due to their population having gone through a population bottleneck about 10,000 years ago.

The **founder effect** is a decrease in gene variation in a population. It results from the formation of a new population from just a few individuals who leave a larger population. A *population bottleneck* occurs when a population declines to a very small number. Both result in decreased genetic variation.

Alleles are regularly lost from populations. However, the process of mutation produces new alleles.

Which of the following is a result of cheetahs having gone through a population bottleneck?

A The cheetah species is more likely to become extinct.

B Mutations occur more frequently in the cheetah genome.

C Individual cheetahs have different alleles for many genes.

D The cheetah population cannot increase past a certain size.

A population bottleneck reduces genetic variation. Natural selection acts on genetic variation. If this variation is low, natural selection is less able to cause a change in allele frequencies in response to environmental change. In other words, populations are less able to adapt to change and the species is more likely to become extinct, so choice A is correct. A bottleneck does not increase mutation rate, it leads to individuals having the same alleles for more genes, and it poses no limit to potential population size, so choices B, C, and D are incorrect.

Speciation

Evolution does not occur only to change existing species. Entirely new species also evolve. As species become extinct, new and different species arise to replace them. **Speciation** is the formation of new, genetically distinct species from populations of existing species.

Speciation refers to the formation of new species and occurs when one population is isolated from another.

Recall the definition of a *population*—a group of organisms of the same species that share a geographic area and breed with each other. Every population shares a gene pool, a set of gene alleles, among its members. Species arise when a population splits or two populations are under different selective pressures. Eventually, members of one population stop mating with each other. Genes and alleles stop flowing between them.

Sometimes, the separation of populations is due to *geographical isolation*. For example, a highway may divide what was a single population of burrowing beetles into two populations. Speciation may also occur in the same area, such as when some parasites move onto a different host species. The parasites on the new host will only encounter others on that same host species. *Reproductive isolation* prevents this population from mating with members of the original population.

Geographical isolation divides two populations through a physical barrier, such as a canyon, river, or highway.

Reproductive isolation prevents members of two populations from mating, even if they inhabit the same area.

As the separate populations evolve along separate paths due to natural selection, they become increasingly different. Eventually, they may be considered entirely separate species.

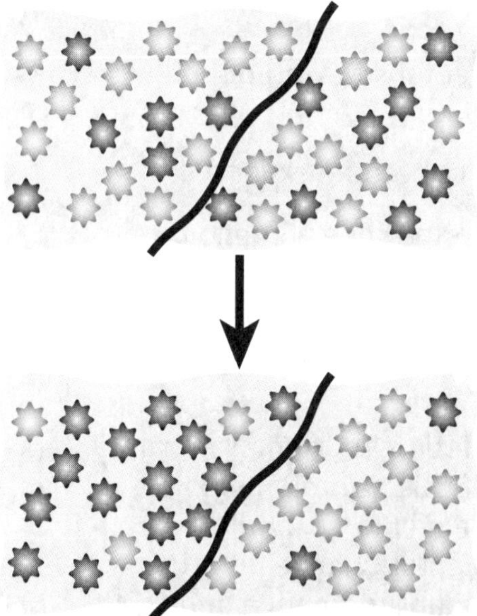

Original population is divided into two genetically similar populations.

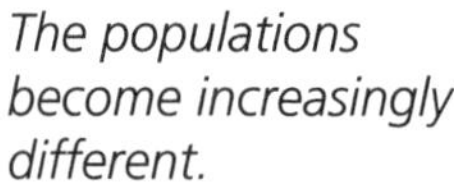

When a single population is divided geographically into two, gene flow between them stops and the new populations evolve along different paths. This may eventually lead to the formation of entirely new species.

One definition of **species** is a group of organisms that can mate and produce fertile offspring. Organisms of different species cannot breed and produce fertile offspring due to **isolating mechanisms.** These are behaviors or physical characteristics that prevent mating and breeding between different species.

Isolating mechanisms can take different forms, and can either prevent organisms from mating or, if they do mate, prevent healthy, fertile offspring from developing. Mating is avoided if members of the two species are active at different times of the day or mate only during different seasons. They may have evolved different mating calls or rituals, or they may mate or breed in different habitats.

If mating does occur, sperm from males of one species may not be able to reach the eggs of females from the other species. Even if gametes do meet, fertilization may not occur or the zygote that results from fertilization may not be viable. Sometimes, closely related species are able to produce hybrid offspring. Usually, the offspring is sterile. For example, the mating of a horse and a donkey produces mules, which cannot produce offspring of their own.

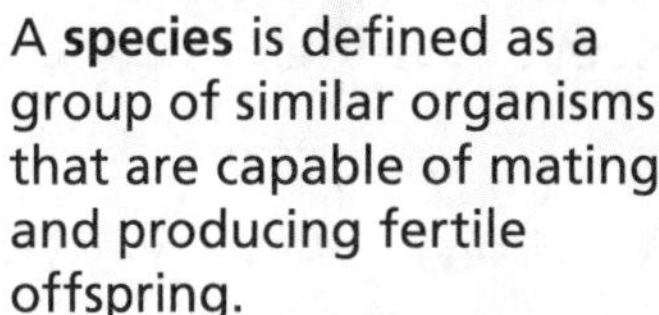

A **species** is defined as a group of similar organisms that are capable of mating and producing fertile offspring.

An **isolating mechanism** is a physical or behavioral trait that prevents a member of one species from mating with a member of a different species and producing fertile offspring.

Horses have 64 chromosomes and donkeys have 62. Their mule offspring have 63 chromosomes.

A new bee species, which pollinates a particular flower, arises from a larger bee population that pollinates a different type of flower. Explain why natural selection would favor the evolution of isolating mechanisms between the two species.

Each bee species is adapted to pollinate a specific type of flower. If bees from the two species mated, their offspring might not be able to pollinate either flower type very well. Isolating mechanisms prevent bees of both species from producing offspring that are less able to survive in their environment. These mechanisms ensure that offspring have the adaptations of their parents and help the parents' alleles to be passed on to future generations.

IT'S YOUR TURN

Please read each question carefully. For a multiple-choice question, circle the letter of the correct response. For a constructed-response question, write your answers on the lines.

1 Which is one way that natural selection differs from genetic drift?

A Natural selection causes the frequencies of alleles in a population to change.

B Natural selection affects smaller populations more often than larger populations.

C Natural selection results from some individuals producing more offspring than others.

D Natural selection depends on some traits helping individuals survive in their environment.

2 A particular gene has two alleles, *G* and *g*. Each allele has a frequency of 50% in a population. Which is **most likely** to preserve these allele frequencies?

A The population doubles in size over several generations.

B A number of individuals with one allele migrate from the population.

C One allele results in a phenotype that better enables organisms to reproduce.

D A population bottleneck temporarily reduces the population size by one-tenth.

3 Recently, bears have been found in the Arctic Circle that are hybrids between grizzly bears and polar bears. Which type of isolating mechanism usually keeps these species from producing offspring?

A mating and breeding in different habitats

B production of a nonviable embryo or fetus

C inability of sperm to reach the egg during mating

D failure of the fertilized egg to implant in the uterus

4 Under which of the following conditions would a dominant allele that coded for a fatal disease **most likely** remain in a population?

A The allele is acted on by natural selection.

B The gene is expressed only in members of one sex.

C The gene is expressed in individuals late in their lives.

D The allele mutates to a nonfatal form during an individual's lifetime.

5 Imagine that DNA replication and cell division were completely error-free and that cell DNA were completely protected from substances that cause mutation. How would natural selection be affected?

A It would become more efficient, since it removes mutations from the populations.

B It would become ineffective, since it depends on variations within populations.

C It would become unnecessary, since organisms would be better adapted to their environments.

D It would become more obvious, since it would improve on organisms with better cell processes.

Use the the graphs below to answer question 6.

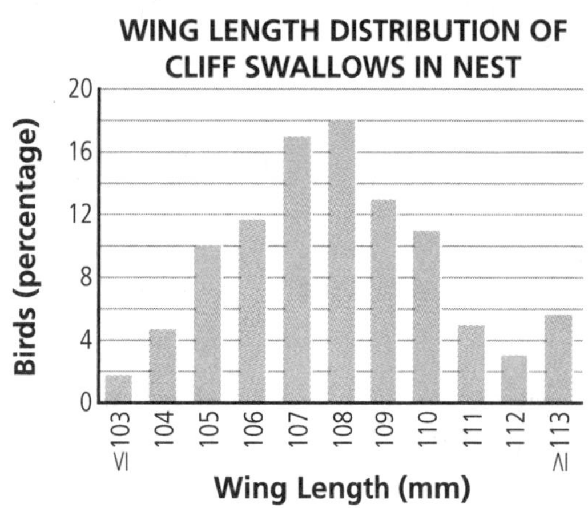

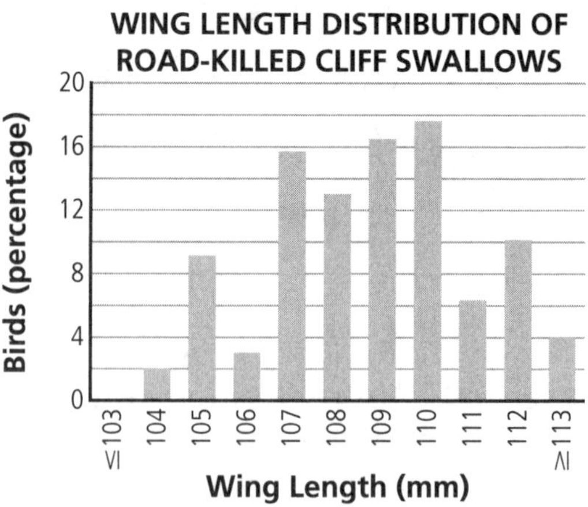

6 Cliff swallows (*Petrochelidon pyrrhonota*) nest on bridges and overpasses along highways. Scientists collected data on a cliff swallow population, examining 134 adult birds found in nests and 104 adult birds found as roadkill. The data is shown in the graphs.

A In order for natural selection to act on the population, what must be true about the phenotypic variation seen in the graphs?

____

____

____

____

B Is natural selection acting on the cliff swallow population? Explain how the data support your response.

____

____

____

____

C Are the frequencies of the alleles that affect wing length likely to remain stable in this population? Explain.

____

____

____

____

The Evidence for Evolution

BIO.B.3.2.1

Throughout Earth's history, species have become extinct, new species have arisen, and populations have been shaped by natural selection. These processes resulted in the enormous diversity of organisms that exist today. What is the evidence that these organisms are all related by descent from a common ancestor?

Evolutionary Relationships

The theory of evolution states that every species on Earth today descended from species that existed previously. Therefore, any two species are related due to the fact that they share a common ancestor species. Some species, such as tigers and lions, share a relatively recent common ancestor. Others, such as tigers and butterflies, last shared a common ancestor early in the history of animal life.

Evolution does not lead to a steady replacement of older species with newer species, as depicted in the upper image below. Instead, it results in a tree of life in which speciation events produce new branches. Over time, new traits evolve in certain species. For example, hair first evolved in an ancient mammal-like species. This trait has been inherited by descendant species: all mammal species alive today have hair. Patterns of similarities and differences among species are evidence of evolution. Scientists use different types of evidence to determine evolutionary relationships, including fossils, anatomy, and DNA.

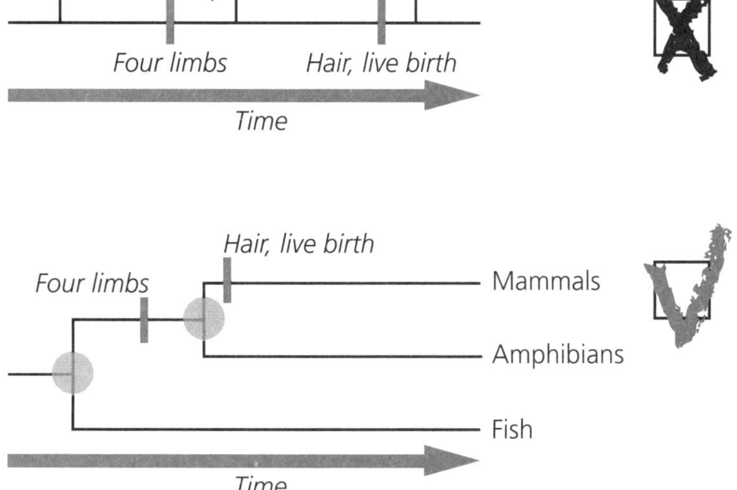

Evolution is not a linear process (top), but a branching process that results in different degrees of relatedness between species (bottom).

Evolution is also called "descent with modification" because it states that species descended from older species, but were modified (changed) in the process.

Both Charles Darwin and Alfred Russell Wallace proposed the idea of common descent at about the same time.

It is important to remember that individuals do not evolve; only populations evolve.

The human species did not evolve from chimpanzees. Rather, humans and chimpanzees shared a common ancestor.

Based on the diagram on page 169, what can be concluded about the last common ancestor of amphibians and mammals?

A It had hair.

B It laid eggs.

C It did not have gills.

D It did not have limbs.

Because hair evolved after the mammal and amphibian lineages had diverged (separated), the last common ancestor did not have hair; choice A is incorrect. Because gills are present in fish and amphibians, they were likely present in the common ancestor of amphibians and mammals, so choice C is incorrect. Because limbs had evolved in the line leading to the last common ancestor of mammals and amphibians, it must have had limbs, and choice D is incorrect. This ancestor must have laid eggs, since live birth evolved after the lineages diverged; choice B is correct.

Evidence from Fossils

In some cases, when organisms die they leave behind evidence of their existence in the form of **fossils.** Perhaps the most well-known example of fossils are dinosaur bones, but a fossil can be any evidence that an organism once existed, such as footprints preserved in mud or a chunk of petrified wood.

By arranging fossils chronologically, through a variety of dating techniques, and by comparing fossils to living organisms, scientists can infer how life on Earth has changed over hundreds of millions of years. Fossil evidence tells us that fishes existed before four-limbed vertebrates and that dinosaurs existed before the first birds. Fossil evidence supports the idea that life on Earth has changed over time and that new species arise from existing species.

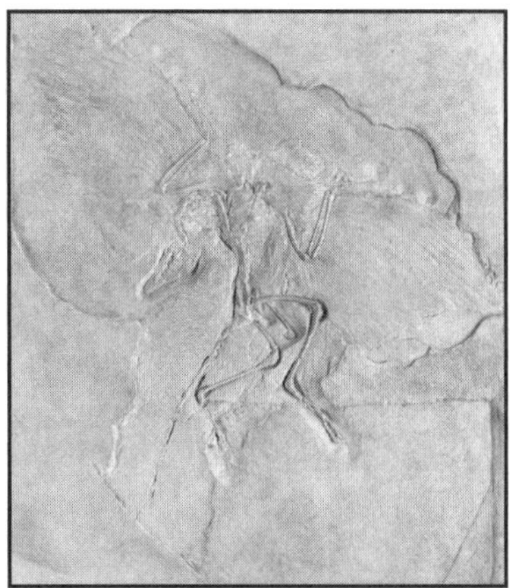

Fossils of *Archaeopteryx* show that the species had characteristics of both dinosaurs and birds.

Fossils are remains or traces of organisms that once lived and have been preserved. Tracks, bones, eggshells, and even entire organisms can become fossilized.

The name *Archaeopteryx* means "ancient wing." Although it was first classified as a bird, it is now considered a dinosaur.

Modern scientists use evolutionary relationships to determine classification. Because birds descended from dinosaurs, they are classified as dinosaurs.

Paleontologists have identified *transitional fossils,* or intermediate forms between older species and their more modern descendants. An example of a transitional fossil is that of *Archaeopteryx,* considered to be an intermediate form between dinosaurs and birds. The first *Archaeopteryx* fossil was discovered in 1861, revealing a creature that shared many features with those of small, bipedal dinosaurs, including a bony tail, well-developed teeth, and three grasping claws on each wing. The fossil also included birdlike characteristics, such as hollow bones, a furcula (or "wishbone"), and impressions of feathers.

Transitional fossils provide evidence for how species have changed over time.

Scientists first thought *Archaeopteryx* to be an ancestral bird, but later fossil finds suggest it is one of several birdlike dinosaurs. Most paleontologists today think *Archaeopteryx* is not a direct ancestor of modern birds, but a relative of this avian ancestor. Still, the fossil evidence is clear—modern birds evolved from a dinosaur ancestor.

Which statement **best** describes the significance of *Archaeopteryx* fossils?

A They revealed the direct ancestor of birds.

B They prove that dinosaurs were feathered.

C They provided the first evidence for evolution.

D They show that birds and dinosaurs have a common ancestor.

Most scientists think *Archaeopteryx* was an evolutionary "dead end," not the direct ancestor of birds, so choice A is incorrect. Scientists have only recently begun to understand the details of how evolution occurs, but many scientists have noted evidence for change over time. *Archaeopteryx* fossils are evidence for bird evolution, but are not the first evidence for evolution, so choice B is incorrect. The fossils show that *Archaeopteryx* was feathered, but one cannot conclude from fossils of a single species that all dinosaurs were feathered, so choice C is incorrect. Fossils show that *Archaeopteryx* had characteristics of both dinosaurs and modern birds, which suggest a close evolutionary relationship between the two groups. The correct choice is D.

Evidence from Anatomy and Development

At one time, scientists inferred evolutionary relationships between species primarily by comparing their anatomies, or the structure of their bodies. Species that share a common ancestor typically have similar structures.

Evolution modifies organism's bodies so that they may adapt needed functions.

Even before the discovery of *Archaeopteryx,* many scientists had suspected that birds evolved from reptiles such as dinosaurs. The tissues that produce feathers in birds are similar to those that produce scales in reptiles. Birds also have scales on their feet, and they lay eggs that are similar in basic structure to reptile eggs.

Scales and feathers are **homologous structures**—that is, their similarities are due to evolution from a common ancestor. Many species that do not share a close evolutionary relationship nevertheless have similar structures. At first glance, fish fins and dolphin fins may seem more similar than scales and feathers. Yet dolphins and fish did not share a recent common ancestor. Their fins are **analogous structures**—they function similarly because they are adaptations to similar conditions: life under water.

Homologous structures share an evolutionary relationship. They will have the same tissues, but in different forms.

Analogous structures perform similar functions.

Scientists can differentiate between homologous and analogous structures by examining them in detail. Unlike analogous structures, which tend to look similar only at the surface level, homologous structures are similar at multiple levels. Though they serve different functions, dolphin fins are structurally similar to human arms. The structures have similar bones (humerus, radius) arranged in similar ways (ball-and-socket joint at the shoulder). This is because both humans and dolphins share a relatively recent common ancestor—a mammal with the same kind of joint and arrangement of bones inherited by both species.

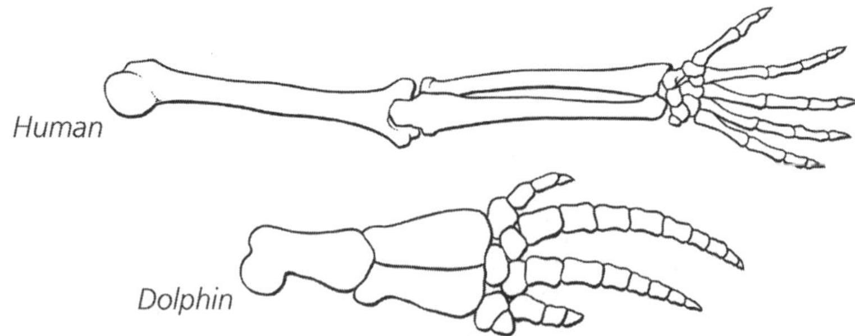

A dolphin pectoral fin and a human arm are homologous structures.

Some homologous structures are **vestigial,** meaning that they have little function or have lost their original function. An example of a vestigial structure is the pelvic bones of snakes, which do not attach to the spine and simply float within the snake's body. (Normally, pelvic bones function to attach the lower limbs to the spine.) The presence of these vestigial structures indicates that snakes evolved from an ancestor with a functional pelvis and limbs. Furthermore, snakes shared a common ancestor with four-limbed vertebrates, such as amphibians and mammals. These evolutionary relationships are shown in the diagram on the next page.

A **vestigial structure** has lost its original function, but suggests that the species descended from an ancestor with the fully intact, functional structure.

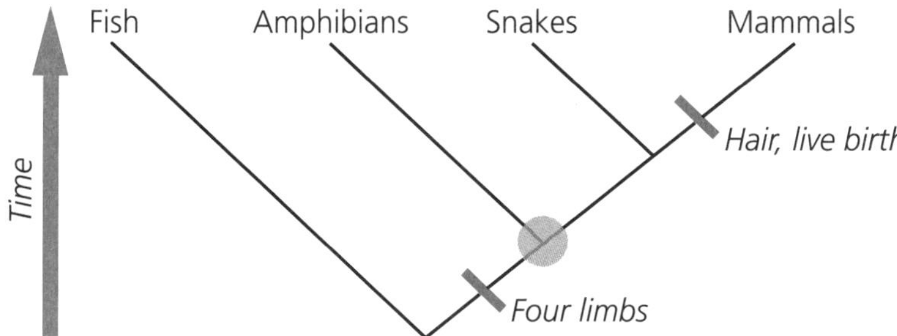

The green dot represents the common ancestor of all present-day amphibians, snakes, and mammals.

Scientists also examine how traits develop in embryos and fetuses. In the developing organism, some characteristics may appear only during early stages. For example, the fetuses of fish, amphibians, snakes, and mammals all develop similar throat structures at a certain stage. These point to evolution from a common ancestor that developed and retained the same characteristic. In fish, these structures support the gills, but in the other animals they disappear as development continues.

Development refers to the process by which a new multicellular organism forms from a single cell.

Which of the following structures are **not** homologous?

A the wings of a fly and the wings of a pigeon

B the gills of a goldfish and the gills of a shark

C the arms of a human and the arms of a chimpanzee

D the roots of a white oak tree and the roots of a red oak tree

Homologous structures are found in organisms that share a relatively recent common ancestor. Goldfish and sharks both evolved from a common fish ancestor, humans and chimpanzees from a common primate ancestor, and white oaks and red oaks from a common oak ancestor. Therefore, choices B, C, and D are incorrect. Flies are insects and pigeons are birds. Thus, they share a much more distant common ancestor. Their wings, though similar in function, are analogous, not homologous. The correct choice is A.

Evidence from Genes and Molecules

Scientists also use proteins, genes, and DNA as evidence for evolutionary relationships. Similarities among living things indicate that life on Earth has a common origin. For example, the *genetic code* is nearly universal, suggesting that it evolved very early in the history of life and was inherited by species from a common ancestor.

The *genetic code* is the way triplets of DNA or RNA bases, called *codons,* are translated as amino acids, the subunits that make up proteins. The genetic code is identical in nearly all species.

The sequences of bases in DNA or amino acids in proteins can also help to determine evolutionary relationships. DNA is passed on through generations, but **mutations** sometimes occur. These lead to differences in otherwise similar DNA sequences. These differences occur at a certain rate and indicate how long two lineages have evolved independently. The greater the number of sequences, the more time has passed since two species diverged from a common ancestor. More similar sequences indicate a more recent common ancestor.

This information can be used to construct "trees" representing evolutionary relationships. Each line or "branch" represents a *lineage*, a line of ancestors and descendants. Two branches separate where a speciation event gave rise to two different species.

A **mutation** is a change in a DNA sequence. Mutations occur more frequently in nongene DNA sequences. They occur rarely in sequences for very important genes that are essential for basic cell function.

Either gene or nongene sequences in DNA may be compared. Gene sequences will have fewer changes than nongene sequences, which can accumulate mutations without affecting phenotype.

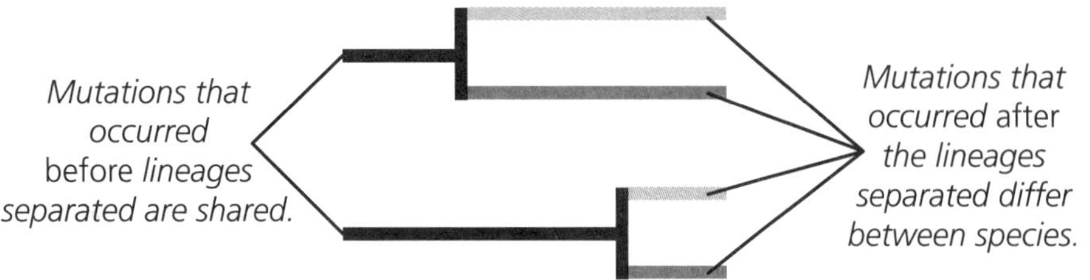

Mutations that occurred before *lineages* separated are shared.
Mutations that occurred after the *lineages* separated differ between species.

The pair of species in the top image diverged from a common ancestor earlier than the pair in the lower image.

Scientists can reconstruct evolutionary history by determining the number of differences in a DNA sequence for pairs of species. Pairs with the fewest differences shared a common ancestor most recently. Pairs with the most differences have been evolving independently for a longer period of time.

The table shows the number of amino acid differences in the cytochrome *c* protein for pairs of animal species. Use this information to determine the evolutionary relationships among these species. Write the name of each species in the correct blank box in the diagram below.

NUMBER OF AMINO ACID DIFFERENCES BETWEEN SPECIES

	Chicken	Horse	Moth	Snake
Horse	11	0		
Moth	29	29	0	
Snake	21	18	29	0
Whale	9	5	27	18

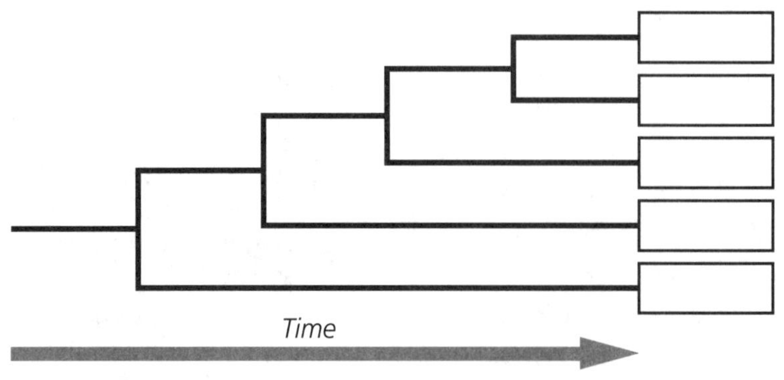

Because the horse and the whale have the fewest number of amino acid differences, they shared a common ancestor until most recently. These species are represented by the top two branches (in either order). The chicken amino acid sequence is more similar to those of the horse and whale than to those of the other species. The chicken is represented by the middle branch. The snake's sequence is more similar to those of the horse, whale, and chicken than to that of the moth. The snake is the fourth branch, which diverges from the other species more recently than it diverges from the moth, the bottom branch.

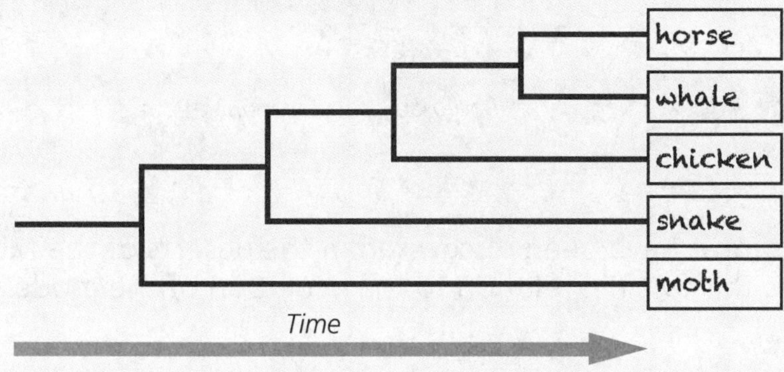

IT'S YOUR TURN

Please read each question carefully. For a multiple-choice question, circle the letter of the correct response. For a constructed-response question, write your answers on the lines.

Use the images below to answer questions 1–3.

COMPARISON OF TWO WHALES

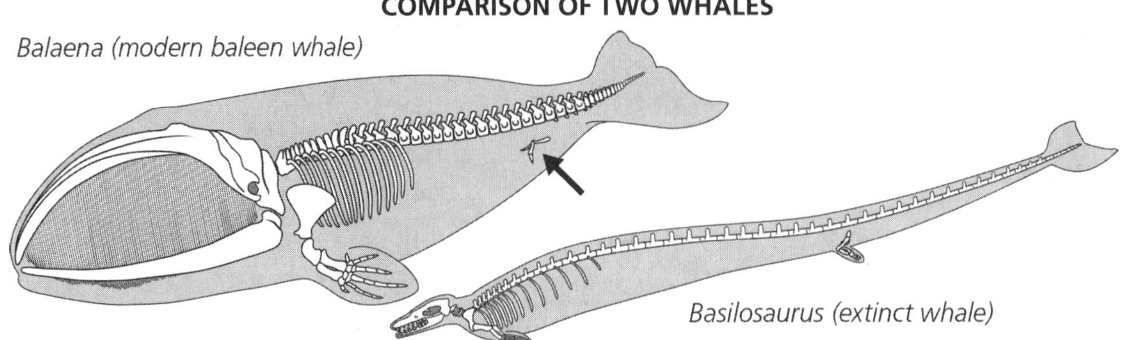

1 Fossils of species such as *Basilosaurus* have been discovered in the deserts of the Middle East. Which term **best** describes this fossil in relation to the evolution of the modern baleen whale?

A analogous

B homologous

C transitional

D vestigial

2 Which statement **best** describes the baleen whale structure that is indicated by the arrow?

A It is a transitional form connecting different types of whales.

B It is analogous to the pelvis and legs of mammals that walk on land.

C It is a vestigial structure that indicates the whale's evolutionary history.

D It is homologous to organs with reduced function, such as the human appendix.

3 Which conclusion about whale evolution can be made from the images?

A Some whales evolved arms and feet to help them swim.

B Whales descended from an ancestor that walked on land.

C Baleen whales evolved independently from toothed whales.

D Whales are ancestors to land mammals with hair and limbs.

Use the images below to answer questions 4 and 5.

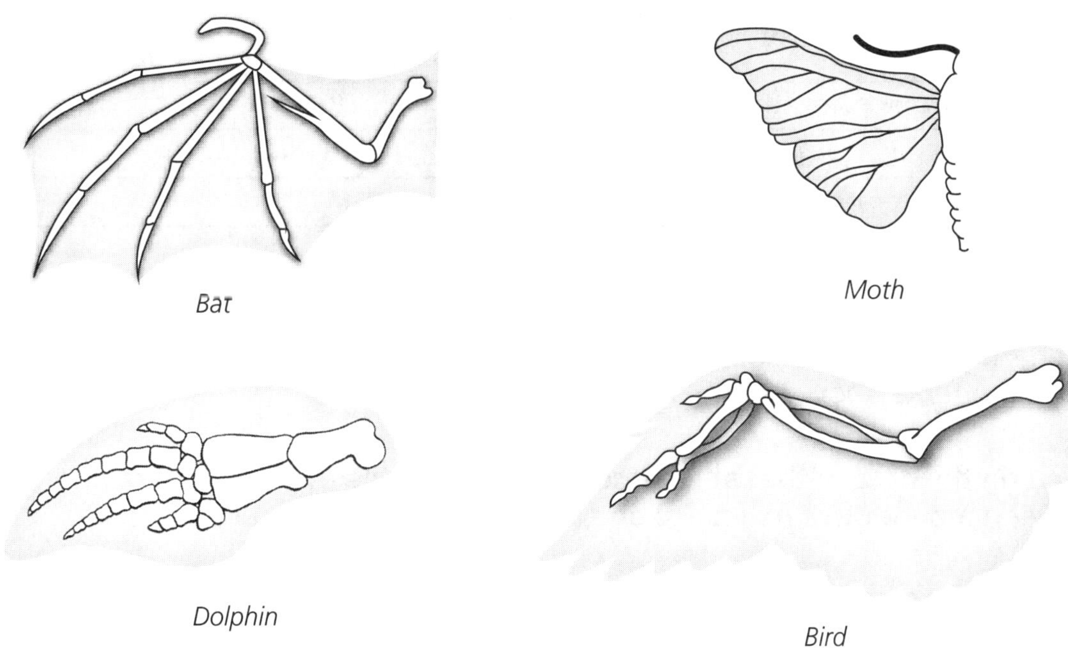

4 Which pair of structures is homologous but **not** analogous?

A bird wing and bat wing

B bat wing and moth wing

C moth wing and dolphin flipper

D dolphin flipper and bird wing

5 Which pair of structures results from natural selection for similar function rather than a shared evolutionary history?

A bird wing and bat wing

B bat wing and moth wing

C dolphin flipper and bird wing

D moth wing and dolphin flipper

Use the table below to answer question 6.

HEMOGLOBIN GENE SEQUENCE DIFFERENCES BETWEEN *MUS MUSCULUS* (MOUSE) AND VARIOUS SPECIES

Species	Number of Bases that Differ from *Mus musculus*
Canis lupus domesticus (dog)	88
Macropus rufus (kangaroo)	158
Ornithorhynchus anatinus (platypus)	161

6 Genes for hemoglobin proteins are found in mammals. The number of base differences between the alpha-hemoglobin gene from mouse and each of three other species is shown in the table above.

A Based on the data in the table, describe the probable evolutionary relationships between mouse (*Mus musculus*) and the three species listed in the table.

B The alpha-hemoglobin gene of *Ornithorhynchus anatinus* (the duck-billed platypus) has 170 base differences from that of kangaroo and 156 base differences from that of dog. What does this evidence suggest about the evolutionary relationship of the platypus to the other organisms?

C A scientist examines the similarities and differences in anatomical characteristics of the four species listed in the table. Explain how comparing both anatomies and hemoglobin genes support descent from common ancestors.

LESSON 3

Scientific Terminology

BIO.B.3.3.1

You may occasionally hear someone say that evolution is "just a theory, not a fact." The speaker may mean to say that evolution is an unproven idea, but the scientific meaning of *theory* is very different from what the speaker intends. To properly understand science, you must know the scientific meanings of terms such as *theory* and *fact.* A *fact* is a statement or piece of information that is accepted to be true. Scientists accept things to be true based on evidence, and many decades' worth of observations, data collection, and experimentation have supported the truth of evolutionary theory. Therefore, evolution is *both* a scientific theory and a fact.

A *fact* is a statement or piece of information that is true. Scientists determine what is true based on available evidence.

Observations and Inferences

Darwin's theory of evolution by natural selection was based on *observations* he made during his journey on the HMS *Beagle.* Darwin took careful notes of the species he saw on the Galapagos Islands and even took specimens of the organisms back to England with him. The several islands of the Galapagos were inhabited by bird species with different adaptations. Some of the finches had long, narrow beaks and others had short, thick beaks. Some lived on the ground, while others lived in trees. Darwin's first observations of the bird led him to infer that they were of very different species. A further *inference* was that the same species would be found on the nearby coast of South America.

An *observation* is made with the senses (sight, hearing, smell, etc.) and can be enhanced with the use of tools such as microscopes.

An *inference* is a conclusion drawn from an observation. To *infer* means "to make an inference."

When Darwin returned from his journey, he made more careful and detailed observations of the bird specimens, even seeking the help of a bird expert. They concluded that, despite their differences, the birds were actually very similar. They were all species of finch, and were found only on the Galapagos Islands. These observations eventually led Darwin to infer that the finches had descended from a single species and adapted in different ways to the environments of the Galapagos.

Large ground finch (*Geospiza magnirostris*)

Medium ground finch (*Geospiza fortis*)

Small tree finch (*Geospiza parvula*)

Warbler finch (*Certhidea olivacea*)

These four species of finches were observed by Charles Darwin on the Galapagos Islands.

Which statement is an inference that can be made from observations of the image on page 179?

A The four finch species have very different beak phenotypes.

B Two of the finch species have beaks with the same general shape.

C The beak of the large ground finch is adapted for crushing large, tough seeds.

D The beak of the warbler finch is more narrow and pointed than that of the small tree finch.

Choices A, B, and D are observations of the finches in the image. Only choice C is an inference—a conclusion based on the observation that the beak of the large ground finch is quite large.

Theories and Hypotheses

Evolution by natural selection is a **scientific theory.** The scientific definition of this term is very powerful. A scientific theory

- explains a broad set of observations about the natural world,
- is supported by evidence and data, and
- provides a set of principles that can be used to make testable predictions and hypotheses.

A **scientific theory** is an explanation of a broad range of observations and provides a framework that scientists can use to analyze and make predictions about the natural world.

A theory explains much more than just a few observations. The theory of evolution explains why we observe so many species on Earth, why different species in different parts of the world are so similar, and why the species found on Earth have changed over time.

Data and evidence support the theory of evolution. This evidence takes the form of the fossil record, comparisons of DNA and proteins, similarities in structures, and shared patterns of development in related species.

The theory of evolution allows scientists to make testable predictions. For example, scientists can predict that a pair of similar species will have fewer DNA differences than a pair of very different species.

While the time scale of evolutionary change makes it difficult to test what will happen in the future, scientists can make predictions about what types of species they will encounter in the fossil record. For example, scientists know that tetrapods, organisms with backbones and four limbs, did not exist until after the Devonian geologic period. During the Devonian, bony fishes diversified and their species colonized the seas.

Snakes, lizards, birds, crocodiles, mammals, and turtles are all *tetrapods,* a group that includes four-limbed animals. All of these, plus fishes, are also *vertebrates,* or animals with a bony spine.

The framework of evolutionary theory told scientists that the common ancestor of all tetrapods is a tetrapod-like fish that existed at the end of the Devonian period. Further, fossils of this ancestor (or a closely related species) may be found in rock layers about 375 million years old.

The evolutionary framework pointed scientists to a location in the Arctic Circle where rocks of the appropriate type and age would be exposed. Their research expedition resulted in the discovery of the fossil species *Tiktaalik*, a *transitional form* between fish and tetrapods.

A *transitional form* is a fossil species that is intermediate between existing species. *Tiktaalik* has a neck, shoulders, and limb bones, like a tetrapod. However, it also has fins, scales, and a fishlike tail.

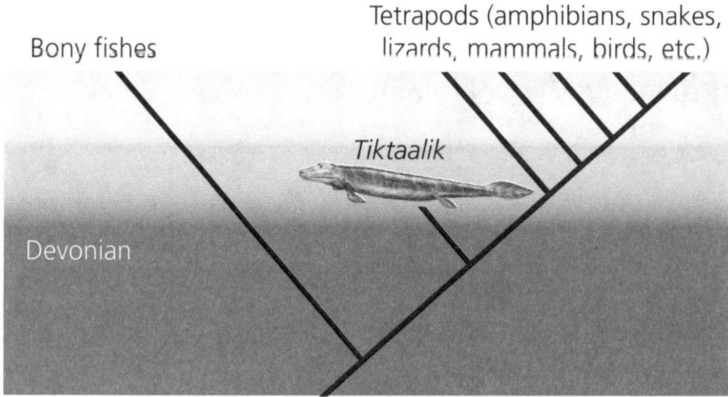

The fossil species *Tiktaalik* represents a transition between fish and tetrapods, four-limbed animals.

Scientific theories also allow scientists to test hypotheses. A **hypothesis** is a testable explanation for observations about the natural world. For example, scientists have observed a species of red crossbill, *Loxia curvirostra*, feeding on the seeds contained in pinecones. The scientists thought that the bird's crossed bill is an adaptation that allows it to open tough pinecones. They hypothesized that a bird with a crossed bill will be able to open more closed pinecones than one with an uncrossed bill.

A **hypothesis** is a testable explanation for observations and data. A good hypothesis is stated in such a way that it is clear what should be tested and measured.

This hypothesis is testable. Scientists tested the hypotheses by trimming the beaks of crossbills they had captured. (Because this part of the beak has no nerve endings, trimming it does not cause the birds pain. Like fingernails, it grows back after trimming.) The scientists observed and recorded the number of seeds that the crossbills were able to remove from open and closed pinecones, both before and after the beak trimming. When their beaks were trimmed, the crossbills were unable to open the tough scales of the closed pinecones. This result supported the scientists' hypothesis.

A hypothesis is valuable even if it turns out not to be supported by the results of an experiment. Hypotheses help scientists to determine which explanations work and which do not work.

Untrimmed, crossed bill

Trimmed bill

An experiment supports the hypothesis that the crossed bill of *L. curvirostra* is an adaptation for feeding on closed pinecones.

Subpopulations of a mouse species differ in coat color. Scientists think that the differences in coat color may be adaptations to different environments. The scientists are able to make life-sized plastic models of the mice, which they can place in the environment and check for signs of removal or attack by predators. State a hypothesis regarding coat color that may be tested by the scientists.

A hypothesis should be stated in such a way that the relevant variables are measurable. An example of a good hypothesis is "More of the models will remain untouched when placed in the environment that matches the coat color than when placed in a mismatched environment."

Principles and Laws

Scientists' understanding of the natural world is informed by scientific laws and principles. A **scientific law** is a statement or equation that accurately describes observations. Unlike a theory, a law does not provide an explanation for the observations. For example, the law of superposition states that, in undisturbed layers of bedrock, a rock layer will be younger than the layer below it and older than the layer above it. The law of superposition does not explain why this is the case—that sediment is deposited from above. The law simply describes the relationship between the relative position of a rock layer and its age.

Laws and other shared understandings can form the basis of **scientific principles.** For example, the Hardy-Weinberg principle states that, if certain conditions apply for a population, the allele frequencies in that population will not change. This principle is based, in part, on the Hardy-Weinberg law, an equation that describes the frequencies of two alleles of a gene in a population.

A **scientific law** describes or summarizes observations, but does not explain them. A law may be in the form of a mathematical formula. (Hardy-Weinberg law)

A **scientific principle** is a concept based on scientific laws and rules that are agreed upon by the scientific community.

The Hardy-Weinberg law is $p^2 + 2pq + q^2 = 1.0$, where p is the frequency of one allele and q is the frequency of the other.

The principle of faunal succession states that rock layers of the same age contain combinations of similar fossils. Which statement is **not** true regarding the principle of faunal succession?

A It can provide support for a theory, such as the theory of evolution.

B It can be used to create a timeline of species that existed through time.

C It leads scientists to expect certain types of fossils in certain rock types.

D It proposes that species have become extinct and new species have arisen.

Scientific laws and principles can support theories, help reconstruct what happened in the past, and lead to predictions about the natural world, so choices A, B, and C are all true and therefore not correct. However, laws and principles do not provide explanations. The principle of faunal succession does not state that extinction and speciation are causes for the occurrence of different fossils in different rock layers. The correct choice is D.

IT'S YOUR TURN

Please read each question carefully. For a multiple-choice question, circle the letter of the correct response. For a constructed-response question, write your answers on the lines.

1 An organism's niche is the role it occupies in an ecosystem. For example, a cheetah's niche in the savanna ecosystem is that of a hunter of gazelles and other medium-sized, fast-running herbivores. The principle of competitive exclusion states that two species cannot occupy the same niche in the same ecosystem. Which statement is true regarding this scientific principle?

A More evidence is required before it can be accepted as a fact.

B Ecological evidence allowed it to move from a theory to a principle.

C Changing the principle to a mathematical formula would make it a law.

D The principle can be used to support a theory explaining how species change.

2 Which term describes an explanation for a wide range of observations, supported by many different lines of evidence?

A hypothesis

B law

C principle

D theory

Use the image below to answer question 3.

Notes taken on a hike through the woods

- *Tree leaves are mostly green. Some are just beginning to turn yellow. They will soon stop producing green chlorophyll and drop from the trees.*
- *A fresh hoof print alongside the trail indicates that deer roam through the forest.*
- *One chipmunk has very full cheek pouches. It is storing food to fatten up for the winter.*
- *Forest is dimly lit, even though the sky is sunny. The thick canopy of tree leaves keeps the understory of smaller plants from growing.*

3 Which of the following is an observation rather than an inference?

A The chipmunk has stored food in its cheek pouches.

B The hoof print alongside the trail looks like a deer hoof.

C The yellow leaves have stopped producing green chlorophyll.

D The thick canopy of tree leaves keeps the understory from growing.

Use the images below to answer question 4.

Battus philenor
Pipevine Swallowtail

Limenitis arthemis astyanax
Red-spotted Purple

Limenitis arthemis arthemis
White Admiral

4 The images show the pipevine swallowtail butterfly (left) and two forms of the species *Limenitis arthemis.* Scientists think that the red-spotted purple form of *L. arthemis* is a Batesian mimic of the poisonous pipevine swallowtail. In Batesian mimicry, a nonpoisonous species resembles a poisonous model species. This adaptation causes predators to confuse the mimic with the model, and avoid it.

Scientists can create lifelike models of butterflies that can be placed in the butterflies' natural settings and periodically checked for signs of damage from predators such as birds.

A Identify at least two characteristics of a good hypothesis.

____

____

____

____

B State a good hypothesis that allows scientists to determine whether the red-spotted purple phenotype is an adaptation for Batesian mimicry.

____

____

____

____

C Explain how the theory of evolution by natural selection helps scientists arrive at a hypothesis for understanding the variation in the *L. arthemis* species.

____

____

____

____

Module B

Continuity and Unity of Life

Unit 8

Ecology

Ecology is the study of the relationships between organisms and their environment. This unit will help you review the ecological levels of organization, the energy flows that take place in an ecosystem, the cycling of matter, and the response of an ecosystem to natural and human-caused change.

1 Ecosystems and Biomes The biosphere is composed of many levels of ecological organization. In this lesson, you will review these levels from individual organisms to populations, communities, ecosystems, biomes, and the biosphere. You will also review the characteristic biotic and abiotic components of aquatic and terrestrial ecosystems.

2 Ecosystem Interactions Energy flows through the many interactions and relationships of an ecosystem. In this lesson, you will review food chains, food webs, and energy pyramids. You will also review the different kinds of biotic interactions that take place, such as competition, predation, and symbiosis.

3 Cycles of Matter Matter as well as energy cycles through an ecosystem. In this lesson, you will review how matter in the form of water, carbon, oxygen, and nitrogen recycles through the ecosystem.

4 Ecosystem Response to Change Ecosystems respond to change in a variety of ways. In this lesson, you will review the natural and human disturbances that cause ecosystems to change. You will also review how limiting factors affect population dynamics and potential species extinction.

LESSON 1

Ecosystems and Biomes

BIO.B.4.1.1, BIO.B.4.1.2

All organisms are interdependent with the living and nonliving things in their environments. The study of the interactions among different types of organisms, and between organisms and their physical environment, is called **ecology.**

Ecology is the study of the relationships between organisms and their enviroment.

Ecological Levels of Organization

Ecologists look at different levels of organization, from individual organisms to the entire planet Earth. The smallest and most specific level is the individual **organism,** such as a ladybug, an oak tree, or a black bear. All the individuals of a single species that inhabit a particular area make up a **population.** All the black bears living in Cook Forest, in Pennsylvania, make up a single population.

Individual **organisms** of the same species make up a **population.** Different populations make up a **community.** The community, along with the nonliving environment, makes up an **ecosystem.**

Other populations also share Cook Forest. All of the populations of different species that share an area make up a **community.** The community of Cook Forest, along with the nonliving elements of the forest (such as soil, water, and sunlight), makes up an **ecosystem.**

Ecosystems around the planet with similar characteristics are grouped into **biomes.** All the biomes on Earth make up the planet's **biosphere,** the largest level of ecological organization.

Similar ecosystems are grouped into **biomes,** which together make up Earth's largest ecosystem, the **biosphere.**

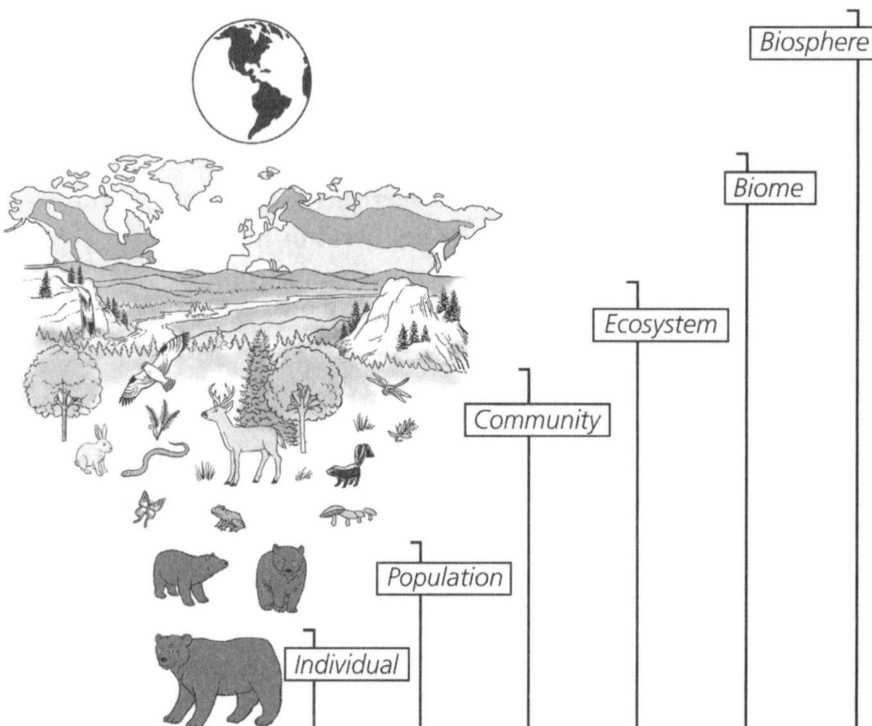

The levels of organization studied by ecologists range from individual organisms to the entire biosphere of planet Earth.

A student wants to observe how changes in the water temperature of a local stream affect the fish living in the stream. Which of the following levels of organization would be **most** appropriate for this study?

A individual

B biosphere

C ecosystem

D community

To answer this question, consider the factors that are involved in the study. The stream probably includes more than one fish, so choice A is incorrect. The student will focus on a single stream, not Earth's entire biosphere, so choice B is incorrect. Remember that an ecosystem includes living and nonliving things and a community is all of the populations in an area. The student is studying the interactions between a nonliving thing (temperature) and the fish in the stream. Therefore, the student is studying aspects of an ecosystem, and the correct choice is C.

Biotic and Abiotic Factors

Ecosystems are made up of both living and nonliving parts. The living parts of an ecosystem are called **biotic** factors. These include populations and communities. The nonliving parts of an ecosystem are called **abiotic** factors. These include temperature, precipitation, sunlight, oxygen, carbon dioxide, and soil.

The biotic and abiotic factors in an ecosystem often interact. For example, trees move water from their roots to the surfaces of their leaves. This water then evaporates and enters the atmosphere. Trees may also keep sunlight from reaching the lower levels of a forest ecosystem, preventing smaller plants and trees from growing.

Biotic and abiotic factors interact to form ecosystems of very different sizes. An ecosystem can be an entire forest, a small stream, or even a human mouth. The table below describes some ecosystems commonly found in Pennsylvania.

The term *bio* means "living." The prefix *a*- means "not" or "non."

Biotic factors are living, while **abiotic** factors are nonliving.

COMMON PENNSYLVANIA ECOSYSTEMS

Ecosystem	Biotic Factors	Abiotic Factors
Temperate upland forest	raccoons, white-tailed deer, oak trees, conifer trees	rich soil, moderate precipitation, warm summers
Pond	largemouth bass, frogs, algae, water lilies	shallow water, dissolved gases
Rotting log	fungi, bacteria, beetles	shaded from sun, damp environment

A sunflower uses sunlight, water, and carbon dioxide to make food through photosynthesis. Is this a biotic–biotic, abiotic–abiotic, or biotic–abiotic interaction? Explain your reasoning.

To answer this question, consider the elements involved in photosynthesis. A sunflower is an organism, so it is a biotic factor. Sunlight, water, and carbon dioxide are all nonliving elements in the environment. Thus, they are abiotic factors. An interaction between a biotic factor and abiotic factors is a biotic–abiotic interaction.

Major Terrestrial Biomes

Earth's biomes can be divided into **terrestrial** (land) biomes and aquatic (water) biomes. Every biome has a characteristic climate, including temperature and precipitation patterns; latitude; altitude; and soil types. Each biome is also characterized by a set of organisms adapted to conditions found there. A particular biome may occur in several different places on Earth.

Terrestial biomes are confined to land.

TERRESTRIAL BIOMES

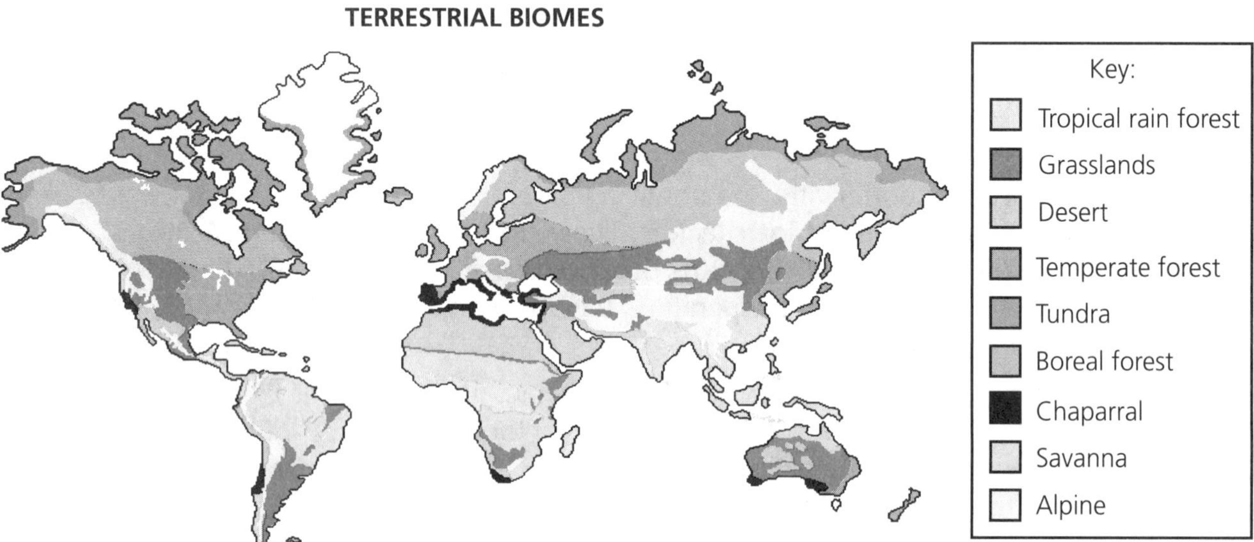

The map shows Earth's terrestrial biomes. Notice that their locations follow a pattern. The tundra biome appears in regions near the Arctic Circle, which surrounds the North Pole. Most deserts occur just to the north and south of the equator, while tropical rainforests are located at the equator. Both latitude and altitude affect the location of biomes.

Latitude is the measure of distance from Earth's equator. Higher latitudes are located farther from the equator and closer to either pole. Biomes at higher latitudes are generally colder. *Tundra,* the coldest biome with a permanent layer of frost beneath the soil, surrounds the North Pole. *Taiga,* or *boreal forest,* is found just south of the tundra biome.

Latitude is measured in degrees that increase from the equator to either pole. The equator lies at 0° latitude; State College, PA, lies at 41° North latitude; and the North Pole lies at 90° N latitude.

Altitude is a measure of a location's distance above sea level. Biomes at higher altitudes are farther from sea level and generally experience colder temperatures. Mountain ranges make up the high-altitude *alpine* biome.

Earth's biomes can be sorted into three categories according to their average temperatures: cold, temperate, and tropical. The tables describe the characteristics of different terrestrial biomes.

COLD TERRESTRIAL BIOMES

Biome	Characteristics	Soil	Organisms
Arctic tundra	short, cool summers; long, cold winters; little precipitation	thin, nutrient-poor, has a permanently frozen layer of soil and ice	small shrubs, grasses, caribou, wolves, polar bears
Boreal forest (taiga)	short, warm, wet summers; long, cold, dry winters	thin, nutrient-poor, acidic	evergreen trees, moose, foxes, bears, chipmunks
Alpine tundra	short, cool summers; long, cold winters; little precipitation	rocky, nutrient-poor	small shrubs, mountain goats, sheep

TEMPERATE TERRESTRIAL BIOMES

Biome	Characteristics	Soil	Organisms
Temperate forest	warm, wet summers; cool, wet winters	thick, nutrient-rich	deciduous trees, deer, squirrels, rabbits, bears
Grassland	hot summers; cold winters; some rain	thick, nutrient-rich	grasses, shrubs, mice, prairie dogs, coyotes
Chaparral	hot, dry summers; mild, rainy winters	thin, nutrient-poor	shrubs, some deciduous trees, foxes, rabbits, coyotes

TROPICAL TERRESTRIAL BIOMES

Biome	Characteristics	Soil	Organisms
Desert	long, hot, dry summers; shorter, dry winters; very little precipitation	sandy or coarse-grained, nutrient-poor	cacti, shrubs, lizards, small rodents
Tropical rain forest	warm all year; long wet season and short dry season	thick, nutrient-poor; acidic	tall trees with wide leaves, vines, snakes, butterflies, chimpanzees
Savanna	hot; fairly dry; alternating wet and dry seasons	thin, relatively nutrient-poor	grasses, shrubs, lions, wildebeests

The United States covers a variety of biomes, including tundra, boreal forest, temperature forest, grassland, alpine, and desert. Pennsylvania is located in a temperate forest biome, although many of its trees have been cut down.

In general, cold biomes are near the poles, temperate biomes are at the mid-latitudes, and tropical biomes are near the equator.

The Rocky Mountains are part of an alpine biome. Though they are located in the mid-latitude region, they experience low temperatures because of high altitudes.

The chaparral biome appears on many continents. It is found on the west coast of the United States and the coastal areas of the Mediterranean, among other places.

Temperate forests are characterized by *deciduous* trees, which have broad, thin leaves that drop every autumn.

Boreal forest, or taiga, biomes have many *conifers,* evergreen trees with needlelike leaves.

The tropical rain forest has the greatest species diversity of any terrestrial biome.

A student who lives in a boreal forest biome travels to a tropical rain forest biome for a yearlong internship. Describe two changes in climate that the student will experience during her internship in the tropical rain forest.

The tropical rain forest biome is generally warm all year, in contrast to the boreal forest biome, which has long, cold winters. Also, the tropical rain forest gets precipitation for most of the year, but the boreal forest has a longer dry season. Thus, the student will probably experience more precipitation during her internship and consistently warmer temperatures throughout the year.

Major Aquatic and Marine Biomes

Because much of the planet is covered by water, many important biomes are **aquatic,** consisting of lakes, rivers, wetlands, and ocean zones. Two major factors affecting aquatic biomes are salinity and sunlight.

Salinity is the salt concentration of water. Ocean, or *marine,* biomes are characterized by saltwater. Some nonmarine biomes may be partially salty, or *brackish.*

Sunlight penetrates only to a certain depth, which depends on the clarity of the water. The types of organisms found in the zones of Earth's oceans are determined by the amount of sunlight penetrating the water. Photosynthetic organisms, such as algae, are located nearer to the coastlines and the surface of the open ocean.

The tables describe the characteristics of different aquatic biomes.

Aquatic biomes consist of bodies of water or ocean zones.

Marine means "ocean." Oceans are vast bodies of saltwater with zones that make up different biomes.

Salinity refers to the concentration of salts in water. Rare saltwater lakes have salinity several times greater than ocean water.

NONMARINE AQUATIC BIOMES

Biome	Location	Characteristics	Organisms
Fresh-water lake	small to large bodies of water surrounded by land	vary greatly in the amount of dissolved oxygen and nutrients, and the types of organisms they can support	aquatic plants, phytoplankton, zooplankton, invertebrates; where there is enough oxygen, fishes
River	moving fresh water	vary in temperature, turbulence, and amount of dissolved sediment	phytoplankton, rooted plants, fishes, and invertebrates
Estuary	transition zone between river mouth and marine biome	brackish (salty) water from mixing with seawater, salinity changes with tides	aquatic grasses and algae, invertebrates, food species such as crabs and oysters
Wetland	shallow basins, in river flood zones, along coasts of lakes and oceans	may be freshwater or saltwater, may be dry part of the year	invertebrates, shore birds, and other predators

Invertebrates are organisms that lack a backbone. They include crabs, clams, oysters, shrimp, lobsters, and snail. Marine invertebrates also include squid, octopus, and jellyfish.

MARINE (OCEAN) BIOMES

Biome	Location	Characteristics	Organisms
Inter-tidal	area between low and high tide lines	periodic changes in exposure to air, salinity, and temperature; pounding force of ocean waves; organisms may bury in sand or mud	large algae; small fishes; invertebrates such as sea stars, mollusks, worms, clams, and crustaceans
Pelagic	vast waters of the open ocean	light in the upper layer, allowing photosynthesis; most organisms in this upper region	phytoplankton, zooplankton, fishes, marine mammals, turtles, and squid and other invertebrates
Benthic and abyssal	seafloor, deepest regions are called *abyssal zones*	no sunlight except on sloping seafloor along coasts; at lowest depths, cold temperatures and high pressure; organic matter drops from pelagic biome	invertebrates such as crabs and worms, and fishes; some adapted to complete darkness
Coral reef	upper layers of tropical pelagic	structure built up of coral skeletons over long periods of time	corals, fishes, and invertebrates; high species diversity

Deep-sea vent ecosystems occur in the benthic and abyssal zones of the ocean floor. Heat from deep below Earth's surface produces chemical reactions that allow *chemosynthetic* organisms to thrive.

In which marine biome does the greatest rate of photosynthesis occur?

A benthic

B coral reef

C intertidal

D pelagic

The largest area is made up of the open ocean. The upper layers of the ocean water receive enough light for photosynthesis to occur. These make up the pelagic biome, so choice D is correct. The benthic zone, choice A, is too deep to receive enough light, and coral reefs, choice B, and inter-tidal biomes, choice C, are much smaller than the pelagic biome.

IT'S YOUR TURN

Please read each question carefully. For a multiple-choice question, circle the letter of the correct response. For a constructed-response question, write your answers on the lines.

1 A scientist is comparing an ecosystem in the savanna biome to an ecosystem in the grassland biome over the course of one year. Which of the following features will he **most likely** encounter in both ecosystems?

A tall deciduous trees

B thick, nutrient-rich soil

C periods of dry weather

D extremely low temperatures

2 Which of the following is a biotic–biotic interaction?

A a snake warming itself on a sunny rock

B a rainstorm washing nutrients from the soil

C a human shivering because of cold weather

D a squirrel gathering acorns from an oak tree

3 Which statement correctly describes a part of an ecosystem?

A A community consists of both biotic and abiotic factors.

B A community is made up of different types of organisms.

C A population is an abiotic factor affecting the ecosystem.

D A population consists of different species living in an area.

4 In which aquatic biome does the salinity of water change with the tides?

A benthic

B estuary

C lake

D pelagic

Use the graph below to answer question 5.

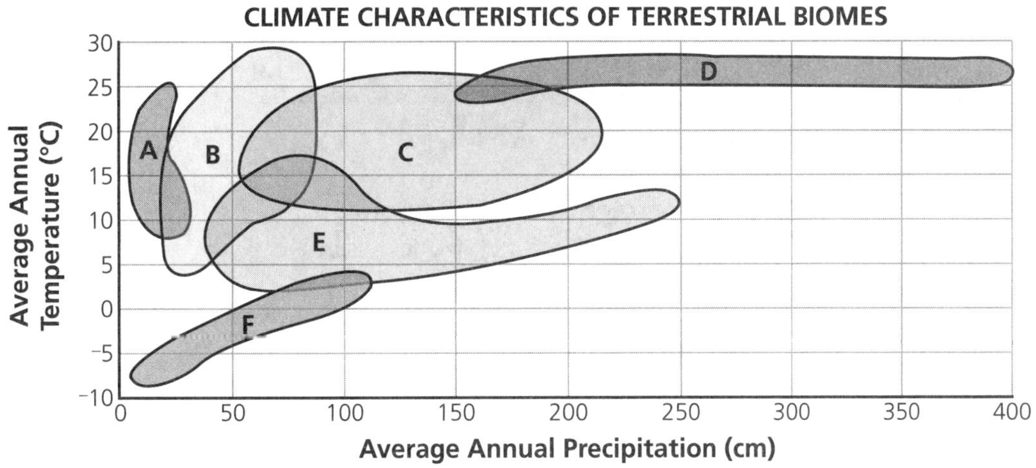

5 The graph depicts average annual temperature and precipitation for six different biomes, labeled A–F.

A Identify the hot desert and grassland biomes. Justify your response based on the data shown in the graph.

____

____

____

____

B Explain how the plants growing in biome C are likely to differ from those found in biome E. Justify your response based on the data shown in the table.

____

____

____

____

C Identify the biome with the greatest altitude or latitude. Justify your response based on the data shown in the table.

____

____

____

____

Ecosystem Interactions

BIO.B.4.2.1, BIO.B.4.2.2

An organism in an ecosystem must interact with the community around it. It may depend on some populations for food, try to avoid becoming food for other populations, and compete for the same resources with a third population. It may associate with a member of another species in a way that mutually benefits both, or to the benefit of only one member of the pair.

Ecological Relationships

The resources in an ecosystem are limited. Populations that require the same resource find themselves in **competition.** Only some individuals will obtain the resource, while others will not. Some populations are predators, capturing and feeding on other species in the community. The predator–prey relationship is called *predation.*

The organisms in a community may interact through symbiosis. A **symbiotic relationship** is one in which individuals of two different species live together in close association. A symbiotic relationship may harm or benefit either species. There are several types of symbiosis, as shown in the table below.

TYPES OF SYMBIOSIS

Interaction	Who Benefits?	Example
Mutualism	Both organisms benefit.	Cleaner fish eat parasites and dead cells from other fish, such as grouper. The cleaner fish get food, and the grouper avoid disease.
Commensalism	One organism benefits; the other organism neither benefits nor is harmed.	Some mites attach to flies for transportation. The mites are able to move from one place to another, and the flies are not affected.
Parasitism	One organism benefits and the other is harmed; usually the harmed organism is not immediately killed.	Fleas feed on the blood of a variety of vertebrates, such as dogs. The fleas get food, but the dogs experience itching and discomfort.

Competition occurs when organisms seek the same limited resource.

Predation describes the use of one animal population as food by another. *Herbivory* describes the use of plants as food.

The prefix *sym-* means "together" and *bio* means "living." In a **symbiotic relationship,** individuals of different species live closely together.

In *mutualism,* both species benefit.

In *commensalism,* one species benefits without harming or benefitting the other.

In *parasitism,* one species benefits at the expense of the other. However, a parasite does not normally kill its host.

Predation, the ecological relationship in which one consumer preys on another, is sometimes described as a +/– relationship. This means that one species benefits (+) at the expense of the other (–). Complete the table with the symbols +, –, and 0 (no effect) to characterize each of the relationships. Are there any –/– relationships in nature?

	Species 1	Species 2
Predation	+	–
Competition		
Commensalism		
Mutualism		
Parasitism		

Competition is a +/– relationship because one species benefits at the expense of the other. Commensalism is a +/0 relationship. Mutualism is a +/+ relationship, and parasitism is a +/– relationship. There are no –/– relationships in nature because, if neither species benefits, the relationship is not favored by natural selection.

Food Chains and Food Webs

The organisms in a community may be classified as producers, consumers, or decomposers. **Producers,** such as plants, algae, and some bacteria, are able to make their own food through photosynthesis. **Consumers** are organisms that obtain energy by feeding on producers or other consumers. Animals are consumers.

Within an ecosystem, all consumer populations depend on other populations for food. The feeding relationships in an ecosystem may be depicted in food chains and food webs. In the food chain below, algae are the producers. Tadpoles are *primary consumers,* which feed directly on producers. Crayfish are *secondary consumers,* because they feed on primary consumers. *Tertiary consumers,* such as the brook trout, feed on secondary consumers. Any consumer that eats the brook trout is a *quaternary consumer.*

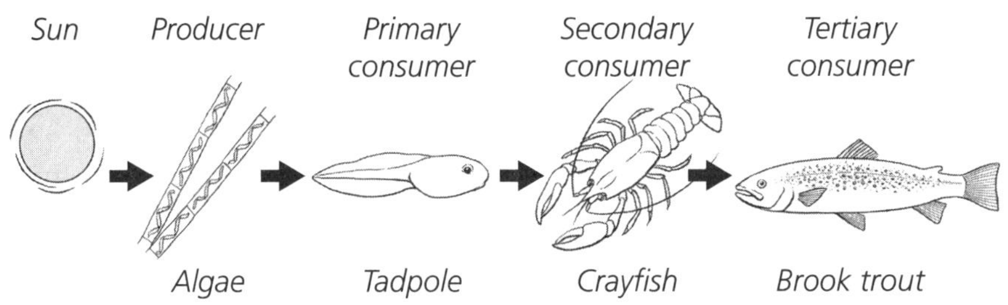

This food chain shows the flow of energy in a Pennsylvania stream ecosystem.

Producers use the energy from sunlight to build sugars and other organic molecules. These molecules are used to build the organisms' bodies and provide energy to **consumers.**

Photosynthesis converts carbon dioxide and water to simple sugars and oxygen gas.

Tertiary means "third-order" and *quaternary* means "fourth-order."

A **food chain** shows the flow of energy from one organism to another, in the direction shown by the arrows. Energy moves from producers to primary consumers, to secondary consumers, etc.

Most consumers in an ecosystem depend on more than one type of organism for food. For this reason, ecologists often use food webs to show feeding relationships. While a **food chain** shows the flow of energy in one linear sequence of organisms, a **food web** shows the complex set of feeding relationships among the many populations in a community.

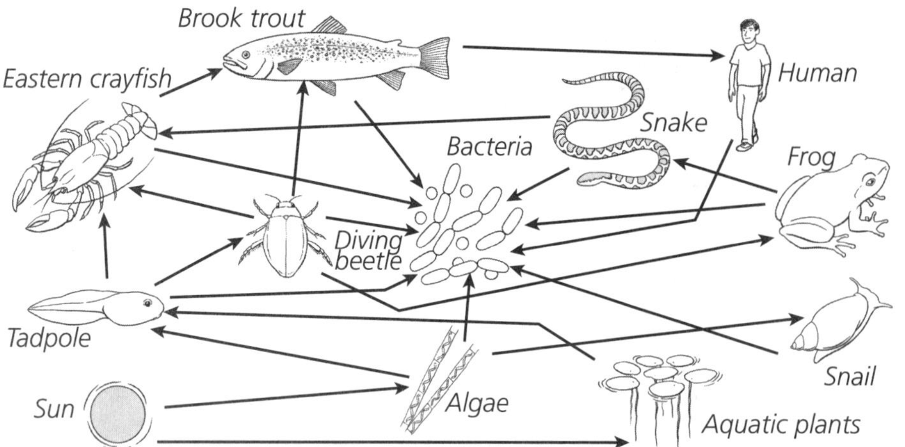

A food web provides a more accurate picture of feeding relationships than a food chain does.

A **food web** show the interrelationships of many food chains. Food webs illustrate that organisms can have more than one role in an ecosystem. In this food web, the Eastern crayfish is both a secondary and a tertiary consumer.

Some organisms die before they are eaten by herbivores or predators. Their bodies are broken down by **decomposers,** which help to recycle matter in an ecosystem. Decomposers obtain energy by breaking down animal wastes, leaf litter, and the remains of dead organisms. Many soil bacteria and fungi are decomposers, as are earthworms and many insect species. As they break down this matter, they release nutrients back into the environment. Decomposers make the matter trapped in dead organisms and waste material available as nutrients to producers.

Producers may obtain energy from the sun, but they also require mineral nutrients from the soil and water. These nutrients are available due to the work of decomposers. A **decomposer** is an organism that obtains its energy by breaking down dead and decaying matter.

Which organism is a primary consumer in the ecosystem shown in the diagram above?

A a snail

B a human

C a diving beetle

D an aquatic plant

A primary consumer eats producers. Choice B is incorrect because humans are quaternary consumers in this ecosystem. Choice C is incorrect because diving beetles are secondary consumers in this ecosystem. Choice D is incorrect because aquatic plants are producers, not consumers. The correct choice is A. Snails feed on algae, which are producers.

Trophic Levels

The initial source of energy for the organisms in a food web is the sun. Producers convert the light energy from the sun to chemical energy stored in their bodies. For example, a blueberry bush uses photosynthesis to build the sugars that make up a plump, sweet blueberry. A chipmunk obtains energy from eating the berries. The chipmunk transfers some of this energy to the hawk that eats it. The blueberry bush, the chipmunk, and the hawk occupy different **trophic levels,** or positions in a food chain.

An organism's **trophic level** is its position in a food chain or web. Producers occupy the lowest, and largest, trophic level, followed by primary consumers, secondary consumers, and tertiary and higher-order consumers.

However, not all the sunlight that the blueberry bush captures is converted into juicy blueberries. The plant's cells require energy to carry out the chemical reactions essential to life. Much of the energy it obtains through photosynthesis is used for life functions, and some is lost as heat. Only some energy is used for growth and stored in the plant's body. Of the light energy that is converted by producers to chemical energy, only a small fraction is transferred to primary consumers as in the form of food.

Of the energy gained by one trophic level, much of it is used to carry out life processes or is lost as heat. Only a small fraction moves on through the next higher level.

Similarly, when the chipmunk consumes the blueberries, not all of the energy it gains will be used to grow or build up fat stores. Much of the energy is required for basic cellular functions. Additional energy is used by the chipmunk to sense its environment, move through the ecosystem in search of food, and maintain a constant body temperature. Unlike the energy stored in body tissues, this energy is not available to the hawk that preys on the chipmunk.

Energy flows from the lowest trophic level, the producers, to the highest-order consumers. However, only a small portion of the energy from one trophic level is transferred to the next higher level. The flow of energy through the trophic levels of an ecosystem is depicted in an **energy pyramid.**

An **energy pyramid** is a model that shows the amount of energy stored in the bodies of organisms at different trophic levels of an ecosystem.

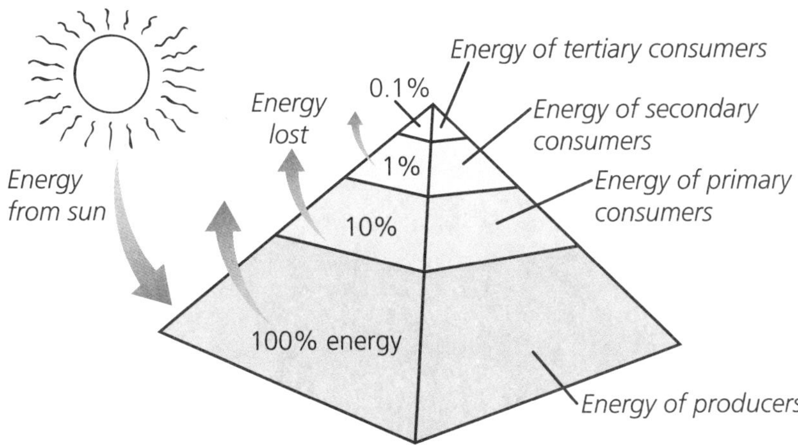

Energy is lost at each trophic level in an ecosystem.

Earth continually receives energy from the sun, but very little new matter reaches Earth from space. Explain why organisms can survive without matter from space, but cannot survive without energy from the sun.

Energy is continually lost at each trophic level as it is converted to other forms. Only some of the energy in one trophic level is stored as chemical energy and consumed by the next higher level. This loss of energy from ecosystems means that new energy must be constantly added to the system. Matter is not lost from ecosystems, but is recycled by decomposers.

IT'S YOUR TURN

Please read each question carefully. For a multiple-choice question, circle the letter of the correct response. For a constructed-response question, write your answers on the lines.

1 Which piece of evidence **best** supports the following statement?

"In an ecosystem, the total amount of matter remains constant, even though its form and location change."

A Producers capture energy from sunlight.

B Most food chains have three levels or fewer.

C Decomposers return nutrients to the environment.

D Multiple food chains can be combined into a food web.

2 Small birds eat insects from the backs of rhinoceroses. The birds obtain food, and the rhinoceroses eliminate biting insects from their skins. Which ecological relationship is **not** represented by this situation?

A commensalism

B mutualism

C parasitism

D predation

3 Which trophic level is generally the smallest in a terrestrial ecosystem?

A producer

B primary consumer

C secondary consumer

D tertiary consumer

Use the diagram below to answer question 4.

CHESAPEAKE BAY FOOD WEB

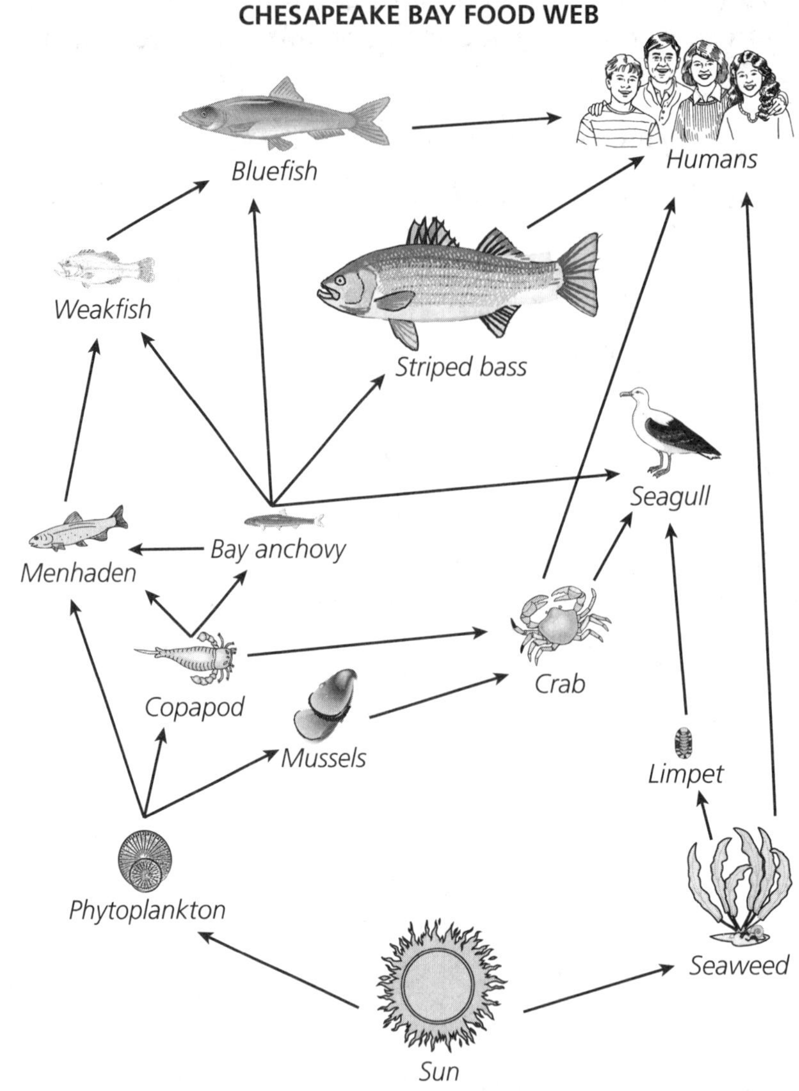

4 The food web shows the trophic relationships among organisms in an aquatic ecosystem. Humans rely on the ecosystem for food.

A Identify a path of energy from the sun to humans, through the ecosystem. Your response should take the form of a food chain.

___

___

___

___

B Compare a person's trophic level when consuming a seaweed salad and when consuming a fillet of striped bass.

C Identify the type of organism missing from this food web and explain its importance to the ecosystem.

Cycles of Matter

BIO.B.4.2.3

Energy from the sun continuously reaches Earth and enters Earth's ecosystems. New matter, unlike energy, rarely enters Earth from outside the planet. The matter that organisms need to grow and survive must be recycled through Earth's ecosystems. Living organisms are made up mainly of just a few elements, the most common being carbon, oxygen, hydrogen, and nitrogen. These are contained in compounds such as water, carbon dioxide, oxygen gas, and nitrogen gas, which move through Earth's atmosphere and biosphere in **biogeochemical cycles.**

Carbon, oxygen, hydrogen, and nitrogen make up most of living matter. **Biogeochemical cycles** describe the movement of elements among biotic and abiotic components of an ecosystem.

Decomposers play an important role in recycling organic matter from dead organisms and waste back into the environment.

The Exchange of Carbon Dioxide and Oxygen

The element oxygen (O) can take the form of oxygen gas, or it may be a component of water, carbon dioxide, nitrogen compounds, or other organic molecules. Oxygen makes up nearly half the mass of Earth's crust, though this mineral form of oxygen is not available to living things. Oxygen gas (O_2) is essential for cell processes. Organisms that carry out *aerobic* respiration consume the oxygen gas in the atmosphere. If it were not replaced, Earth's atmosphere would eventually be depleted of oxygen.

Both plants and animals carry out *aerobic* (oxygen-requiring) respiration.

Respiration also releases carbon dioxide (CO_2) into the atmosphere. Plants and other photosynthetic organisms balance these changes to the atmosphere, helping to keep its mixture of gases stable. Photosynthesis uses carbon dioxide, removing it from the air, and produces oxygen gas as a by-product. The net result of photosynthesis and respiration by Earth's organisms is a stable atmosphere of about 20% oxygen gas.

Oxygen gas makes up about 20% of the air while carbon dioxide makes up less than a fraction of 1%.

Earth's early atmosphere lacked any significant amount of oxygen gas. The evolution of photosynthetic bacteria created the oxygen-rich atmosphere that allowed life as we know it to evolve.

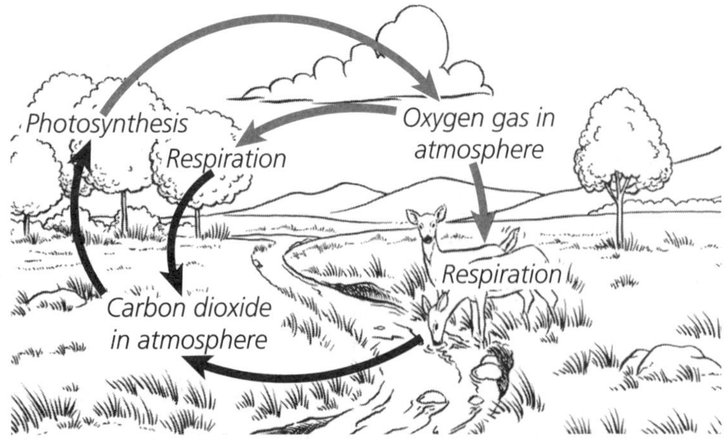

Oxygen gas and carbon dioxide in the atmosphere are exchanged by the processes of photosynthesis and aerobic cellular respiration.

Warmer temperatures cause the stomates in plant leaves to close to help plants conserve water. This reduces the amount of air entering and exiting plant leaves. How would the composition of Earth's atmosphere change if average global temperatures increased?

A Plants would take up less carbon dioxide and release less oxygen.

B Plants would take up less carbon dioxide and release more oxygen.

C Plants would take up more carbon dioxide and release less oxygen.

D Plants would take up more carbon dioxide and release more oxygen.

Gases in air inside the leaves are used in photosynthesis. Limiting the exchange of gases in the plant leaf with the atmosphere reduces the rate of photosynthesis. After the cells of the leaf have used the available carbon dioxide and produced oxygen, air exchange is required in order for photosynthesis to continue. Closing the stomates causes plants to take up less carbon dioxide, so choices C and D are incorrect, and release less oxygen, so choice B is incorrect. Choice A is correct.

The Carbon Cycle

Photosynthesis removes the carbon dioxide from the atmosphere, and respiration replaces it. However, the carbon cycle involves additional processes. Respiration converts **organic** carbon, in the form of carbohydrates, fats, and proteins, to carbon dioxide, an inorganic compound. Photosynthesis reverses the process to produce organic carbon.

Organic carbon may also be locked away deep beneath Earth's surface. The carbon in dead organisms and wastes may form layers of sediment on Earth's seafloor. As these layers continue to build up over millions of years, high pressure converts them to carbon-rich fossil fuels.

Fossil fuels are extracted from within Earth's crust and processed to make gasoline and oil. The burning of fossil fuels, as well as organic matter such as wood, releases carbon dioxide into the atmosphere. The processes that make up the carbon cycle are shown in the diagram on the next page.

An **organic** compound contains the elements carbon (C) and hydrogen (H). Carbon dioxide is not an organic compound.

While photosynthesis balances the carbon dioxide produced by respiration, fossil fuels do not form quickly enough to balance the carbon dioxide released by their burning.

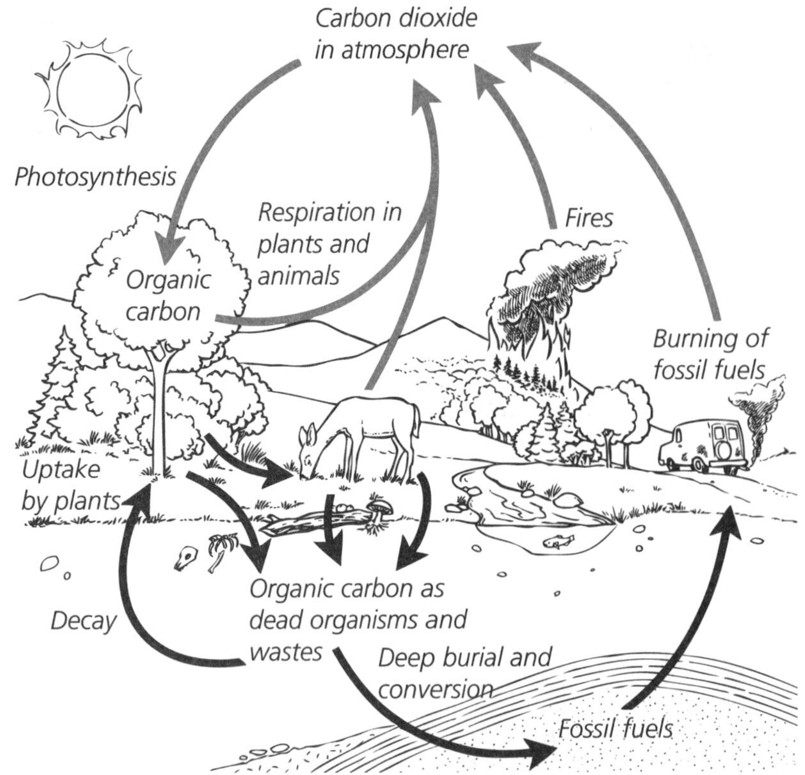

The element carbon is converted between carbon dioxide and organic forms by the processes of the carbon cycle.

The *carbon cycle* is the movement of carbon between the atmosphere, Earth's crust, and living things. It converts carbon between organic and inorganic forms.

Tree trunks are strengthened by cellulose and lignin, carbon-containing polymers that provide rigidity and support. Tree trunks maybe used as nests by animals such as squirrels, which also consist of organic carbon compounds. Describe **two** paths by which the carbon in a squirrel can become part of the structure of a tree trunk.

The squirrel may be eaten by a hawk, which uses the organic carbon for energy, converting it to carbon dioxide. Or, the squirrel may be buried and converted to fossil fuel. When the fossil fuel is extracted and burned millions of years later, the carbon is again released as carbon dioxide. Carbon dioxide in the air can be taken up by trees and converted to organic compounds that make up the tree trunk.

The Nitrogen Cycle

Nitrogen, one of the elements that make up proteins and nucleic acids, is essential to living things. Earth's atmosphere consists of 78% nitrogen gas, N_2. However, this form of nitrogen cannot be used by most organisms. The strong triple bond between the two nitrogen atoms in a molecule of nitrogen gas is difficult to break. Breaking apart molecules of nitrogen gas is necessary if the element is to be incorporated into amino acids, nucleotides, and other biological molecules.

The *nitrogen cycle* is the movement of nitrogen between the atmosphere, the soil, and living things. It is made possible by bacteria that chemically convert nitrogen gas (N_2) to different compounds.

The only organisms capable of doing this are prokaryotes. Nitrogen-fixing bacteria in the soil convert nitrogen gas to the nitrogen compound ammonium. This *nitrogen fixation* allows other bacteria to produce nitrites and nitrates, which plants take in through their roots. Animals obtain nitrogen by consuming plants and other organisms.

Some plants, such as legumes, associate with nitrogen-fixing bacteria. These bacteria reside in *nodules*, round structures that grow on the plants' roots. The bacteria produce ammonium, which the plants then convert to nitrates and other compounds. In return, the plants provide the bacteria with nutrients from photosynthesis.

The diagram below shows the nitrogen cycle. Notice that nitrate in the soil can be converted back to nitrogen gas.

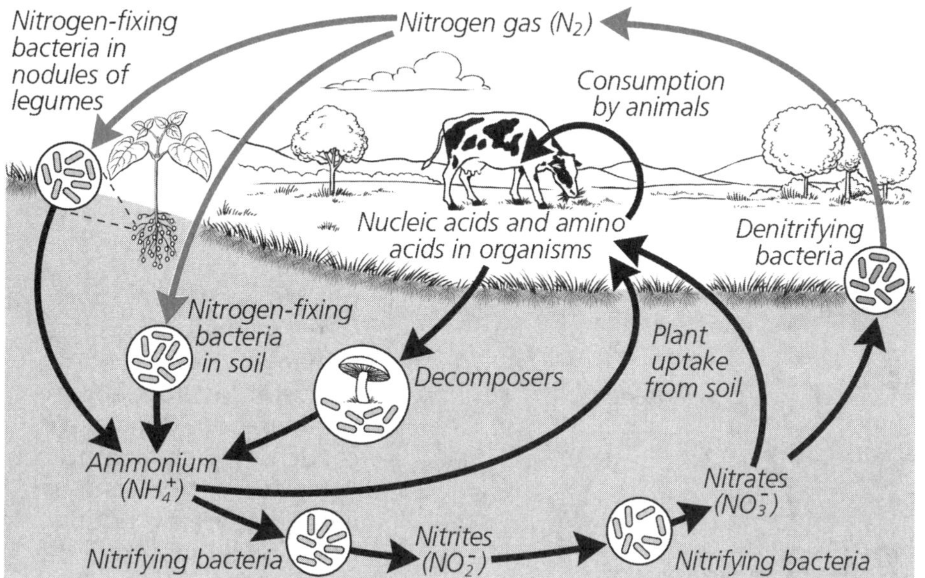

The element nitrogen is converted from nitrogen gas in the atmosphere to compounds that can be used by organisms.

DNA is made up of sugars, phosphate groups, and nitrogen bases. Which process is **not** involved in moving a nitrogen atom into the DNA in a cell of a cow?

A decomposition of plant matter

B digestion of plant matter by the cow

C nitrogen fixation in root nodules of a plant

D conversion of nitrate by denitrifying bacteria

Choices A and C help to change nitrogen compounds to forms that can be taken up by plants. Choice B is required for the cow to incorporate nitrogen into its body. Only choice D moves nitrogen compounds in soil to nitrogen gas in the atmosphere, a form that cannot be used by organisms.

Farmers may plant nutrient-depleted soils with legumes, which contain nitrogen-fixing bacteria in their roots. This helps to replenish the nitrogen in the soil.

Another source of ammonium is the decomposition of organisms and their wastes.

Artificial fertilizers are made by converting nitrogen gas to nitrate, an energy-intensive process. They often contain phosphorous (P) and potassium (K) along with nitrogen.

A small amount of nitrogen gas is converted to nitrate by lightning in the atmosphere.

The Water Cycle

Water is essential to living things. Fresh water moves between the atmosphere, Earth's surface, and organisms in a process called the *water cycle*. Water evaporates from Earth's surface due to heating by the sun. Most water evaporates from oceans, which cover most of the planet, and from lakes, rivers, and wetlands. Water also exits the surfaces of plant leaves through small pores called stomata. The evaporation of this water, called *transpiration*, is also important to the water cycle.

Water evaporates from oceans, seas, and salt lakes, but salts do not.

Transpiration is the evaporation of water from the surface of plant leaves. This water was originally taken up from the ground by the plant's roots.

The resulting water vapor in the atmosphere may, under certain conditions, form clouds. Water vapor condenses into very fine droplets of liquid that remain in the atmosphere as clouds. When cloud droplets become too large, they fall as *precipitation* (rain, snow, sleet, or hail).

Most precipitation falls into the ocean. Precipitation that falls on land and moves over it, flowing down slopes, is called *runoff*. Runoff may enter lakes, rivers, streams, and oceans. Precipitation may also soak into the ground. If it enters a natural reservoir inside the bedrock, it becomes *groundwater*. The diagram below illustrates the water cycle.

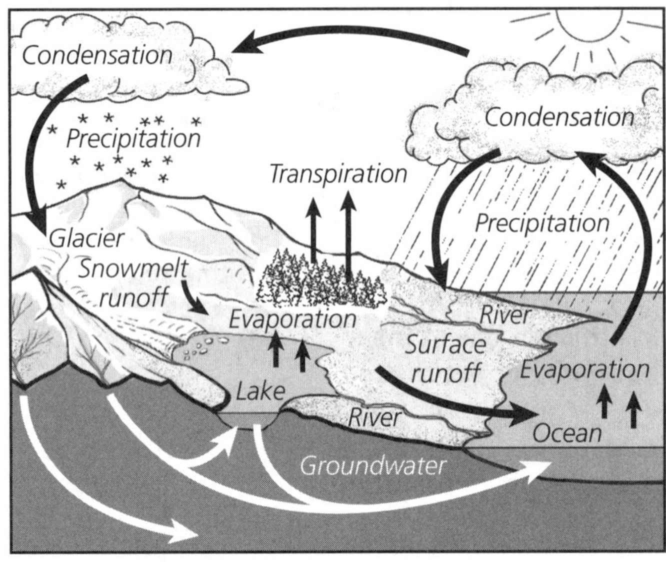

Water is constantly recycled through the water cycle.

Heat causes *evaporation*. When a liquid evaporates, it changes to a gas. A temperature drop leads to *condensation*. When a gas condenses, it changes to a liquid form. Droplets of liquid water form clouds. When water falls from the clouds, it is *precipitation*.

Runoff is liquid water that runs over land and flows into a body of water.

Groundwater remains in underground reservoirs.

A previously barren landscape is slowly changed to one filled with grasses and trees. How does the addition of plants affect the water cycle?

Water from the ground moves into plant roots and exits through the leaves in the process of transpiration. This encourages the water to evaporate and enter the atmosphere over the landscape area.

IT'S YOUR TURN

Please read each question carefully. For a multiple-choice question, circle the letter of the correct response. For a constructed-response question, write your answers on the lines.

1 Which statement describes the function of producers in Earth's biogeochemical cycles?

A Producers add nitrogen to the atmosphere and remove oxygen from the atmosphere.

B Producers remove carbon dioxide from the atmosphere and add oxygen to the atmosphere.

C Producers add carbon dioxide to the atmosphere and remove oxygen from the atmosphere.

D Producers remove nitrogen from the atmosphere and add carbon dioxide to the atmosphere.

2 Water changes phase over the course of the water cycle. Which process in the water cycle **most** directly results from condensation?

A the formation of clouds and precipitation

B the flow of runoff into a river and ocean

C the movement of water from plants to the atmosphere

D the entrance of precipitation into groundwater reservoirs

3 The carbon dioxide in the atmosphere is an inorganic form of carbon. Organic compounds contain both carbon (C) and hydrogen (H). Which process in the carbon cycle changes carbon to an organic form?

A respiration

B photosynthesis

C burning of fossil fuels

D burial of dead organisms

4 A multicellular consumer can obtain nitrogen for use by its cells in which of the following forms?

A nitrites

B nitrates

C amino acids

D nitrogen gas

Use the graph below to answer question 5.

OXYGEN IN EARTH'S ATMOSPHERE THROUGH GEOLOGIC TIME

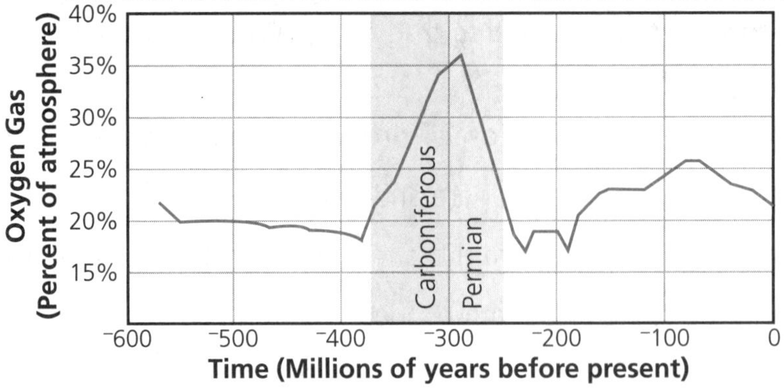

5 The graph depicts the proportion of oxygen gas in Earth's atmosphere over the past 600 million years, the time during which multicellular life has existed. Two geologic periods are highlighted.

A Identify a ten-million-year period in Earth's geologic history when the rate of oxygen uptake by respiration equaled its production by photosynthesis. Justify your response.

B Explain how the processes of Earth's biogeochemical cycles resulted in the change observed for the Carboniferous geologic period (~300–375 million years ago).

C Explain how the processes of Earth's biogeochemical cycles resulted in the change observed for the Permian geologic period (~250–300 million years ago).

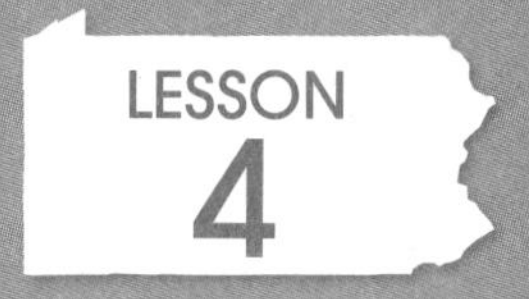

Ecosystem Response to Change

BIO.B.4.2.4, BIO.B.4.2.5

Earth is home to a variety of ecosystems, from scorching deserts to the freshwater Great Lakes. However, ecosystems can change over time in response to both biotic and abiotic factors, whether natural or caused by human activity.

Ecological Succession

Ecosystems depend largely on the plant communities that characterize them. A grassland ecosystem can support a different set of organisms than a temperate forest. Changes in the plant community affect both biotic and abiotic factors in an ecosystem. The orderly process by which an ecosystem changes over time is known as **succession.** Succession can occur after a disturbance, such as a wildfire, leaves nothing but bare soil. Succession can also occur in an area that has no soil to begin with.

Primary succession occurs on surfaces that did not previously support plant life, such as bare rock. Rock may become exposed as a result of volcanic eruptions or melting glaciers. The first species to become established are generally lichens and mosses. Lichens can *weather,* or break down, rock and add organic matter to the ground, forming new soil. Mosses lack true roots and absorb water from their surroundings, allowing them to grow where there is little soil.

These organisms change the bare rock environment to one with soil, allowing the seeds of other types of plants to germinate and grow. Over time, the ecosystem gains a new community of plants.

Secondary succession occurs in areas that previously supported life, such as an area affected by wildfire or abandoned farmland. In contrast to primary succession, plants may quickly take root in the bare soil. Grasses are usually the first to grow in this type of ecosystem. The grasses change the ecosystem's biotic and abiotic characteristics, for example, by providing shade and nutrients. These changes allow shrubs and other plant types to grow. Eventually, the new plant community replaces the grasses.

The new plant community, in turn, changes the ecosystem to make it more suitable for small trees. Each successive plant community changes the ecosystem, making it less suitable to the current community and allowing another community to replace it. Eventually, a community consisting of large trees remains stable for many hundreds of years. This stage in succession is called the *climax community.*

An ecological *community* consists of all the different populations in an ecosystem.

In each stage of ecological **succession,** a plant community changes the ecosystem, making it more suitable for different plant species. A new plant community then replaces the existing one, changing the characteristics of the ecosystem.

Soil is a combination of weathered rock particles and decayed organic matter.

If soil is depleted of nitrogen, species that hold symbiotic nitrogen-fixing bacteria in their roots can survive and add nitrogen back to the soil.

In secondary succession, grasses establish themselves on bare soil. Over time, larger plants move in and replace smaller plants.

Fire can also change the plant community of an ecosystem. Periodic wildfires had prevented succession from changing the tallgrass prairie ecosystems of the central United States to forest. Although fire burns the vegetation above the ground, grasses have root systems below ground. After a fire, grass regrows from these roots. Both wildfires and intentional fires created by Native Americans, along with heavy grazing by buffalo, maintained the tallgrass prairie ecosystems for many hundreds of years. In the absence of fires and grazing, ecological succession may eliminate tallgrass prairies.

Some pine trees are adapted to periodic wildfires. Their tightly sealed cones open only when heated, allowing new pine trees to germinate in the soil of the altered ecosystem.

Controlled fires are still used today as a tool for managing ecosystems.

In which environment can grasses begin to grow more easily, one with bare soil or one with many small shrubs? Is the same true for small shrubs? Explain.

Grasses represent an early stage in ecological succession and grow better in bare soil. Small shrubs, in contrast, grow better on land where grasses are growing. This difference allows shrubs to replace grasses in ecological succession.

Population Dynamics

Population sizes change over time. Births and the addition of new members from other populations cause it to increase in size. Deaths and individuals leaving a population cause it to shrink. The balance of these factors determines whether a population increases or decreases, and how quickly it does so. The study of these changes is known as **population dynamics.**

The populations making up an ecological community are interdependent. Some populations depend on others for food: *herbivores* depend on producers and *predators* depend on their prey. Therefore, an increase or decrease in one population can result in a corresponding change in another population.

A *population* is the group of organisms of the same species that share an ecosystem.

Population dynamics depend on numbers of births, deaths, individuals moving into the population, and individuals leaving it.

One example is the pattern observed in predator–prey cycles. As the prey population decreases, less food is available for the predator population. As a result, the predator population also decreases. With fewer predators in the ecosystem, the prey population is allowed to grow. Then, more food becomes available for the predators, whose population increases again. The following graph demonstrates the predator-prey cycle for hare and lynx populations in Northern Canada.

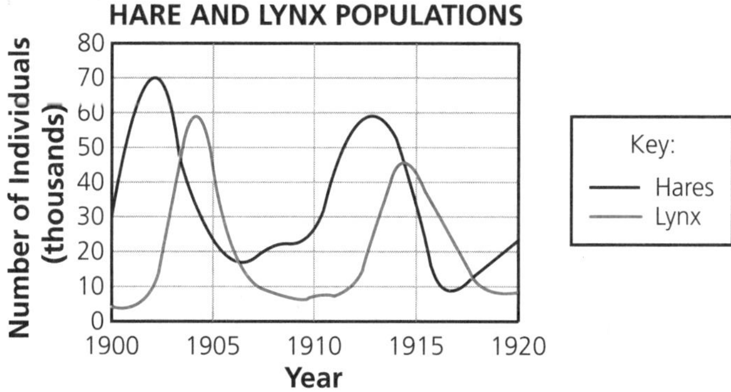

An *herbivore,* a type of primary consumer, is an animal that feeds exclusively on plants.

A *predator* is an animal that hunts other animals, called prey.

The populations of predators and their prey often follow a cycle, with changes in one population resulting in changes in the other.

Some scientists think that the cycles observed in the graph above are driven by changes in the plants available in the ecosystems. Hares feed on plants. Describe the changes in plant abundance over time that would result in the population changes shown in the graph.

If the availability of plants (producers) drives the changes in hare and lynx populations, then plants should be very abundant around the years 1900 and 1910. The high availability of food for the hares would cause the hare populations to increase, diminishing the amount of plant material (1900–02, 1910–13), and then decrease (1902–06, 1913–16). The lynx populations would increase later than the hare population, peaking in 1904 and 1914.

Nonnative Species and Community Disruptions

The small fish called the round goby was first reported in Pennsylvania waters in 1996. The population of this introduced species has since increased in the Great Lakes. Round gobies blend in with rocks and pebbles, lying in wait for prey. They are sensitive to movements of water and can feed even in complete darkness. These features enable the round goby to successfully compete with similar **endemic** Great Lakes fish, such as the mottled sculpin.

The round goby is a **nonnative species.** Nonnative species, often endemic to other regions of the world, may be introduced by shipping or as discarded pets. Nonnative species have several characteristics that allow their populations to grow at the expense of native species.

Endemic species are those found in their original ecosystems.

Nonnative species are living outside their normal range and compete with native species. They are sometimes called *invasive species.*

Many nonnative species are aquatic organisms that arrived on or in ships traveling from one part of the world to another.

Generally, nonnative species

- have fewer predators or no predators in their new ecosystem;
- use more of the ecosystem's resources, or use available resources more effectively; and
- may reduce other endemic populations directly, through predation.

Removing or reducing a population can also impact an entire ecosystem. For example, sea otters are an endangered species that live in the coastal waters of the northern Pacific Ocean. Sea otters were once hunted for their dense fur coats, and still face threats to survival. Where sea otter populations thrive, their kelp forest ecosystems maintain a high degree of *biodiversity.* Sea otters feed on sea urchins, spiny sea creatures with no eyes or limbs. Sea urchins eat algae such as kelp, which are very large algae that provide a habitat for many species. A decline in the sea otter population can eliminate a kelp forest, reducing it to a community of sea urchins and small, red algae, but few other species.

One proposed solution for reducing invasive fish populations is for people to catch the fish and eat them.

Biodiversity is the variety of life forms in an area. It may be measured in terms of genes, species, or entire ecosystems. The number of different species in an area is one important aspect of biodiversity.

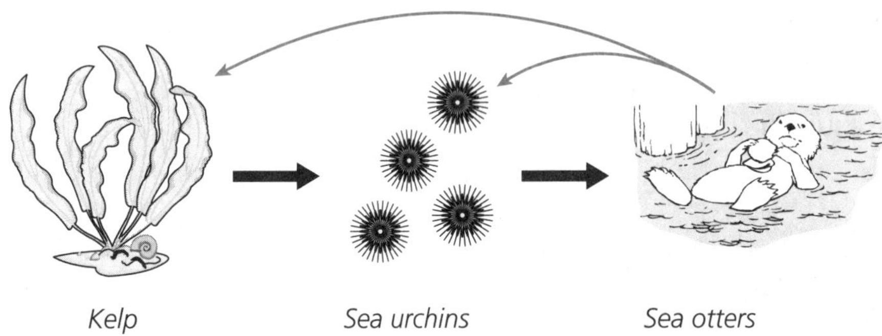

The green arrows represent effects of the sea otter population on the rest of the food chain in the kelp forest ecosystem.

Study the diagram above. Which statement correctly describes the effects of the sea otter population on the sea urchin and kelp populations?

A Otters have a negative effect on both sea urchins and kelp.

B Otters have a negative effect on sea urchins and a positive effect on kelp.

C Otters have a positive effect on sea urchins and a negative effect on kelp.

D Otters have a positive effect on both sea urchins and kelp.

The sea otters limit the sea urchin population. This is a negative effect, so choices C and D are incorrect. By limiting sea urchins, the otters maintain high kelp populations. This is a positive effect, so choice A is incorrect and choice B is correct.

Limiting Factors and Population Growth

The size of a population can be limited by predators, prey, and competitors in the ecosystem. In addition to these biotic factors, abiotic factors can also limit population growth. **Limiting factors** prevent populations from becoming too large. For example, the availability of prey species limits the population sizes of predators, such as wolves or lions. The inability of sunlight to penetrate into deeper ocean waters limits the growth of phytoplankton in this part of the ocean.

The combined effects of different limiting factors determine the size for a population in an ecosystem. Due to limits on prey and land, for example, an area may be able to support only a small population of wolves. The largest number of individuals in a population that an ecosystem can support at a given time is called its *carrying capacity.*

Populations generally grow at a high rate when many resources are available. As fewer resources become available, population growth slows. The graph below shows the growth of a population as it reaches its ecosystem's carrying capacity. Growth is rapid at first, but then slows.

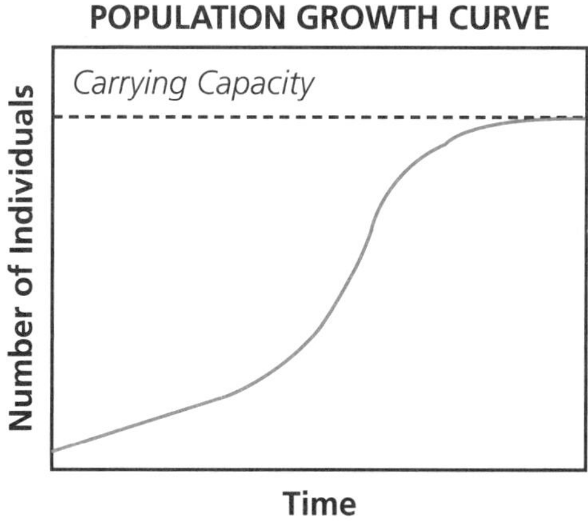

A population may sometimes grow past its carrying capacity, but the ecosystem will not sustain this larger population for long. Eventually, population is limited by a lack of resources and drops back down toward its carrying capacity. This is shown in the graph below.

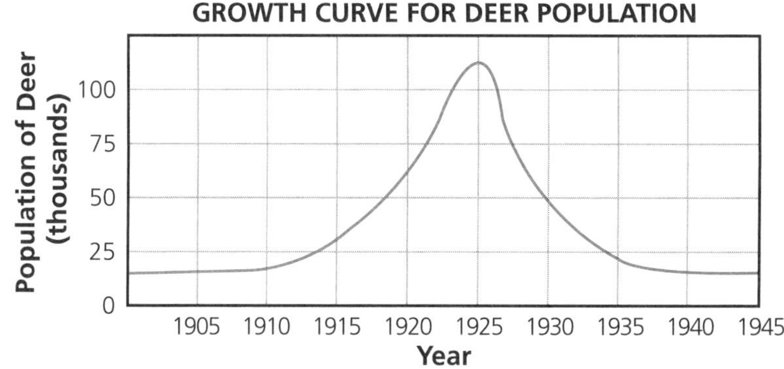

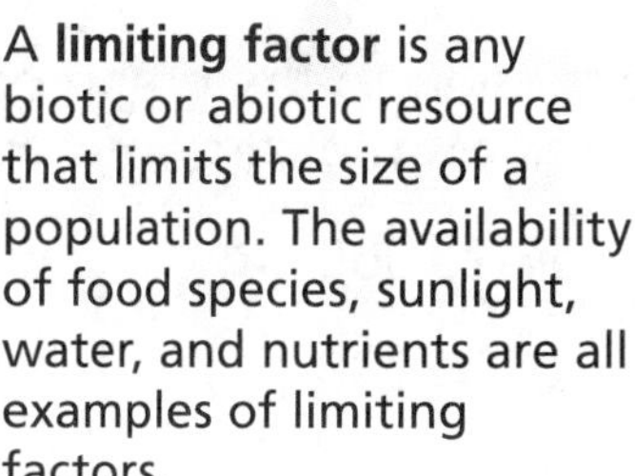

A **limiting factor** is any biotic or abiotic resource that limits the size of a population. The availability of food species, sunlight, water, and nutrients are all examples of limiting factors.

Remember that *biotic* factors are living and abiotic factors are nonliving.

Carrying capacity is the maximum population size an ecosystem can support. The carrying capacity of an ecosystem limits the sizes of populations in it.

Populations grow more rapidly when plenty of resources are available for each individual. They grow slowly or not at all when there are more individuals competing for resources.

The carrying capacity of an ecosystem does not always remain the same. For example, the elimination of predators such as wolves can increase the ecosystem's carrying capacity for deer.

According to the graph on page 215, which number **best** estimates the carrying capacity for the deer?

A 20,000

B 55,000

C 80,000

D 105,000

The actual number of deer starts off at about 20,000, undergoes a rapid increase and decrease, and stabilizes again around 20,000. This number best reflects the ecosystem's carrying capacity for the deer. Choice A is correct.

Agricultural Runoff and Eutrophication

Depletion of an ecosystem's resources can limit population sizes. However, adding nutrients to an ecosystem may also lead to changes that unbalance populations. Producers are limited by the availability of nutrients, such as nitrogen and phosphorous. These nutrients are often added to farmland in the form of fertilizer. If added carefully, fertilizer increases the nutrients available to crops and has little effect on neighboring ecosystems. However, precipitation may sometimes dissolve the nutrients in the soil, carrying them to nearby bodies of water. This *agricultural runoff* can disrupt aquatic ecosystems through the process of *eutrophication.*

Algae populations increase in response to added nutrients in the water. This rapid growth leads to an *algal bloom,* which gives a bright green or, sometimes, red color to the water. The thick algae layer blocks light from the lower depths of the lake, reducing photosynthesis. Also, once the algae have used up the excess nutrients, their population returns to carrying capacity. The resulting dead organisms begin to decompose, causing the numbers of decomposers (mainly bacteria) to increase. Decomposers further reduce the levels of dissolved oxygen in the ecosystem. Algal blooms, by reducing the dissolved oxygen in an aquatic ecosystem, can lead to the death of larger organisms, such as fish. The flow chart on the next page summarizes the process described here.

Eutrophication refers to the changes that occur to an aquatic ecosystem as a result of added nutrients. *Agricultural runoff* is a cause of eutrophication.

The natural eutrophication of lakes occurs over hundreds of years, but eutrophication due to pollution occurs quickly.

Excess nutrients can also come from sewage produced by livestock or water treatment plants.

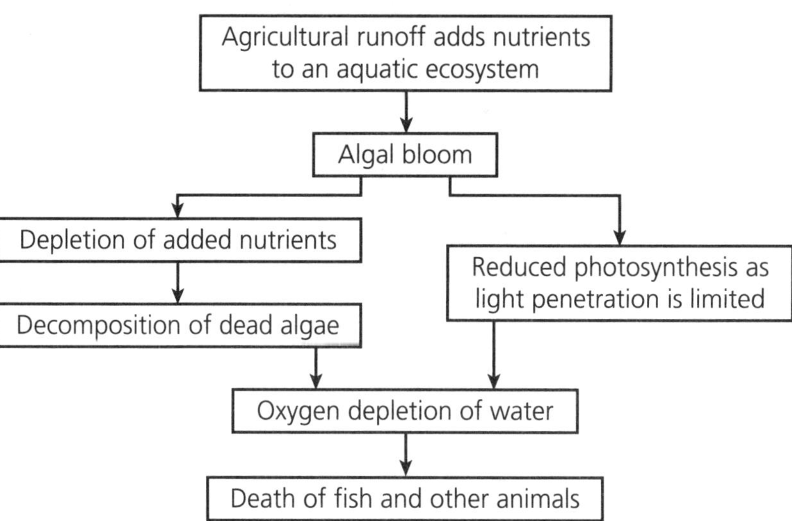

In the 1960s, Lake Erie suffered from severe eutrophication. Bulldozers were used to remove the dead algae that washed up on the lake's beaches.

Duckweed is a type of small, fast-growing aquatic plant that floats at the water's surface. Duckweed requires nitrogen and phosphorous to grow. Explain how duckweed can aid a lake that has excess nutrients from agricultural runoff.

When added to the lake, the duckweed absorbs the nutrients from the water and grows rapidly. Then, the floating duckweed can be removed from the lake's surface, removing the excess nutrients from the lake water. (The duckweed may then be fed to livestock.) By preventing decomposition of the plants in the lake, healthy levels of dissolved oxygen are preserved.

Atmospheric and Climate Change

Temperature and moisture are among the abiotic factors that distinguish Earth's diverse biomes. Such factors determine where populations of different species occur in the biosphere. Temperature and other climate conditions result from the effects of the sun's energy on Earth's surface.

As shown in the figure on the next page, electromagnetic radiation from the sun travels through space to Earth's atmosphere. Some of this energy is absorbed by Earth's surface and converted to heat. Some is reflected by atmospheric particles on Earth's surface, back into space. Crucially, some of the reflected energy, instead of escaping the atmosphere, is instead absorbed by *greenhouse gases*—the carbon dioxide, water vapor, and methane present in trace amounts in Earth's atmosphere. This energy is radiated back to the surface, raising Earth's average global temperature about 30°C. This natural process is known as the *greenhouse effect.*

Greenhouse gases are atmospheric gases such as water vapor, carbon dioxide, nitrous oxide, and methane that trap heat energy.

The *greenhouse effect* is a natural process in which certain gases in the atmosphere retain heat radiating from Earth's surface.

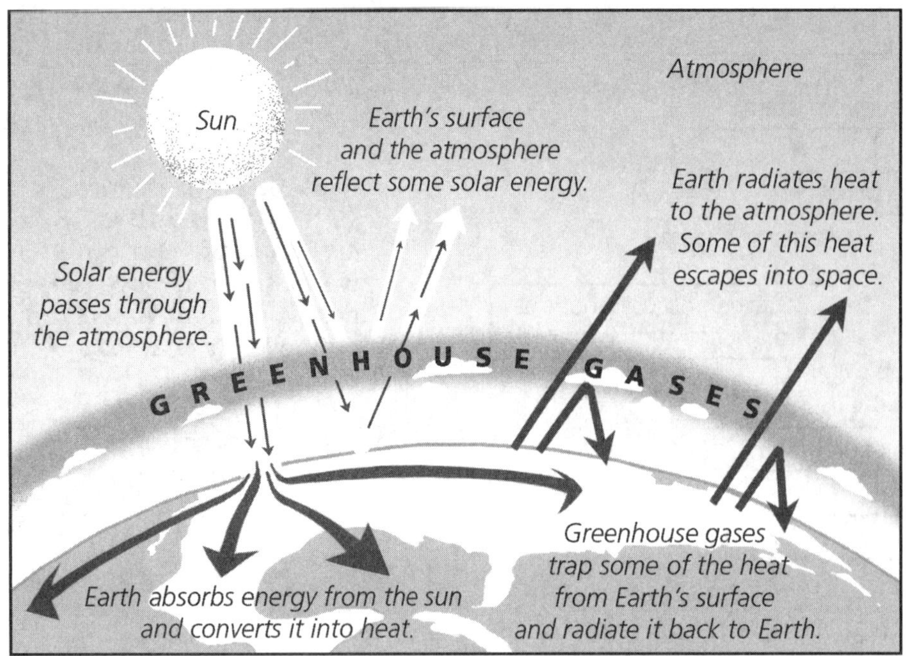

Some of the solar energy that reaches Earth is reflected back into space, and some of the energy is trapped by greenhouse gases.

Many human activities, from energy and food production to transportation, raise greenhouse gas levels in the atmosphere. Fossil fuels contain carbon, which is released as carbon dioxide when the fuel is burned. Cattle and other livestock release methane gas as waste. Increasing the concentration of greenhouse gases prevents more energy from escaping Earth's atmosphere. This can raise the average global temperature, a process known as *global warming*, which contributes to climate change.

Global warming is an increase in average temperatures worldwide.

Increasing average temperatures even a few degrees Celsius will have large effects on Earth's ecosystems. For example, fish populations, which are adapted to certain temperatures, are moving closer to the poles as ocean temperatures rise. Melting polar ice caps and ice sheets cause sea levels to rise, flooding the coastal areas that hold many of Earth's unique ecosystems.

A rise in Earth's average global temperature can also increase droughts, floods, and the severity of hurricanes and other storms. Drought conditions increase the occurrence of wildfires, which can destroy entire ecosystems if vegetation is extremely dry. Increased evaporation due to higher temperatures moves more water into the atmosphere, which in turn makes heavy precipitation and floods more likely. Finally, warmer ocean waters provide more energy to tropical storms and hurricanes, increasing their strength and allowing them to cause greater damage to ecosystems.

Earth naturally goes through long-term climate cycles. For this reason, the planet has experienced both ice ages and warmer, interglacial periods. The causes of these climate cycles are still not completely understood, although most scientists think that variations in Earth's orbit and axial tilt play important roles.

Another important atmospheric gas is ozone, which is highly reactive when struck by ultraviolet (UV) radiation. UV rays from the sun penetrate Earth's atmosphere and stimulate the production of vitamin D in human skin cells; overexposure to UV rays, however, can damage a person's cells and is a primary cause of skin cancer.

The *ozone layer* in the upper atmosphere absorbs nearly 99% of the sun's UV radiation before it reaches Earth's surface. In the 1980s, scientists discovered significant thinning in the ozone layer over Antarctica. These ozone "holes"—which have since been detected throughout the atmosphere—are caused by human-made compounds, particularly *chlorofluorocarbons* (CFCs). CFCs were commonly used as cooling agents in refrigerators and as propellants in aerosol sprayers; when released into the air, they break apart into atoms that can destroy ozone molecules.

The *ozone layer* is a region of the upper atmosphere in which high concentrations of ozone gas absorb much of the sun's ultraviolet radiation.

As the ozone layer thins, increasing levels of UV radiation penetrate the atmosphere and reach Earth's surface. In addition to the dangers they pose to humans, UV rays have been shown to degrade plastic materials and harm certain crops and marine organisms, such as plankton. In response, governments have enacted laws to limit the use of ozone-depleting substances.

Cattle ranching is important to the US economy. How can cattle ranching cause the average global temperature to increase?

A Methane gas released by cattle radiates heat back to Earth.

B Grazing causes Earth's surface to absorb more solar radiation.

C Cattle eat plants that remove methane from the atmosphere.

D Carbon dioxide in the atmosphere reacts with cattle waste to produce greenhouse gases.

Choice B is incorrect because climate change is due to changes in the composition of the atmosphere, rather than changes to Earth's surface. Choice C is incorrect because plants remove carbon dioxide, rather than methane, from the atmosphere. Choice D is incorrect because carbon dioxide itself is a greenhouse gas. During their digestive processes, cattle produce and release methane gas, which is a greenhouse gas. Greenhouse gases help warm the planet by radiating heat back to Earth. Choice A is correct.

Habitat Destruction

Human-caused changes to ecosystems can destroy **habitats,** the areas where species can find the resources they need to survive and reproduce. Large, wooded areas with plenty of deer and moderate temperatures are habitats for wolves, while warm, sandy beaches are habitats used by sea turtles to lay their eggs.

A **habitat** is an ecosystem area that provides the resources a species needs to survive and reproduce. Different species have different habitat requirements.

Because species rely on their particular habitats to survive, protecting habitats is essential to conserving wildlife and maintaining biodiversity. Habitat destruction is a leading cause of the extinction of endangered species.

Changes such as the eutrophication of lakes, *deforestation* of wooded areas, and rising sea levels can eliminate habitats. Pollution of natural areas can also make habitats unsuitable. *Pollution* can include any human-caused change to an ecosystem that negatively affects the populations that inhabit it. In addition to chemicals, excess noise and light can also be forms of pollution.

Deforestation is the clearing of all trees from an area.

Pollution is the addition of substances, objects, or other factors that cause harmful changes to an ecosystem.

Describe a type of human-caused environmental change that can affect the activity of the species listed below.

Case A: Male tree frogs sing to attract female tree frogs.

Case B: Flowers bloom in response to the period of darkness each day.

Case C: Spotted owls nest in the trunks of old-growth trees.

In case A, noise pollution can disrupt the mating of tree frogs, which require a habitat where male songs can be heard. In case B, light pollution from streetlights can disrupt plant flowering. In case C, deforestation can eliminate the habitat required for spotted owls to nest.

IT'S YOUR TURN

Please read each question carefully. For a multiple-choice question, circle the letter of the correct response. For a constructed-response question, write your answers on the lines.

1 Light penetrates the clear water of the open ocean more deeply than it does lake water. Phytoplankton is found deeper in the open ocean than in freshwater lakes. What does this observation **best** indicate?

A Phytoplankton provides nutrients to consumers in the ecosystem.

B Phytoplankton reduces the light available to organisms at lower depths.

C Phytoplankton populations are limited by their ability to photosynthesize.

D Phytoplankton population growth is limited by the presence of marine salts.

Use the graph below to answer question 2.

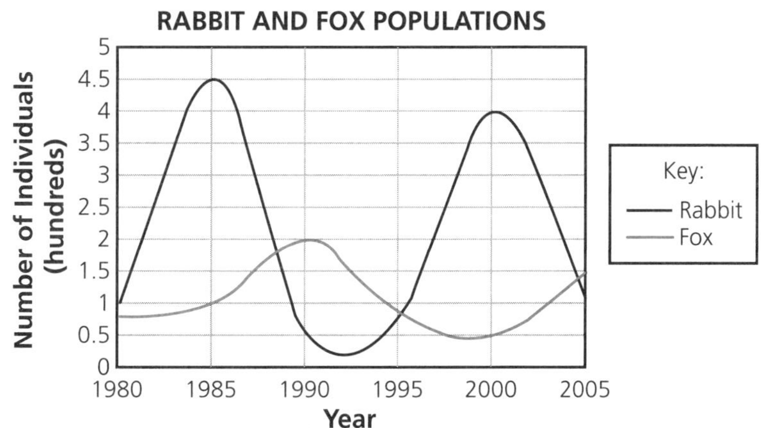

2 What **most likely** caused the change in the rabbit population from 1995 to 2000?

A more parasites

B fewer predators

C more competition

D fewer plant resources

Use the diagram below to answer question 3.

PARTIAL FOOD WEB OF EASTERN US FOREST

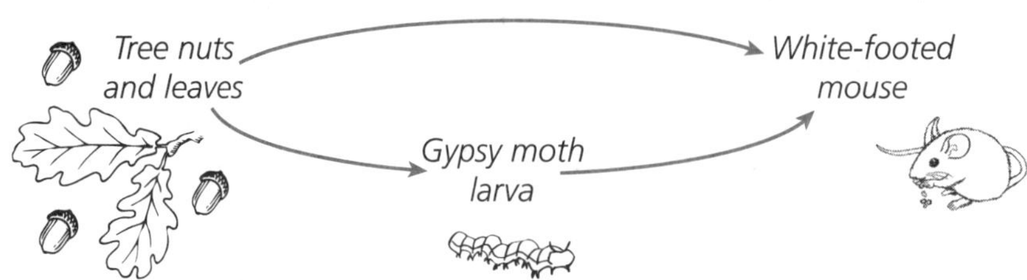

3 American chestnut trees once dominated forests of Pennsylvania and the eastern United States. These tall trees shaded the forests, the nuts they produced were a food source for many species, and their wide trunks provided timber. In about 1900, the chestnut blight fungus spread from imported chestnut trees to American chestnut trees. Although the fungus did not affect the imported chestnut trees, it harmed the American chestnuts, which now grow only as shrubs and do not produce nuts. Oak and other tree species have replaced the American chestnut in many forests. These species do not grow as tall as the healthy American chestnut, which could reach heights up to about 30 meters. American chestnut populations also produced similarly high quantities of nuts each year. In contrast, oak populations produce abundant acorn crops one year, and smaller crops the next.

The diagram above shows part of an eastern US forest food web.

A Consider forest ecosystems where American chestnut trees dominated, before the introduction of the chestnut blight fungus. Describe one factor that limited the populations of oak trees in these forests.

____

____

____

____

B Compare the white-footed mouse population in a forest dominated by American chestnut and in a forest dominated by oak, in terms of changes from year to year.

____

____

____

____

C Gypsy moth larvae eat the leaves of oak and chestnut trees. An outbreak of gypsy moth larvae, which occurs when their population grows too large, can destroy trees. Explain how restoring the American chestnut to eastern US forests would affect the likelihood of a gypsy moth outbreak.

____

____

____

____

Use the table and graph below to answer question 4.

BENTHIC MACROINVERTEBRATE POLLUTION TOLERANCE

Organism	Pollution Tolerance (0 = least tolerant; 10 = most tolerant)
Beetles	5
Bloodworms	9
Mayflies	3
Mosquito larvae	7
Stoneflies	1

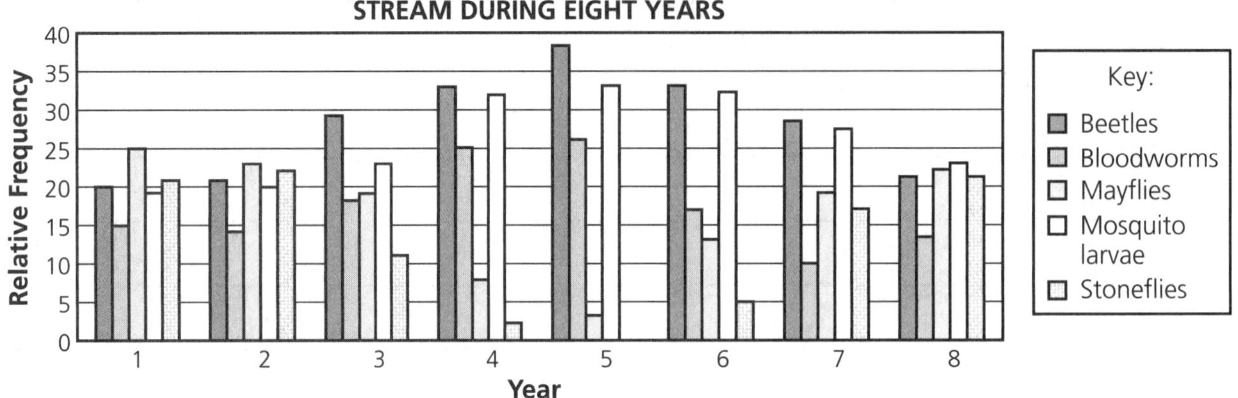

4 Benthic macroinvertebrates are organisms that live on and within a streambed. These organisms differ in their sensitivity to various pollutants, as shown in the table. Ecologists can measure the water quality of a stream by comparing the numbers of these organisms. The bar graph shows stream data taken over an eight-year period.

A Compare the types of benthic macroinvertebrates you would expect to find in a healthy, unpolluted stream to those in a heavily polluted stream.

____

____

____

____

B Describe how the level of pollution in the stream changed over the eight-year period of the study. Explain how you determined this.

____

C Do the stonefly and mayfly populations affect the stream's carrying capacity for the other organisms? Explain.

5 Forests of American beech and sugar maple trees are a type of climax community found in parts of western Pennsylvania. Which statement is **most likely** true concerning these plant species?

A Their roots change environments of bare rock to fertile soil.

B Their seeds grow best in bare soil with little other plant life.

C They reduce the ecosystem's carrying capacity for grasses and shrubs.

D They alter the ecosystem so that it is better suited for other plant species.

6 Flooding can impact aquatic ecosystems by increasing turbidity. Turbidity refers to the amount of solid material suspended in water. Turbid water appears cloudy or muddy. What is the **most likely** effect of increased turbidity on an aquatic ecosystem?

A The water contains less dissolved oxygen.

B Large fish are able to take in more energy.

C The water contains fewer dissolved nutrients.

D Small fish are more easily caught by predators.

Module B Review Continuity and Unity of Life

Please read each question carefully. For a multiple-choice question, circle the letter of the correct response. For a constructed-response question, write your answers on the lines.

1 Which statement describes a cell's chromosomes at the beginning of prophase of meiosis I?

A The DNA in each homolog has been exchanged.

B It contains half the normal chromosome number.

C The sister chromatids are joined at the centromere.

D Each sister chromatid has a unique combination of alleles.

Use the graph below to answer question 2.

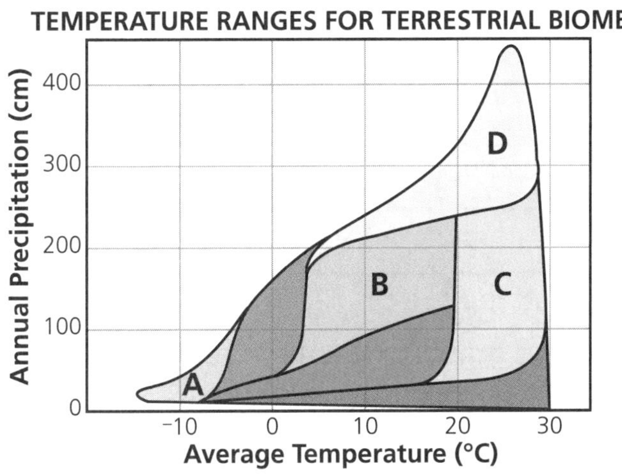

2 The graph above depicts the ranges of average annual precipitation and temperature for Earth's terrestrial biomes. Which shaded area of the graph represents the biome with the greatest species biodiversity?

A area A

B area B

C area C

D area D

Use the graph below to answer question 3.

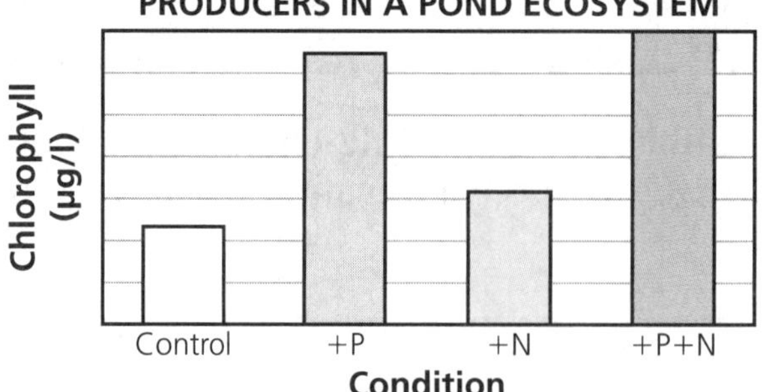

3 A pond ecosystem contains photosynthetic single-celled and multicelled algae, as well as small aquatic plants. Scientists tested the effects of adding nitrogen (N) and phosphorous (P) compounds to the pond. Pond conditions were allowed to return to normal after each treatment and before the next treatment was performed. The graph describes their results.

A Explain how the eukaryotic algae and plants in the pond acquire nitrogen in the control condition.

____

____

____

____

B Use the data shown in the graph to identify the major limiting factor(s) in the ecosystem. Justify your response.

____

____

____

____

C Explain how the addition of nitrogen and/or phosphorous may disrupt the pond ecosystem, even when the excess nutrients have been taken up by producers.

____

____

____

____

4 Some of the cells of an animal undergo both mitosis and meiosis. Which statement describes a difference between meiosis and mitosis?

A Mitosis involves DNA replication, but meiosis does not.

B Crossing-over occurs during mitosis, but not during meiosis.

C Sister chromatids separate during mitosis, but not during meiosis.

D Mitosis produces cells with normal chromosome numbers, but meiosis does not.

5 In humans, the genes *HERC2* and *OCA2* are both located on chromosome 15. These genes, along with others, determine eye color. Which conclusion can be drawn about eye color in humans?

A Eye color is a polygenic trait.

B Eye color is a sex-linked trait.

C The genes for eye color are co-dominant.

D Each gene for eye color has multiple alleles.

6 Turner syndrome is a rare disorder that occurs in females, who are born with only a single X chromosome. Which of the following identifies the type of chromosomal mutation that causes Turner syndrome?

A deletion

B duplication

C nondisjunction

D translocation

Use the diagram below to answer question 7.

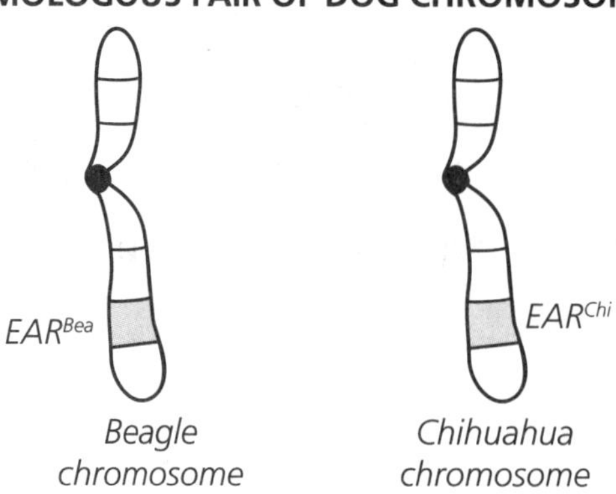

7 A pure breed of dog is a line of parents and descendants that share similar traits. Purebred dogs of different breeds may be crossed to produce hybrids.

A hybrid puppy has one beagle parent and one Chihuahua parent.

A A dog's gametes contain 39 chromosomes. Describe the number and parental origin of the chromosomes in cells of the hybrid puppy's body.

____

____

____

____

B Beagles have floppy ears but Chihuahuas have ears that stand upright. All hybrid puppies exhibit upright ears. Assume that this trait is controlled by a single gene, called EAR. Complete the Punnett square to show the cross between the purebred beagle and Chihuahua parents. Identify the dominant and recessive alleles.

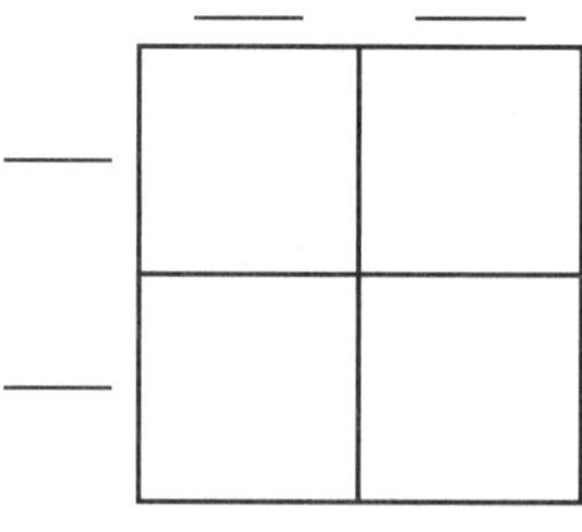

____

____

C When grown, the hybrid puppy is crossed with another beagle-Chihuahua hybrid dog. Will the offspring that result from this cross have the same ratio of beagle and Chihuahua alleles as their parents? Explain in terms of the processes that form gametes.

8 Viruses cannot transcribe or translate their own genes, but can invade host cells that do so. Coxsackie viruses can affect the skin, the lining of the mouth, or the internal organs. Some coxsackie viruses contain genes for proteins that disrupt the function of the Golgi apparatus. How do these viral proteins affect the host cell?

A They inhibit the translation of mRNA in the host cell.

B They cause the host cell to transcribe viral DNA only.

C They allow the transport of viral proteins into the host cell.

D They prevent the host cell from secreting synthesized proteins.

Use the sequence below to answer question 9.

ORIGINAL GENE SEQUENCE

. . . — GGA — GGC — TAT — ATC — AGA — . . .

9 Several of the codons from a gene are shown above. Which of the following sequences is the result of a frame-shift mutation to the original sequence?

A GGA — TAT — ATC — AGA — CGC

B GGG — GCT — ATA — TCA — GAG

C GGC — GGT — TAT — ATA — AGA

D GGA — GGC — TAC — ATC — AGG

Use the table below to answer question 10.

POSSIBLE COMBINATIONS OF HEMOGLOBIN ALLELES

Genotype	Phenotype
$Hb^N\ Hb^N$	normal red blood cells
$Hb^N\ Hb^S$	50% of red blood cells are affected
$Hb^S\ Hb^S$	all red blood cells are affected

10 Sickle cell anemia is a genetic disease that affects the shape of the hemoglobin molecule in red blood cells. The hemoglobin molecule is controlled by two alleles: Hb^N (normal hemoglobin allele) and Hb^S (sickle cell allele). The table above shows the possible combinations of these alleles. Based on the table above, which of the following **best** describes the alleles that control the hemoglobin molecule?

A Hb^S is dominant to Hb^N.

B Hb^N is dominant to Hb^S.

C Hb^N and Hb^S are co-dominant.

D Hb^N and Hb^S are both recessive.

11 Green alder is a shrub whose roots contain small, round structures called *nodules.* Bacteria of the genus *Frankia* grow inside the nodules, feeding on sugars produced by the plant. *Frankia* species are able to convert nitrogen gas (N_2) to ammonia (NH_3).

Several hundred acres of farmland, with bare, nutrient-poor soil, are abandoned.

A Identify the ecological interaction between green alder and *Frankia* bacteria in its root nodules. Justify your response.

B Describe the role of green alder in changing the abandoned land.

C Will a plant community made up mainly of green alder continue to include a large proportion of this plant population as time passes? Explain.

Use the diagram below to answer questions 12 and 13.

CHESAPEAKE BAY FOOD CHAIN

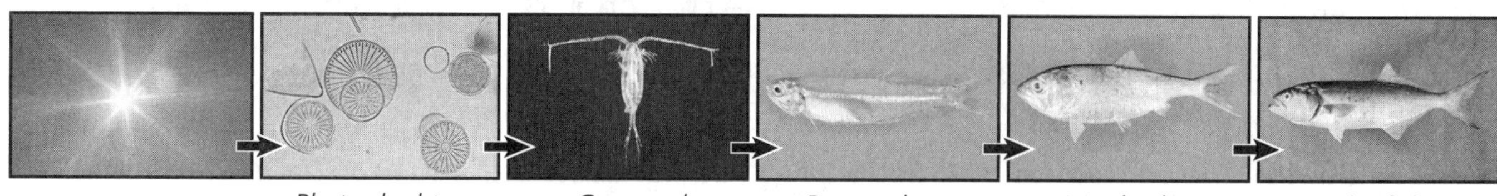

12 **The food chain above shows interactions in the Chesapeake Bay ecosystem. Which statement correctly identifies the trophic level of one population in the ecosystem?**

A Bluefish are primary consumers.

B Menhaden are secondary consumers.

C Phytoplankton are primary consumers.

D Bay anchovies are secondary consumers.

13 **Which statement correctly describes the amount of energy available to other fish populations, as compared to the menhaden population?**

A Less energy is available to the bluefish because energy is lost by the menhaden.

B More energy is available to the bluefish because they occupy a higher trophic level.

C More energy is available to the bay anchovies because energy is lost by the menhaden.

D Less energy is available to the bay anchovies because they occupy a lower trophic level.

Use the graph below to answer question 14.

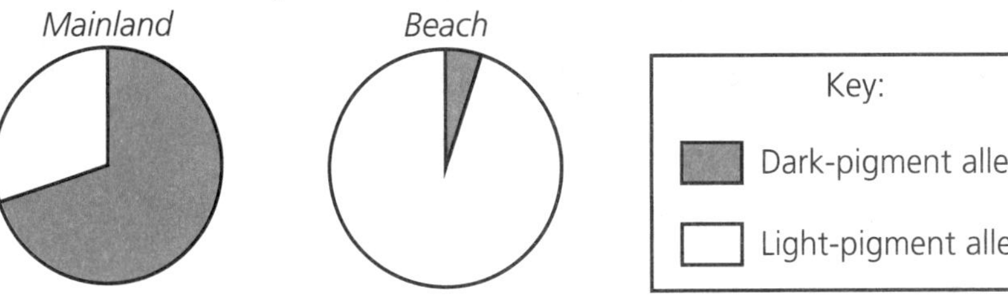

14 Oldfield mice are small rodents that nest in burrows dug into the ground. Different populations of oldfield mice inhabit the southeastern United States. Mainland populations live in forested areas with dark soils. These mice have brown and gray coats. Populations that live on sandy beaches have light tan and yellow coats. Coat color in oldfield mice is influenced by the *MC1R* gene, which controls pigment production. The graphs describe the frequencies of two alleles of this gene in beach and mainland populations.

A Explain why the allele frequencies for the beach subpopulation differ from those of the mainland subpopulation.

____

____

____

____

B Describe two factors that would allow the mainland and beach oldfield mouse populations to eventually become separate species.

____

____

____

____

C Mainland oldfield mouse populations existed before the beach populations. Explain how the *MC1R* allele more commonly found in beach populations originated.

____

____

____

____

15 A genetic mutation occurs in a gamete that eventually forms an offspring. If the resulting phenotype is neutral, how will the mutation affect the population of organisms?

A It will improve the overall fitness of the population.

B It will increase the number of alleles in the population.

C It will reduce the effects of natural selection on the population.

D It will decrease the number of heterozygous individuals in the population.

16 Gregor Mendel was an Austrian monk who determined how traits are inherited in pea plants. Mendel's first law of inheritance states that the two alleles for a gene in an individual will be packaged in different gametes. Half the gametes will contain one allele, and half will contain the other allele.

Which statement **best** describes Mendel's first law?

A The law has more evidence to support it than a theory.

B The law describes a pattern of inheritance observed in nature.

C The law explains why alleles segregate into different gametes.

D The law is based on inferences rather than direct observations.

17 Which of the following statements describes an interaction between two abiotic factors in an ecosystem?

A Wind carries sand particles and deposits them on a beach.

B A tomato plant absorbs sunlight to carry out photosynthesis.

C A squirrel buries excess food in the soil to save for later meals.

D Decomposers feed on a dead organism and release nutrients.

18 Which statement **best** explains why the replication of DNA is called semiconservative?

A Chromosomes replicate about halfway through the cell cycle.

B One strand of a DNA double strand forms later than the other.

C Complimentary base pairing conserves some genetic information.

D Offspring inherit half of the DNA in the cell nucleus from each parent.

Use the graph and diagram below to answer question 19.

DIFFERENCES IN ENOLASE PROTEIN SEQUENCE

Species	Number of Amino Acid Differences from Yeast (a Fungus)
Human	21
Chicken	23
Tomato	30
Corn	29

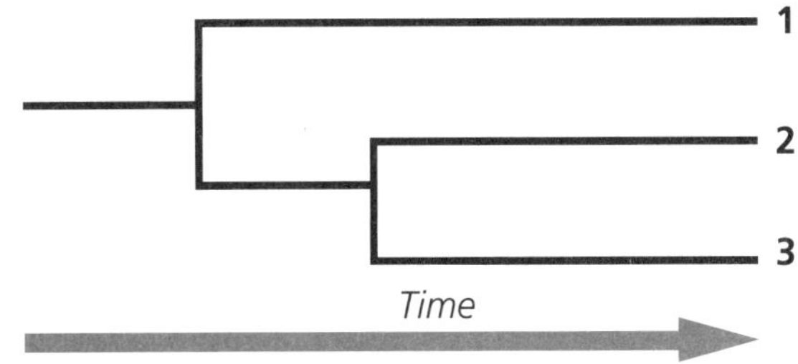

19 The enolase protein is involved in cellular respiration. The table above compares a portion of the enolase protein between yeast and different organisms. The diagram represents evolutionary relationships among three groups of organisms. According to information in the table, how should the diagram be completed?

A Plants should be placed in position 2.

B Animals should be placed in position 1.

C Animals and fungi should be placed in positions 2 and 3.

D Plants and animals should be placed in positions 2 and 3.

20 Scientists have inserted the gene for human insulin into bacteria. They first insert the insulin gene into a circular plasmid, and then insert the plasmid into bacteria cells. The insulin produced by bacteria is used to treat human medical conditions.

A Explain how the insulin gene can be removed from human DNA and combined with the plasmid DNA.

____

____

____

____

B Describe one way that the transcription or translation of the insulin gene differs in bacteria and human cells.

____

____

____

____

C Describe one way in which the transcription or translation of the insulin gene is similar in bacteria and human cells.

____

____

____

____

A

abiotic — a nonliving thing in an ecosystem

active transport — the movement of particles from an area of low concentration across a membrane to an area of high concentration, using ATP as an energy source, to build up a concentration gradient

adenosine triphosphate (ATP) — a small, soluble molecule that provides energy for reactions throughout the cell; ATP releases energy when a phosphate bond is broken

adhesion — the tendency of water molecules to stick to other surfaces

allele — a version of a gene due to a variation in the nucleotide sequence

allele frequency — how often an allele occurs in a population, its relative frequency

analogous structures — structures in different organisms that have the same function but are different in form and inheritance

aquatic — associated with water

B

biogeochemical cycles — the movement of abiotic factors such as carbon, oxygen, nitrogen, and water between living and nonliving parts of an ecosystem

biome — the similar ecosystems of a large geographic area with species adapted to that environment

biosphere — the ecosystem of the planet Earth, made up of all biomes

biotic — a living or once-living thing in an ecosystem

C

carbohydrate — a macromolecule made of carbon, hydrogen, and oxygen that cells use for energy

catalyst — a substance that speeds up a chemical reaction without being changed itself

cell — the basic unit of life

cell cycle — the stages of a cell's life leading to division and duplication; interphase, nuclear division, and cytokinesis

cellular respiration	a process that breaks down organic molecules such as glucose and captures the released energy in ATP
chloroplast	an organelle in plant cells that captures sunlight and transforms it to chemical energy
chromosome	a single piece of DNA, made up of genes
cloning	the practice of reproducing an organism that is genetically identical to the original
co-dominance	a type of inheritance in which two alleles representing homozygous phenotypes are equally expressed
cohesion	the tendency of water molecules to stick to each other
community	the populations of different species that inhabit a particular area
competition	when two organisms or species compete for limited resources, such as territory, food, water, or mates in the same environment
concentration	the amount of a substance, the solute, dissolved in a given volume of water or another substance, the solvent
concentration gradient	a gradual difference in the concentration of a substance in a solution as a function of distance
consumer	an organism that gets its energy by feeding on other organisms
crossing-over	the exchange of genetic material between homologous chromosomes in meiosis I that results in unique sister chromatids
cytokinesis	the final stage of the cell cycle, during which the cytoplasm divides to form two daughter cells

D

decomposer	an organism that gets its energy by breaking down dead or decaying matter, making nutrients available for other organisms
deoxyribonucleic acid, DNA	the molecule that stores genetic information in living things
diffusion	the movement of molecules or ions down a concentration gradient until it reaches equilibrium
DNA replication	the process by which DNA makes an exact copy of itself
dominant	a type of inheritance that is expressed when only one allele or both alleles shows the genotype; i.e., homozygous or heterozygous genotype

E

ecology — the study of the relationships between organisms and their environment

ecosystem — the community of living organisms and nonliving elements of an area

endemic species — a species living in the area where it originated

endocytosis — the process by which extracellular materials are taken into the cell by forming a membrane vesicle around it

endoplasmic) reticulum (ER) — a membrane-bound organelle that produces and transports materials for use inside and outside a eukaryotic cell. *Rough ER* has ribosomes and is involved in the production of proteins; *smooth ER* has no ribosomes and is involved in the production of lipids and hormones.

endosymbiosis — a theory that early eukaryotic cells were formed from simpler prokaryotes

energy pyramid — a model that shows the amount of energy stored in the bodies of organism at different trophic levels of an ecosystem

enzyme — a protein catalyst

eukaryote — an organism made of one or more complex cells with DNA contained in a nucleus and specialized membrane-bound organelles

evolution — the change in allele frequencies over time that results in new species developing from existing species

exocytosis — the process by which substances are released from the cell into the extracellular environment via vesicles that fuse with the plasma membrane

F

facilitated diffusion — the transport of substances across the plasma membrane with the assistance of transport proteins; does not require energy

food chain — a model that shows the flow of energy from one organism to another

food web — a model of interrelated food chains that shows the flow of energy between organisms

forensics — the use of science and technology to investigate and solve crimes

fossils — the preserved remains and traces of organisms that once lived on Earth

founder effect — the decrease in genetic variation when a new population arises from a small number of individuals

frame-shift mutation — the addition or deletion of one or more nucleotides that changes the order in which they are grouped into codons

freezing point — the temperature at which a liquid changes phase to become a solid

G

gametes — specialized cells used in reproduction; sperm and egg cells

gene — a sequence of nucleotides on a stretch of DNA that contains the information needed to make a protein

gene expression — the process through which the information in a gene is used to produce a protein or RNA

gene splicing — a laboratory method of cutting apart and recombining genes to produce recombinant DNA

gene therapy — the use of genetic engineering to change the DNA in genes causing a disease for the purpose of therapy

genetic drift — a change in allele frequency in a population due to chance events

genetic engineering — the practice of using technology to insert, delete, or alter genetic material directly

genetically modified organism (GMO) — an organism that contains DNA from other organisms; also called *transgenic organism*

genotype — the combination of alleles for a particular gene

Golgi apparatus — an organelle in eukaryotic cells that processes materials for release from the cell

H

habitat — an area within an ecosystem that provides an organism with the resources it needs to survive

homeostasis — the process of maintaining a stable internal environment

homeostatic mechanism — a method by which an organism regulates its internal environment, such as thermoregulation

homologous structures — a similar structures in different organisms that are the result of inheritance from a common ancestor

hypothesis — a testable explanation for observations and data

I

impermeable not allowing the passage of a substance

incomplete dominance a type of inheritance in which the heterozygous phenotype is a blend of two alleles, neither dominant nor recessive

interphase the longest stage of the cell cycle, during which the cell grows, replicates its DNA, and prepares to divide

isolating mechanism a physical or behavioral trait that prevents mating between species

L

law, scientific a statement or equation that summarizes observations without explaining them

limiting factor any biotic or abiotic resource, such as food, sunlight, or nutrients, that limits the size of a population

lipids organic compounds composed of carbon and hydrogen and relatively little oxygen that are insoluble in water

M

macromolecules large, complex molecules made of chains of smaller molecules; includes lipids, carbohydrates, proteins, and nucleic acids

meiosis the process of cell division that produces gametes

migration the movement of individuals into and out of a population that results in a change of allele frequencies

mitochondrion a membrane-bound organelle where energy transformation takes place

mitosis the second stage of the cell cycle, during which the nucleus is divided

monomers small, building block molecules that combine through chemical reactions to form large polymers

multicellular made up of many cells with specialized functions

multiple-allele a type of inheritance in which more than two alleles exist for a gene, resulting in many combinations of possible genotypes

mutation a permanent change in a DNA sequence

N

natural selection the process in which alleles for traits that give an advantage in survival and reproduction are more likely to be passed on to offspring

nondisjunction the failure of chromosomes or chromatids to separate during meiosis or mitosis

nonnative species a species living outside the area where it originated, introduced either intentionally or accidentally by humans; also called *invasive species*

nucleic acids DNA and RNA; biological macromolecules made of carbon, hydrogen, nitrogen, oxygen, and phosphorus that convey genetic information

nucleus a membrane-bound organelle in eukaryotic cells that contains genetic material

O

organ a structure composed of two or more tissue types, that performs a specific function

organ system a group of organs that work together to perform a specific function

organelle a specialized part of a cell with a specific function

organic compounds molecules that contain carbon and hydrogen and make up all forms of life

organism an individual living thing, such as an animal, plant, fungus, protist, or bacteria

osmosis the movement of water from an area of higher water concentration through permeable membranes to an area of lower water concentration; a form of passive transport

P

passive transport the movement of a substance across the plasma membrane without any input of energy

phenotype the expression of a trait

photosynthesis the process that converts light energy from the sun into chemical energy stored in compounds such as glucose

plasma membrane a phospholipid bilayer that encloses a cell to separate it from its environment and controls the passage of materials into and out of the cell

polygenic trait a trait determined by many different genes

population a group of individual organisms that occupies an area and shares a gene pool

population dynamics the study of changes in population numbers due to births, deaths, and individuals moving into and out of a population

principle, scientific a concept based on scientific laws and rules agreed upon by the scientific community

producer an organism that uses sunlight as its energy source

prokaryote a unicellular organism lacking a nucleus and membrane-bound organelles

protein a macromolecule made of carbon, hydrogen, oxygen, and nitrogen that performs structural and regulatory functions for cells

R

recessive a type of inheritance that is expressed only if both alleles show the genotype, i.e., a homozygous genotype

ribosome a cellular organelle made of protein and RNA where protein synthesis takes place

S

selective breeding the practice of breeding organisms with desirable traits; also called *artificial selection*

semiconservative replication the process by which a double strand of DNA separates and each strand serves as a template for replication, producing new DNA that consists partially of new material and partially of the original

sex-linked trait a trait determined by genes on either the X or Y chromosome

speciation the development of new species as a result of genetic isolation from a main population

species a group of similar organisms that are capable of mating and producing fertile offspring

specific heat the amount of heat energy needed to increase the temperature of one gram of a substance one degree Celsius

succession a series of predictable sequential changes in an ecosystem over time

symbiotic relationship — a relationship between two organisms that live together; both organisms may benefit, or one may benefit and the other is harmed, or one may benefit and the other neither benefits or is harmed

system — a set of components that interact to produce something greater than the sum of its parts

T

terrestrial — associated with land

theory, scientific — an explanation for a broad range of observations based on data, that provides a framework that can be used to make predictions about the natural world

tissue — an anatomical structure made of similar cells that perform a specific function

transcription — the process in which the genetic information in DNA is copied onto a strand of mRNA

translation — the process in which the instruction on a strand of mRNA is used to produce a protein

translocation — a chromosome alteration in which genes are moved or exchanged between chromosomes

transport protein — a protein in the plasma membrane that is involved in the movement of molecules and ions into and out of the cell

trophic level — the position of an organism in a food chain or web, as a producer, consumer, or decomposer

U

unicellular — made up of a single cell

V

vestigial structure — a structure that has lost its original function but suggests that an organism has descended from an earlier organism in which the structure was functional